GROUP
DISCUSSION
as Learning Process
A SOURCEBOOK

GROUP DISCUSSION

as Learning Process
A SOURCEBOOK

ELIZABETH W. FLYNN
JOHN F. LA FASO

EDUCATOR FORMATION BOOKS Director:
Richard J. Payne

PAULIST PRESS
NEW YORK N.Y. • PARAMUS N.J.

Design: Marion Faller
Cover Drawing: Rita Corbin
Photography: © 1971 by Marion Faller

Library of Congress Catalog Card Number: 74-170013

Published by Paulist Press
Editorial Office: 304 W. 58th St., N.Y., N.Y. 10019
Business Office: 400 Sette Drive, Paramus, N.J. 07652

Printed and bound in the United States of America

Contents

Who Should Use this Book, and How

This book is designed to be of practical assistance to anyone interested in improving his abilities for group discussion leadership and participation and his knowledge of learning-discussion groups. Group management is an interdisciplinary field, and in teaching courses in leadership we, the authors, found no single text that provided us with the tool we needed. We have tried to develop a book to serve our needs and the needs of others confronted with the constantly increasing necessity of doing a better job of leading groups and training others to do so.

While giving a solid basis of theory, so that those working with this book will have more than a "bag of tricks", it also gives practical, detailed help in the many facets of group leadership, including training in the development of suitable questions for use with any kind of material in any media. It is addressed to those working with learning groups and problem-solving groups including students from the last two years of high school through grad-

uate programs, and groups of adults in educational or organizational programs. Almost any group of people, from the family through schooling, business, or government, finds itself confronted from time to time with the need to study a problem, seek a solution and make a decision. Proper use of this book should be helpful.

We hasten to point out to you that this is a *book.* Since we have great faith in the value of the *discussion process,* we naturally do not think that this book alone will be as helpful to you as this book *plus* a group. If you sit quietly at home and read it, you will find it interesting—you may even pick up a few things of value. But it will never help you as it could unless you use its insights and recommendations in an actual group setting. As presented here the material has been used primarily at the graduate level, but it is equally applicable at the undergraduate level. We believe the learning involved in going through the training process would prove very beneficial to students, enabling them to profit more from their other studies. Training can be given outside the academic setting, and the authors have used the material in this way.

The book is organized so that the first seven chapters are concerned with theory and the last seven with practical application. In working with the text, we believe it is best to combine theory and practice at each working session, studying paired chapters in advance and putting them into practice within the training group or class sessions. Brief introductory materials are included so that the class can get to work as a discussion training group at its first session.

To simplify the task of those working with the text, we have used as examples of discussion materials some of the most generally known selections from the Bible. It is not necessary to use as practice material any particular selections or media. Examples of questions, their development and use, would be meaningless unless the reader had ready access to the sources. A trainer or instructor working with other materials can develop similar examples with his group. The GUIDEBOOK gives further examples and indicates typical ways in which questions can be developed as well as the kinds of problems encountered in developing and using questions. The GUIDEBOOK also contains exercises and recommended plans and procedures for taking a group through the entire training process.

Each chapter is followed by a listing of sources for further information, and a very complete annotated bibliography is included. We have tried to make the index thorough and practical for our own use, and believe it will prove equally helpful to others.

We believe that there are some theories that are not neutral in themselves, containing implicit premises that run counter to a truly human view of man as a thinking, feeling individual, entitled to respect, trust and concern. We believe that our premises and their resultant conclusions are fairly explicit

in this work. We lean toward a cooperative rather than a competitive group orientation, and hence away from what we would consider excessive individualism. It is our belief that the character and quality of the interpersonal relationships in a learning environment affect the learning and growth of the individual members. As we see it, education necessitates attitudinal change, and therefore must include the integration of knowledge. Therefore the educative process must deal with affective factors as well as cognition and skill training. We believe that education cannot and should not try to be a value-free process, but that values should not be imposed. This places an obligation on the educator or group leader to help group members discover and develop their own values and find ways to relate their behavior productively toward their values and goals. We are convinced that a classroom is a group, that much education is best forwarded through participatory group procedures, and that the educator should function at times as a discussion leader. It is our opinion that most adult education should include group discussion, and that such discussion is possible on many intellectual levels. We think many adult action groups fail to achieve their goals because they slight or avoid the learning discussion phase of their group life.

We do not favor the "leaderless group", believing that trained, knowledgeable, democratic leadership is an asset to the group, although insufficient of and by itself. We believe it is possible to train leaders, and that one of the tasks of a leader is to train group members to share responsibility and to assume at least some of the functions of leadership, while as titular head he still maintains a certain separateness and difference from other group members. In so doing he obviously retains a certain amount of power, and he must be careful to use this power for the good of the group members. We think it is possible for him to achieve the satisfaction of his own goals of responsibility, growth and productivity in this role. Without such satisfactions he is in danger of subverting the group goals to his own ends through conscious or unconscious manipulation. We are aware of the strength of social pressures in a cohesive group, and therefore of the dangers of coercion and the need to protect the minority opinion.

We believe that much that goes on under the name of "discussion" is a poor or distorted version of the possibilities of the process. Many potentially productive and effective groups suffer from lack of knowledge and skills of group operation and leadership; this is most often an unnecessary waste of time and talent. A poor group can improve, a good group can be a better one; non-leaders can become leaders and poor leaders can become good leaders.

Materials for First Session

A

WHAT IS DISCUSSION?

Discussion is a natural human activity—an interesting, exciting and creative experience. Discussion is a shared pursuit of responsive understanding—of yourselves, of each other, and of the material under discussion. Discussion can lead to personal growth and the creation of community.

WHAT DO LEADERS DO?

A warm, open and enthusiastic attitude on the part of the Leader is the catalyst that aids the development of these attitudes in group members. Leaders are present to help themselves and other group members (1) make a thoughtful examination of the meaning of the material and of the problems it presents, (2) clarify their thinking and feeling about the problems, (3) decide their individual response. It is not presumed that Leaders necessarily know more about the subject under discussion, but that they are trained and prepared to lead this discussion and offer this special kind of assistance to the group. The Leader will help the group by discouraging side conversations, which are destructive of productive discussion, and by discouraging the citing of outside authorities. Bringing in outside references removes discussion from the shared material which provides the common basis, and discourages participants from thinking through the problems for themselves.

WHO DECIDES THE RIGHT ANSWER?

Don't expect pre-packaged answers. Neither the Leader nor a member of the group will summarize or provide a conclusive answer at the end of the discussion. Each of you will try to find personally satisfying answers; your pursuit of answers may continue long after this discussion ends. The discussion provides information and deepened understanding, but the real answers will be your personal response to life and the world.

HOW DO I PREPARE FOR A DISCUSSION?

Read the presentation for this session at least twice, first for general comprehension and second for attention to specifics. On the second reading, underline words and phrases you consider important, and make notes in the margins of anything you do not understand, questions you would like to ask your group, and examples and applications that occur to you. Think about the reading, using your own words to describe your thoughts and feelings. What problems are dealt with?

What answers are suggested? What important ideas does it convey? How? How would you explain it to someone else? Do these ideas conflict with other ideas or feelings you have? Are problem situations presented? How would you behave in such situations? Why?

Discussions may be based on other forms of presentation: films, lectures, sociodrama and so forth. If your presentation is not in written form, you may find it helpful to jot down a few brief notes.

B

DURING THE DISCUSSION . . .

SPEAK TO THE SUBJECT. The presentation, your own ideas and feelings about it and about the statements of others are the subject of the discussion. Limit your comments to those you can support from these sources.

SPEAK TO THE QUESTION. Make every effort to answer questions directed to you, asking for time to think about your answer, if you wish. If you believe you have no comment to make, feel comfortable about saying so. Do not worry about having the "right" answer—most questions Leaders ask may be answered in many ways.

SPEAK TO ONE ANOTHER. Although the Leader directs a question to you, your answer is offered for the assistance of the whole group in its pursuit of responsive understanding. Speak clearly and loudly enough for all to hear, addressing your remarks to the group, rather than to the Leader. It is not necessary to wait until you are called on to speak. Your relevant comments and questions are important to the group.

SEEK FOR YOUR OWN UNDERSTANDING AND RESPONSE. This discussion concerns you—your ideas, feelings and actions. Do not accept another's answer as your own unless it makes sense to you. Do not hesitate to disagree, but before you do, be sure you understand the other's meaning. If you feel a question is so worded that it shows misunderstanding of the presentation or of a previous statement by another group member, feel free to say so.

SEEK TO AFFIRM THE OTHER. Listen carefully to others, showing your interest in and acceptance of the viewpoints they express.

SEEK TO UNDERSTAND THE OTHER. If you do not understand a member's comment, question him or try to restate what he has said in your own words, checking for comprehension.

SEEK DIALOGUE NOT MONOLOGUE. Discussion is a shared search, and should not be a platform for a few more articulate members. Attempt to bring more quiet members into the discussion by directing comments or questions to them.

HAVE FUN! Although discussion is an important and serious human enterprise, it is also an experience in the real joy of true communication. Relax, and enjoy yourself!

GROUP
DISCUSSION
as Learning Process

A SOURCEBOOK

1.
Group Discussion and Leadership

OVERVIEW

Face-to-face discussion groups have from their inception, or soon develop, some form of organization, standards or norms, goals and procedures. They also demonstrate a participation pattern and varying levels of communication and cohesiveness. Your group already has an imposed organization in regard to leadership—your trainer or instructor is the appointed head. It is possible that further *formal organization* may develop within this group through role differentiation. This might occur if, for instance, the group decided it should have a secretary to notify absentees of assignments or changes in time and place arrangements.

The nature of this group is such that many of its *procedures* are already determined for it by the parent organization or the trainer. Other procedures will develop, however, as decisions have to be made, for the group will face the problem of *how* these decisions will be made—by vote, by consensus, or by appointing someone to decide for it. Group procedures may be simple or complex but they exist in every group and the aim should be to find those most appropriate for implementing the group goals, while also according with its norms and satisfying its members.

Many of the standards or *norms* for the initial meeting of the group were also determined by the trainer who, by controlling the participation pattern, decided to a considerable extent who should speak, when, and how long, and indicated that interrupting is a "bad" thing. As time goes on, the group may change these norms to some extent, and will develop others. The behavior of group members both in the group situation and outside it will be affected by these norms.

group goals

It is probably obvious that members arrived with *individual goals*, but more work may be required before they develop a *group goal*. It is true that members probably share a goal of "learning something about discussions", but there is usually less agreement on what discussion is, whether all the members want to be discussion Leaders, and even less agreement in the short-range goals of individual sessions or exercises. Ideally group goals should be distinct and intelligible, realistic, and such that all members feel a commitment to them.

participation

The group's first session probably demonstrated an imbalanced *participation pattern*. Seldom does any group achieve a completely balanced pattern, with each member speaking for exactly the same amount of time as every other, nor would this be desirable, but within reason, balance is a desirable goal. Many who spoke may have addressed their contributions to only one or two members, rather than to the group at large, thus producing other short-term patterns of participation.

communication

Members of the group spoke, but not all speaking is *communication*. When the message sent is not the message received, the interchange cannot be considered totally satisfactory. Non-verbal communication may have played a part in the discussion, but received little attention—frowns, nods, head shaking, postural changes are conscious or unconscious messages.

emotion

What signs of *emotion* did you recognize in the group? Do you remember observing any initial tension, excitement, irritation? Were you aware of any of these feelings in yourself? Did you notice the beginnings of antipathy or liking between various members? Did this seem to have any effect on the degree of agreement or disagreement with some of the ideas expressed? How did it affect the participation pattern?

leadership functions

In order for a group to be effective and productive, certain *leadership functions* must be performed. It is the duty of the Leader to help his group provide these functions, and aid them in the necessary training so that leadership is shared through the sharing of these *task* and *social-emotional* functions.

WHAT IS A GROUP?

group, defined

First, what do we mean by a "small group"? How does it differ from an audience, a mob, people riding together on a bus, all the blue-eyed members of your community? We can define a small group as not more than twenty-five people who recognize themselves and one another as members and who meet in a face-to-face situation to accomplish some purpose they believe better fulfilled in this way. The kind of group we will be working with has as its purpose some change in its individual members which they believe is best accomplished through the medium of discussion. The change sought is learning.

interaction

These people act upon and react to each other—this is *interaction*. Though they bring individual, personal goals to the group, they have a common group goal in the pursuit of which they need one another's help. There is sufficient continuity and stability in their

membership

membership so that at least the members themselves have some way

by which they can tell who is and who is not a member. The group can

system be considered as a *system*, in that when it is in action it has an identifiable border, is composed of interrelated parts, behaves in a unified manner and has a history, however short.

If the group is larger than twelve to fifteen persons, there is

subgroups a tendency for discussion to take place in small *subgroups*, and for less interaction to take place in the group as whole.

WHAT IS DISCUSSION?

As we previously described it, "Discussion is a natural human activity—an interesting, exciting and creative experience. Discussion is a shared pursuit of *responsive understanding*—of yourselves, of each other, and of the material under discussion." This statement shows some of the characteristics and goals of discussion. We may add that it is *purposeful* conversation among members of a small group with the assistance of a *Leader*, based on a *Presentation*, to develop understanding of a matter of *importance*, in a *climate* of mutual *trust* and *respect*, with the goals of *community* and *individual decision* and *response*. It is *problem-solving* in the sense that any learning experience is the seeking of answers to problems of understanding and action. Any discussion of important questions involves change not only in ideas but also in attitudes, and thus ultimately in behavior. The solutions to problems under discussion will not be pre-determined, and the changes in attitudes grow from the very personal response to the *learning environment* or total situation.

problem-solving A basic pattern for problem-solving was described by John
patterns Dewey in 1910: [1]

1. the recognition of a problem;
2. locating and defining the problem;
3. suggesting possible solutions;
4. considering the consequences;
5. accepting a solution.

This pattern was later expanded to include:

6. testing and evaluating of the tentatively accepted solution.

Since Dewey's original proposal several problem-solving patterns were developed which offered minor modifications, primarily adding further evaluative and testing procedures. It is now recognized that the early pattern was an oversimplified model for much problem-solving, since it failed to take cognizance of emotional and motivational components, and would seem to eliminate the fact that evaluational processes accompany each step. Guilford[2] points out the basic similarity of these patterns, including the model for "creative production" as proposed by G. Wallas in 1926.[3] Guilford, using his structure of intellect concepts, proposes a more comprehensive model for problem-solving in the individual which he believes also serves for most creative production.

In our pursuit of understanding, we often use Dewey's model both as a group and as individuals. However, we must remember that not all problems are fruitfully resolved by methods of strict logic, and not all human concerns are reducible to mathematical formulae. It is an irrational habit to try to reduce everything to bones and dust. Many problems in our lives are characterized by a somewhat lumpy imprecision, and an attempt to whittle them down to slip neatly into a category-box and henceforth be treated as nicely squared off units may result in considerable distortion. The solving of problems so maltreated will result in no solution at all.

phases of discussion

The *phases of discussion* indicate how the discussion process roughly parallels the problem-solving model. The Presentation might be a reading in political science, a short story about priorities in personal values or a film on urban problems. The group's discussion will move through the phases of:

1. understanding the meaning of the Presentation and the life problem to which it may offer possible answers;

2. understanding of the group members' positive and negative intellectual and emotional reactions to the problem itself and to the Presentation;

3. comparing and checking new information and reactions with what the group members already know;

4. considering the implications and consequences;

5. deciding what they, as individuals, feel, believe and must do.

If consideration of these phases is neglected, the discussion will probably be inadequate.

Ambrose Bierce defined discussion as "a method of confirming others in their errors." [4] Many poorly planned or led discussions have caused some people to doubt the value of the process. Many factors enter into a worthwhile discussion. Suppose we were to observe two discussions in progress. We will watch them through a glass window in a soundproof room, and thus will not be able to hear what is said. In the first discussion group the Leader looks happy and enthusiastic and the group is comprised of obviously eager participants, gesticulating and talking together with considerable animation. When we look in on the second group, the Leader looks less happy and it is obvious the group is considerably less vocal, less active, and seemingly less enthusiastic. There seem to be times when no one is saying anything.

What is the difference between these two groups? What is wrong with the second group? Answer—we have no way at all of making such judgments. If we observed them over a period of time, we could make some judgment as to the participation pattern, and we might be able to make a few other judgments as to group cohesiveness from observation of non-verbal behavior, but we could not say anything about the value of one discussion as opposed to the other.

Suppose now that we meet the Leaders of these two groups as they leave their meeting room. If we talk with the Leader of the first group, he might say, "Oh, we had an excellent discussion!

Everyone was involved, and they all had a good time!" The Leader of the second group might say, "Well, I don't know—it seemed to me to be hard work all the way, and I'm not sure they enjoyed it." Now what can we say? Answer—nothing. An inexperienced or untrained Leader may be a poor judge. He is often content if his group just talks, and may give little consideration to what is said. He is also apt to worry if the group seems somewhat quiet and slow to respond at times. Before we could judge the quality of these discussions we would have to know a good deal more. The first group may have had a great discussion—or it may have had a poor one, and the same is true of the second group.

process
 Since discussion is a *process*, each of the phases affects and is affected by all the other phases. Furthermore, as a process, it is always difficult to describe its elements in a list. Lists imply a strict chronology, a set of rigid pre-planned steps. Although information and reflective thought are a necessary prerequisite to the development of alternative solutions and decision, it is possible for these elements to be present in a different order. In some discussions, one or more of the phases might be only fleetingly present. It is important to remember that the fifth phase, "deciding what they, as individuals, must do", does not imply a group decision for action, or that unanimous agreement or consensus is sought. If this is thought to be

coercion
 the aim of learning-discussions, coercion and manipulation by the Leader or the group will enter the picture. It is not always possible

to reach the fifth phase in a particular discussion. However, in talking about discussion we will treat these phases as though they appeared in this order, with a regularity and progression which would seldom appear.

LEARNING GROUPS

A learning group or a learning-discussion such as we are primarily concerned with differs from what is commonly called a decision-making group or an action-group in a number of ways. The latter groups are under pressure of both agenda and time, and these factors must be considered in goals and procedures. A learning group has an agenda, but is far more flexible, more responsive to the needs of its members, and the group does not have the same kind of decision deadlines. It need not press for unanimity at all times, and can respect the wishes of the individual who wants to delay his decision. Most *decision-making and action activities* are necessarily *preceded by a learning-discussion*. The final step or outcome differs in that it is a *group* decision based on individual decisions. In a learning group the outcome consists of *individual* decisions.

WHAT CONSTITUTES LEADERSHIP?

leadership functions

Describing the Leader and his activities as a group or set of *functions* which can and should be shared among the members came rather later in the study of group leadership. Between World Wars I and II, there was a tendency to think of leadership

"traits" theory

"traits", and of the Leader as a person who possessed the largest number of these traits in the highest degree. Such traits as "courage", "high intelligence", "strong personal attractiveness", "aggressiveness" and "flexibility" were attributed to Leaders as definitive of leadership. However, when research showed that in twenty different experimental studies researchers were able to demonstrate only 5% of the traits examined as common to four or more studies, it was realized that the recognition of such traits was not a satisfactory way to predict leadership ability.[5] The traits which appeared most often in the Leaders examined were initiative and intelligence and it is certainly true that a modicum of these is usually necessary for effective leadership.

situation

A later study by Stogdill showed that while these and a few other factors such as socio-economic status and dependability seemed to bear some relation to leadership, ". . . the evidence suggests that leadership is a relationship that exists between persons in a social situation, and that persons who are leaders in one situation may not necessarily be leaders in other situations."[6] Other studies have

special knowledge or skill

indicated that the situation plus the special knowledge or skill of a particular person were the factors resulting in the emergence of a Leader.[7]

**training for
leadership**

shared leadership

Although traits, situation and special knowledge or skill do apply to many occasions of leadership, no one factor or combination of factors seems adequate to explain or even describe the broad spectrum of "leadership". Evidence is available and common sense shows that many Leaders are trained for their work, that one who was at one time not a Leader does become one. We are able to identify a number of common Leader-like behaviors or functions serviceable in leadership. Recent work in the field has concentrated largely on what the Leader *does*, noticing which activities serve a functional purpose for the group. Students of groups have compiled lists of functions which must be performed for group health and productivity, and then have gone on to identify who actually does these things. From this point of view they see that many things the Leader "must do" are actually often done by others. During the time these functions are being performed, the performer may be called "the Leader". We may say that at such times he steps into or assumes the *role* of the Leader. Thus group members share the functions of leadership.

Leader's responsibilities

All groups have certain responsibilities to their members and usually in some way to the larger community. *Leaders serve their groups by assuming those responsibilities which other group members are temporarily or permanently unable to conveniently handle.* What are these responsibilities or *functions* which the appointed Leader wants to share with other members? Why should the Leader want to share them? Some are shared by group members without conscious effort or training. Others are gradually assumed by group members as the group grows or matures.

We often make a basic division in leadership functions between "task functions" and "maintenance, or social-emotional functions." These groups of functions are not always clear-cut in actual group operation, but elements of any given contribution or action

task functions

may be abstracted and categorized under such headings. Certain individuals in a group often assume a greater degree of responsibility than others for the performance of the group task. For instance, in a learning group they may offer a needed piece of information, or seek it from others; they may discover and seek to resolve seeming contradictions; they may suggest several new ways of looking at a problem. The participant who makes such contributions may well have an unsettling effect on other group members, and may seem to challenge their ways of thinking or their values. This, in turn, can cause a lack of cohesiveness in the group.

social-emotional functions

Other individuals in the group may be found to encourage or support opinions and values expressed in the group, to promote feelings which hold the group together, or to perform small practical services for the group. These members are performing social-emotional functions for the group.

"omniscient and omnipotent Leader"

In some groups a few persons may perform almost all of these functions, and in a new and untrained group a great many functions may devolve upon the appointed Leader. However, to perform all of these functions well is just about impossible, and it is impractical to seek for the "omniscient and omnipotent Leader". We prefer a functional approach to leadership which views group effectiveness as a totality, and places on the Leader responsibility for developing the necessary means toward this end.

group effectiveness

The effective group works productively toward the achievement of group and individual goals. Effectiveness also implies a climate of trust and community in a situation which promotes group and individual growth. In an effective group the necessary leadership functions are performed, and their performance is shared.

In 1948 Benne and Sheats drew up a list of leadership functions which were later categorized by Gibb and Gibb for use in training.[8] Since then similar lists have been compiled by many in the field. During your training you will become increasingly aware of these necessary functions, and each Leader will probably create a list of his own to use in diagnosing group problems and checking on group needs and performance. It is not necessary to try to thoroughly understand or remember all of these functions at this stage in your training. As you read through the following list, some functions will seem so obvious as not to need mention; others may seem overly complex. Many are phrased in what may be unfamiliar jargon. It will be helpful to read through the list now and refer to it occasionally during your training until you find it is quite familiar, or you have developed a list which you prefer.

list of leadership functions

1. *Initiating* (change)   (primarily task)
   getting something started; arousing interest; suggesting new directions; guidance of transitions; pointing out moments of choice (see also *Information input*)

2. *Information input*   (primarily task)
   providing resources: data, opinions, ideas; special materials,

devices such as films, role-playing, etc.; stimulating group think-ing and guiding exploration by: reflection (mirroring), deflec-tion, questioning, clarifying and issue-sharpening; rephrasing and elaborating contributions; seeking definitions; linking: harmo-nizing and ordering information and opinion; pointing out simi-larities and differences; coordinating (see also *Regulating*).

3. *Evaluating* (primarily task)
testing validity of contributions; reality testing of suggestions; recognizing contradictions; determining opinion (see also *De-cision-making*).

4. *Decision-making* (primarily task)
resolving controversy (intrinsic conflict); recognizing conflict (extrinsic conflict), and allowing for it; seeking consensus where needed; assisting individual decisions through clarification, acceptance, encouragement (see also *Evaluating*).

5. *Regulating* (gate-keeping) (both task and maintenance)
setting and maintaining goals, norms, standards, agenda; keep-ing on track; one point at a time; side-tracking true irrelevancies; clock-watching; summarizing.

6. *Climate-making* (primarily maintenance)
listening with understanding; treating all contributions with respect, including encouraging expression of minority opinion; encouraging expression of personal feelings; supporting and en-couraging reticent; handling over-aggressive; harmonizing and integrating emotion; tension relief (including making and laugh-ing at jokes, providing silence, etc.); performing chore for group or individual.

7. *Training* (aiding individual and group growth)
(primarily maintenance)
helping group achieve balance between work on task and on social-emotional aspects (see also *Climate-making*); helping group to understand and accept both; structuring situations for under-standing; helping group to understand and promote good cli-mate; aiding planning for diagnosis of dynamic difficulties; seeing problems as "group problems", not "problem individ-uals", and helping group recognize this; providing means of feedback (delayed or indirect); record-keeping, observers, group feedback; encouraging experimentation with roles, responsi-bilities.

behavioral roles   Because many of these functions are quite easy and natural ways of behaving, a number of group members perform one or more of these functions spontaneously. Particularly in the early stages of a group's life a few people may become more or less identified with certain of these functions, and may even be thought of as carrying out the *role* of "The Initiator", or "The Evaluator". At this early period there is apt to be a form of role differentiation in which some members of a group may perform most of the task functions and others most of the social-emotional functions. We have talked previously about the "roles" of Leader and participant. These were assigned roles. The above use of "role" is somewhat different, since we are classifying all of these functions as leadership functions, regardless of the performer. As a group matures, each member's repertoire of functions increases, and the stereotyped roles of "The Initiator" and so on should less easily be pinned to particular individuals. It is part of the job of the appointed Leader to assist in this maturing process.

FOR SOURCES AND FURTHER INFORMATION, CONSULT THE FOLLOWING WORKS:

1. Dewey, John, HOW WE THINK, p. 107, Boston: D. C. Heath & Co., 1933.
2. Guilford, J. P., THE NATURE OF HUMAN INTELLIGENCE, pp. 313-16, N.Y.: McGraw-Hill Book Co., 1967.
3. Wallas, G., THE ART OF THOUGHT, London: Watts, 1926; 1945.
4. Bierce, Ambrose, THE DEVIL'S DICTIONARY, pp. 37-8, N.Y.: Hill & Wang, Inc. 1957.
5. Bird, C., SOCIAL PSYCHOLOGY, N.Y.: Appleton-Century, 1940.
6. Stogdill, R. M., "Personal Factors Associated with Leadership: A Survey of the Literature", JOURNAL OF PSYCHOLOGY, XXV (Jan., 1948) 19-48.
7. Jenkins, W. O., "A Review of Leadership Studies with Particular Reference to Military Problems, PSYCHOLOGICAL BULLETIN, 44 (1947) 54-79.

see also: BULLETIN #2, National Training Laboratories, Washington, D.C.
8. Benne, K. D. and P. Sheats, "Functional Roles of Group Members", JOURNAL OF SOCIAL ISSUES, 4, 2 (1948), 41-9. These authors do not speak of "functional" and "dysfunctional" behaviors, but characterize the latter as functions performed to meet individual needs at the expense of other people's need-meeting.
see also: Gibb, J. R. and L. M. Gibb, APPLIED GROUP DYNAMICS, National Training Laboratories, 1955. Slater, Phillip E., "Role Differentiation in Small Groups", AMERICAN SOCIOLOGICAL REVIEW, 20 (1955) 300-310. Cartwright, Dorwin and Alven Zander, GROUP DYNAMICS (RESEARCH AND THEORY) (3rd ed.), pp. 304-9, N.Y.: Harper & Row, 1968.

2.

The Learning Group Member

OVERVIEW

The individual enters the group with a variety of recognized and unrecognized *motives*, *attitudes* and *values*, and his *behavior* and *learning* in the group are influenced by these and by his *reference groups*, his past *history* and *psychological structure*. His learning occurs through *communication* and involves change through the introduction of information, the development of *balance* in attitudes and *congruence* in concepts and results in *internalization* of ideas and ways of thought and feeling.

WHY DOES SOMEONE ENTER A GROUP?

motivation, or goal-seeking

That this seems a perfectly sensible question shows that in everyday life we expect people to have a reason for what they do. In other words, we expect that their behavior is motivated or goal-directed. It can be said that every individual who enters a group voluntarily, or even involuntarily, does so because he has a need for something. Usually he has several needs, and is probably not aware of all of them. His needs bring him to the group and also affect the way he behaves in the group, but there is no simple, direct way of pointing to a specific type of behavior, including that individual's statements, and labeling the need or needs involved.

needs

Motivated or goal-seeking behavior is usually thought to derive from innate needs or a combination of these needs and external stimuli, but it is also probable that some of our "needs" are learned.

learned motives

Learning in itself can "create" motives, as shown by Thorndike whose Law of Effect states that actions which lead to a satisfying state of affairs tend to be repeated.[1] Motivation is a general term used to cover needs, drives, wants, desires and wishes.[2]

factors affecting motivated behavior

When we consider a particular individual and attempt to understand his motivated behavior, we are confronted with many factors. He is liable to experience more than one motive at any given time, and feel its force in varying degrees, and some of these motives may work well together while others create disharmony. The way he actually behaves under the push or pull of these motivational forces is modified by his psychological environment as well as by his own training, mode or style of thought processes, usual ways of expressing himself, and the opportunities presented to him.[3] O. H. Mowrer, a contemporary psychologist, regards fear as a secondary or learned drive which results in a strong tendency to avoid behavior which previously generated a fear-creating situation. The individual's unique history has developed patterns of avoidance of objects and situations not in themselves dangerous, but somehow felt to be so. These fears, of course, affect learning.[4]

fears

motivation and learning

We tend to believe it would be helpful if we could find a simple explanation of the relationships between an individual's needs, his behavior, his motivation, his environment and his learning, but we are confronted with considerable complexity. Theorists who have posited one or two basic drives or motives as the basis, and therefore the explanation, of all human behavior, leave too much unexplained.

Our original question, "Why does someone enter a group?" may be a perfectly sensible question, but we are not going to find a "perfectly sensible" answer. The participant may join the group with a primary interest in the interpersonal relationships or in the task which the group sets for itself or, more usually, with some combination of these reasons, but this in itself does not tell us very much.

interpersonal relationships

The individual's pursuit of interpersonal relationships may derive from any one of a number of motives, or be a combination of several. Michael Argyle gives a provisional list of seven: (1) non-social drives which can produce social interaction, (2) dependency, (3) affiliation, (4) dominance, (5) sex, (6) aggression and (7) self-esteem and ego-identity.[5]

learning as group task

The task or purpose of our discussion groups is known to be "discussion for learning", and certainly many people are motivated to enter such groups with this goal in mind. Many people recognize that they can learn more readily in the group situation than by working alone. The adult or teenager who is seriously interested in learning may also realize that more real learning will occur if he puts himself in a situation in which he will be expected to participate than in one in which he might be simply a passive audience.

subject matter

shared values

If we now refine our question to, "Why does this individual enter this particular group?", we see that, in addition to all of the above factors, at least two more enter: (1) the particular subject matter of the discussion, and (2) the probability of shared attitudes and values. Given the usual range of possibilities, an individual is more likely to enter a group in which he anticipates that the material to be studied will come close to his interest level and capabilities, and that at least some of the group members will look at things much as he does or share his value system to some extent.

WHAT DOES THE INDIVIDUAL BRING TO THE GROUP?

When a discussion group gathers for the first time a good deal more behavior of individuals is observable than behavior of a group. Each person present brings with him his own motives, ideas, feelings, habits, and ways of communicating. They will not disappear because he is now in a group, although some of these may change in time. Furthermore, when he enters a group the individual is surrounded by an invisible cloud composed of an amazing array

of people from his past and present, and each of them is exerting some force upon him. They each carry not only their own personalities and their emotional relationships with our group member, but a wealth of ideas, opinions, orders and prohibitions. Our individual is already a member of many other groups, including the one he was born into—his family. These groups are of varying degrees of importance to him, but those which have helped form his beliefs and life pattern, and those to which he owes his value structure or to which he feels a strong attachment form his *reference groups*.

reference groups

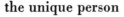

Everything from his grandmother's family parties—happy, noisy, with rich ethnic overtones—to his position as Secretary of the local Boy Scout Troop Committee is whispering through his mind. Though it is only occasionally that one of these reference groups or its members will actually be present to his conscious mind, they will be constantly murmuring and bobbing about him, pushing him one way and pulling him another, criticizing him, punishing him, praising him for every statement he makes and even every thought he thinks or emotion he feels. In his behavior in the group he is not, nor could nor should be, totally free from these influences.

the unique person

In addition to those common human needs he shares with other members and the thick tangle of shared and unshared reference groups, there is something else here—the unique person. He has his own way of seeing the world, his own hopes and fears, his own desires and goals and standards for himself and others. In perceiving the world about him, and in mentally working with these perceptions, he has a unique internal structure or network. Even the young child has built up an increasingly complex system, filter or set

for handling his perceptions and his life. If this were not the case, everyone's report of experience would be identical and any given question would elicit the same response from everyone, given the same data.

Our individual may be highly imaginative, artistic; he may be very practical, pragmatic; he may be rigidly logical and analytical; he may take everything very literally or see things symbolically and mythically. He has his own image of himself, as he believes he is, and as he would like to be. He wants to expand his world, and at the same time make it more comfortable, make it hang together better. He wants to be creative, to give to others, and at the same time to find others giving to him. He wants to get rid of some of his feelings of anger, and to find true community. He wants to be truly, freely, happily, comfortably *himself*. But he is not always sure of what "himself" is, nor quite sure that he likes that self.

ATTITUDES

One way of looking at our group member is as a being with attitudes. The concept of attitudes is so important that some social psychologists say the individual may be thought of as "an organization of attitudes".[6] Allport's definition of attitude is "a mental and neural state of readiness, organized through experience, exerting a directive or dynamic influence upon the individual's responses to all objects with which it is connected."[7] Krech and Crutchfield have proposed a definition which amplifies the meaning of the first part of Allport's definition, and is helpful in seeing the many aspects of "attitude". They speak of an attitude as ". . . an enduring organization of motivational, emotional, perceptual and cognitive processes with respect to some aspect of the individual's world."[8] By learned satisfactions or dissatisfactions we develop responses toward or away from objects of thought. Because one of the ways in which our "thinking" goes on is by recognizing relationships and thus classifying and grouping objects, these responses also become grouped and help us judge new objects when they come to our attention. "(A)n individual's attitude toward a class of objects is determined by the particular role those objects have come to play in facilitating responses that reduce the tension of particular motives and that resolve particular conflicts among motives."[9] Attitudes include both cognitive and affective elements.

concept, attitude, opinion and belief

You may have an attitude toward dictionaries, for instance, as well as a concept of dictionaries. Although the words "attitude", "opinion" and "belief" are often used interchangeably, these descriptive terms usually imply shades of difference. You may have an *opinion* that one particular dictionary is preferable to several others. Your *attitude* toward dictionaries may be that they are interesting, useful reports on how words are usually used, or that they are difficult to use, worthless collections of definitions which are "clear only if known". You may have a *belief* that they are the necessary means of preserving correct language and constitute a very valuable collection of prescriptive rules. All of these attitudes obviously include one or more concepts.

The individual is not always aware of his attitudes, nor of his behaviors which manifest them to others. Attitudes are not observable in the same way as overt behavior. The "aggressive Democrat" may be said to have an unfavorable attitude toward Republicans. On the other hand, if he is characterized by a general aggressiveness, this is a personality trait, and the seeming strength of his attitude toward Republicans may easily be wrongly evaluated. The man in the NEW YORKER cartoon who "hated everybody regardless of race, creed or color" was evidencing "personality", not attitude.[10]

When we say that someone has a "poor attitude" about something, we usually mean that his attitude is negative toward something about which we have strong positive attitudes. When we talk with a friend about a controversial subject, we often shade our conversation somewhat depending on whether we believe he does or does not share our attitude about the matter. When we read a book, to some extent the truism holds that "we all read our own book". If you went to a department store accompanied by a three-year-old, a sixteen-year-old, and a visitor from India you would actually all "see" different things, your perception being in part a function of your attitudes. In other words, attitudes color facts, affect perception, judgment, memory and communication.

ATTITUDE CHANGE AND COMMUNICATION

John, for instance, might have an extremely negative attitude toward Germans, and yet be quite polite to a particular German seated next to him at a dinner party. His conflicting positive feelings toward his charming hostess, whom he wishes to please, might cause him to behave pleasantly toward Dr. Hess. On the other hand, if John has a warm friendly attitude toward Germans, this might have been difficult to infer if the subject under discussion at the table had been "student participation in university administration", and if this is a subject on which both hold strong but opposite opinions and attitudes.

central attitudes   Some attitudes are more important than others for an individual; these more central attitudes will naturally influence more of his behavior and influence it more strongly. Suppose John, together with a negative attitude toward Germans, had a strong positive attitude toward professors, and knew Dr. Hess was a professor; he might listen more attentively to his views on student participation and give them a more objective hearing. The outcome might be that he would not only modify his attitude toward student participation in the direction of the German professor's views, but might even modify his attitude toward Germans. This might indicate that his attitude toward professors was a more central one than his attitude toward Germans. Probably it would also indicate a positive attitude toward new information, or an "open-mindedness" in certain areas.

Suppose Mary had been seated opposite John. Mary has no strong feelings and little background information on the subject under discussion. As she listens, she finds both presenting good arguments and apparently presenting an equal number of facts to back up their arguments. She has no strong positive or negative attitudes toward Germans or professors, but John is in her discussion group, and she has a friendly, admiring feeling toward him, or a positive attitude toward John.

If Mary's attitude toward student participation were to be measured after this discussion, it might be found to be tipped slightly toward John's view. As a *passive audience* she is less apt to be influenced by this conversation than if she herself had participated in it. If her previously neutral attitude, or "no-attitude", were modified, it would be primarily because of her positive attitude toward John. The information she received was *ambiguous*, in that the messages were *conflicting*. However, the total *situation* may have reinforced her positive feelings toward John, if the party was pleasing and the food good. She is more likely to listen attentively to John and remember his arguments. She is therefore apt to believe that John understands the situation better than his opponent, that he was not being "rude" when he disagreed, but merely "forceful in his arguments", and this may increase her positive feelings toward John. We could describe the factors involved in the process of *persuasion* as, (1) initial attitude, (2) state of previous information, (3) situation, including (a) properties of the messages, (b) properties of the communicators, or *source*, with the conflicting messages, and (c) other situational factors such as climate.

If John had been working on the same campus as Dr. Hess, and been involved in the problem, he would have had *direct information*. However, in this conversation he was receiving indirect information or *socially mediated information,* a characteristic of persuasive communication. Socially mediated information, or "secondary perceptions", are common to a great deal of communication, whether or not it is intentionally persuasive.

The likelihood that John will change his attitude toward student participation in this situation in which Dr. Hess is presenting him with *contrary or disconfirming information* is particularly dependent on two characteristics of the *transmission situation* (item "3" above): (1) the properties of the persuasive message, and (2) the source, or agent transmitting the message. The German professor has a somewhat fortunate transmission situation: (1) in regard to his message, since he was talking to one person only, he could hand-tailor his arguments as he picked up *feedback* from John; (2) John's positive attitude toward professors may have helped him accept some of the professor's arguments.

If John has a favorable attitude toward new information in the area of higher education, for instance, he is more readily able to change. This information probably has altered his view of the problem so that he sees it in a new way—sees new facets of it which he did not see before. What has occurred is often considered to be a *change in the object of judgment,* rather than a change in the judgment of the object.

This tale of John, Mary and Dr. Hess shows a few ways in which attitudes, motives and situations, including such things as the communicators and the message, influence *learning behavior*. It also shows to some extent the complexity introduced by communications of a persuasive nature. "(A)s soon as we begin to consider the social mediation of information the relevant objects in the situation begin to multiply, and description of attitude change rapidly becomes more complicated." [11] The following summary of the principles involved in attitude change is based on that of Newcomb, Turner and Converse: [12]

1. new information brings change in perceived content of objects; i.e., in the object of judgment.

2. attitudes toward one object change as the cognitive content of other, associated, objects changes.

2.1 if an attitude toward a goal is changed, attitudes towards associated means may change.

3. interdependence of individual's attitude toward a group or person and toward an object about which both parties have attitudes; e.g., reference group influence.

4. interdependence of attitude toward source and source evaluation, and acceptance of message.

5. influence of attitude change perceived in other recipients of the message.

It might also be noted that Mary's change in attitude, if any, was partly a function of the fact that her previous "attitude" was

direct information

socially mediated information

contrary or disconfirming information

feedback, direct

"change in the object of judgment"

learning behavior

principles involved in attitude change

not really an attitude, and she had little previous information. If John indicated some change in his attitude, it is possible that Mary, as a passive audience, might have been influenced to swing over with him.

CONCEPTS AND CONGRUENCE

Let us suppose John is now in his discussion group, reasonably relaxed, open-minded and interested in learning. What other factors will determine the extent to which his knowledge, attitudes and actions will be affected by his discussion group experience? As a recipient of communications, his learned skills of perception, including touching, smelling, seeing and hearing, his ability to read with comprehension and to grasp other objects presented to his senses all affect his learning. All of these involve his store of *available concepts*.

available concepts

Your concept of something is your general idea of understanding of it, your own particular organization of past instances or experiences of it. Concepts are classes of meaning, rather than individual, specific instances, and may cover various levels of generality, such as dictionaries, reference books, books, communication media. The number, variety and refinement of a person's concepts have a considerable effect on the ease with which he can perceive, or take in, examine and use information. His concepts form perhaps the major part of his mental set. The lack of suitable concepts may make it difficult to even recognize or hear a new idea.

resistance to change

James Harvey Robinson in THE MIND IN THE MAKING points to the internal conflict which makes acceptance of new ideas difficult: "We like to continue to believe what we have been accustomed to accept as true, and the resentment aroused when doubt is cast upon any of our assumptions leads us to seek every manner of excuse for clinging to them. . . . (I)f we are told we are wrong we resent the imputation and harden our hearts. . . . It is obviously not the ideas themselves that are dear to us, but our self-esteem, which is threatened." [13] Hovland *et al.* point out, "A persuasive communication will often create a conflict between the motives aroused by the new incentives it offers on the one hand and whatever motives the individual may have for holding his initial opinions on the other." [14]

imbalance, dissonance

More may be involved here than hating to be "wrong". We are uncomfortable when we are aware of this conflict in our motives, or an *imbalance* or *dissonance* in our attitudes, ideas or actions. If the information does not "fit" with our present store of concepts and attitudes, we will somehow seek to remedy this. There is evidence which seems to indicate that the problem of accepting, or learning, "other side" arguments may well be due to the lack of a suitable cognitive structure rather than to repression. Without "appropriate subsuming concepts in attitude structure", [15] it is difficult to fit in the new information and easier to forget it. [16] As pointed out by Newcomb *et al.* this principle of balance does not apply to all our attitudes, but to those which are central. Furthermore, it does not mean we cannot have mixed reactions toward some object of thought, "liking" it in one way and "disliking" it in another. It is more accurate to speak of a "strain" or a "trend" toward balance, rather than of the achievement of and persistence in a perfect state of equilibrium.[17]

Some people seem to have a greater tolerance than others for imbalance, just as some people have a greater tolerance for ambiguity, but for many people in discussion groups, there is a tendency for discomfort due to imbalance both because the subject matter often involves values and thus is recognized as important for them, and because of their feeling toward the group and toward individual members of the group. If Mary's feelings toward John were to become stronger, but she felt strong disagreement with his ideas on student participation, she would experience discomfort in her relationship with him, due to imbalance.

values and attitude change

The more closely an attitude is related to a person's life values, the more disturbing imbalance will be. Cooper and Mc-Gaugh define value as "an attitude which is dominated by the individual's interpretation of the stimulus object's worth to him in the light of his goals." [18] One's attitudes form a network, or a series of networks, more or less well organized and articulated. At the heart of many of these networks is a value, and one's values may also be related in a similar network. Allport, Vernon and Lindzey in 1951 identified what they saw as six possible life values: theoretical, economic, aesthetic, social, political and religious.[19] For most people, one of these life values is dominant, but others may have importance for him. We tend to view our experiences and order our behavior in accord with our life goals, as we see the situation. The more vital a particular attitude is to the existence or pursuit of a value, the more threatening is an object, idea or event which might cause a change in that attitude.

Normally, balance is restored in attitude systems by adjustments in attitudes which are less important or less "close" to a value. When an attitude is changed which is related closely to a value, this may cause a change in many related attitudes. In the case of John, for instance, it might be possible that his attitude toward Germans, professors and students might shift as the result of a change in his attitude toward the student participation issue.

Festinger's Theory of Cognitive Dissonance

As John tries out his new ideas in some of his old conversational situations, he may find himself embroiled in internal conflict. Some of his old "facts" may fit poorly with some of his "new" ones. Leon Festinger developed his theory of cognitive dissonance to explain what sometimes happens in such situations, and speaks of a "strain toward consistency". He says, "Any time a person has information or an opinion which considered by itself would lead him not to engage in some action, then this information or opinion is dissonant with having engaged in the action. When such dissonance exists, the person will try to reduce it either by changing his actions or by changing his beliefs and opinions. If he cannot change the action, opinion change will ensue. This psychological process, which can be called dissonance reduction, does explain the frequently observed behavior of people justifying their actions." [20]

dissonance reduction

Both the principle of balance, which is concerned with the relationship of two or more interdependent attitudes of some importance to an individual, and the principle of dissonance reduction, concerned with the harmonizing of beliefs and opinions with actions, including the action of "speaking out in favor of", are important factors in learning and response in discussion groups.

INTERNALIZATION

The kind of learning in which we are most interested has been characterized as *internalization*. Kelman distinguishes compliance, identification and internalization.[21] In the first, the individual will give outward expression of acceptance of an idea, as John might have done during his dinner conversation, simply to be polite and please his hostess. *Identification* occurs when the individual adopts the behavior of another person or group because he associates such behavior with a satisfactory role relationship which forms part of his self-image. Mary, for instance, might adopt John's viewpoint in the sense of identification because of her relationship with him. In this case it would not be because the new ideas presented to her were really convincing in themselves, but because for her *John* is "convincing". She would really believe in these opinions, but her belief would be tied to her feelings toward John, and were this relationship to change, this in itself would be sufficient to change her attitude toward student participation. Even if her relationship with John remained stable, the effect of his communication might *fade*, unless his arguments in themselves are congruent with other ideas and values she holds. Kelman says, ". . . opinions adopted through identification . . . remain tied to the external source and dependent on social support. They are not integrated with the individual's value system, but rather tend to be isolated from the rest of his values—to remain encapsulated." [22]

compliance

identification

fading

internalization

Internalization results when the idea or attitude really becomes one's own, integrated into one's total mental structure, satisfying, rewarding and useful in itself. Kelman points out that when internalization is involved, the person who had adopted a recommended opinion because he found it both relevant and congruent, will modify the material to fit his own unique situation. He adds, "(C)ongruence with a person's value system does not necessarily imply logical consistency. Behavior would be congruent, if in some way or other, it fitted into the person's value system, if it seemed to belong there and be demanded by it." [23]

The three processes of compliance, identification and internalization are not mutually exclusive and would seldom occur

incentives   in a pure form. In all three forms, some sort of *incentive* is necessary in order for any kind of acceptance of a new idea. The incentives may be of two kinds. Certainly of major importance is the *quality of the reasons or arguments* presented in favor of the new idea or opinion. If these seem to the hearer reasonable or logical, they will appear more acceptable to him than previous contradictory arguments or opinions, and therefore he would be more comfortable accepting than rejecting them. The second kind of incentive involves *anticipated rewards or punishments*, and the hearer will naturally tend to accept the new idea if it seems to offer possible rewards, particularly if the old idea now presents itself to him as possibly carrying with it the danger of some sort of punishment, such as social disapproval.

The incentives for internalization are of both types, but the rewards and punishments become less tied to specific persons or groups and more part of the individual's own psychological structure. The internalized ideas become part of his own filter system ʼr set by which he perceives and accepts the world, and often have ·elationship to some part of his value system. They now affect ᵇavior.

FOR SOURCES AND FURTHER INFORMATION, CONSULT THE FOLLOWING WORKS:

1. McKellar, Peter, EXPERIENCE AND BEHAVIOUR, Baltimore: Penguin Books, 1968. Re McDougall's theory of 1908, see p. 241.
   see also: Hunt, J. McV., "Motivation Inherent in Information Processing and Action", in MOTIVATION AND SOCIAL INTERACTION: COGNITIVE DETERMINANTS, ed. O. J. Harvey, pp. 94, 62, N.Y.: Ronald Press, 1963.
2. Berelson, Bernard and Gary A. Steiner, HUMAN BEHAVIOR: AN INVENTORY OF SCIENTIFIC FINDINGS, p. 239, N.Y.: Harcourt Brace, 1964.
   see also: Borger, Robert and A. E. M. Seaborne, THE PSYCHOLOGY OF LEARNING, p. 48, Baltimore, Md.: Penguin Books, 1966.
3. Lindzey, Gardner, "The Assessment of Human Motives", in ASSESSMENT OF HUMAN MOTIVES, p. 23, N.Y.: Holt, Rinehart and Winston, 1958.
4. McKellar, Peter, EXPERIENCE AND BEHAVIOUR, p. 254-55.
5. Argyle, Michael, THE PSYCHOLOGY OF INTERPERSONAL BEHAVIOR, p. 14, Baltimore, Md.: Penguin Books, 1967.
6. Newcomb, Theodore M., Ralph H. Turner, and Philip E. Converse, SOCIAL PSYCHOLOGY, p. 153, N.Y.: Holt, Rinehart and Winston, 1965.
   see also: Berelson and Steiner, HUMAN BEHAVIOR, pp. 557-85.
7. Allport, G. W., HANDBOOK OF SOCIAL PSYCHOLOGY, ed. C. Murchison, p. 810 Worcester, Mass.: Clark University Press, 1935.
8. Krech, D. and R. S. Crutchfield, THEORY AND PROBLEMS OF SOCIAL PSYCHOLOGY, p. 152, N.Y.: McGraw-Hill, 1948.
9. Sarnoff, I., "Social Attitudes and the Resolution of Motivational Conflict", in ATTITUDES, eds. Marie Jahoda and Neil Warren, p. 279, Baltimore, Md.: Penguin Books, 1966.
10. Jahoda, Marie, and Neil Warren, ATTITUDES, p. 10.
11. Newcomb, *et al.,* SOCIAL PSYCHOLOGY, p. 102. NOTE: The term "valence" has been used by Lewin and others to designate the attracting or repelling force which a person or object has for an individual. Field theory uses the concept of valence, and would speak of the "valence assigned" to an object as its "value" for that individual. Many others do not use the term, but include the concept in "attitude content". Although the term is useful, particularly in field theory, and avoids occasional circumlocutions, we have avoided the complication of introducing yet another possibly ambiguous term. One of the difficulties in its use is that some writers use it for any stimulus object while others use it only for social objects, that is, groups or persons. See Lewin, K., PRINCIPLES OF TOPOLOGICAL PSYCHOLOGY, N.Y.: McGraw-Hill, 1936.
12. Newcomb *et al.,* SOCIAL PSYCHOLOGY, pp. 109-110.
    see also: Katz, D., "The Functional Approach to the Study of Attitudes", PUBLIC OPINION QUARTERLY, 1960, 24, pp. 163-204. Katz posits four kinds of functions which form the motivational basis for attitudes: (1) instrumental, adjustive, or utilitarian (social reward); (2) ego-defensive (defends self-concept); (3) value-expressive; (4) knowledge (predictability, consistency and stability in perception of world). These are interrelated, but in attempting to change attitudes, appeal must be made to the primary motivation.
13. Robinson, James Harvey, THE MIND IN THE MAKING, p. 42, N.Y.: Harper, 1921.
14. Hovland, Carl I., Irving L. Janis and Harold H. Kelley, COMMUNICATION AND PERSUASION, p. 283, New Haven: Yale University Press, 1953.
15. Fitzgerald, Donald and David P. Ausubel, "Cognitive vs. Affective Factors in the Retention of Controversial Material", in STUDIES IN EDUCATIONAL PSYCHOLOGY, ed. Raymond G. Kuhlen, pp. 423-28, Waltham, Mass.: Blaisdel Publishing Co., 1968.
16. Carroll, John B., "Words, Meanings and Concepts", STUDIES IN EDUCATIONAL PSYCHOLOGY, ed. Raymond G. Kuhlen, Waltham, Mass.: Blaisdel Publishing Co., 1968.
17. Newcomb, Theodore M., Ralph H. Turner, and Philip E. Converse, SOCIAL PSYCHOLOGY, pp. 125-36, N.Y.: Holt, Rinehart and Winston, 1965.
    see also: McGuire, Wm. J., THE SCIENCE OF HUMAN COMMUNICATION, ed. Wilbur Schramm, N.Y.: Basic Books, Inc., 1963. McGuire sees the individual's belief system as made up of interrelated propositions, some of which are illogical due to wishful thinking. See p. 51.
18. Cooper, Joseph B. and James L. McGaugh, INTEGRATING PRINCIPLES OF SOCIAL PSYCHOLOGY, p. 244, Cambridge, Mass.: Schenkman Publishing Co., 1963.
19. Allport, G. W., P. E. Vernon, and G. Lindzey, STUDY OF VALUES, Boston: Houghton Mifflin, 1951.

20. Festinger, Leon, "The Theory of Cognitive Dissonance", THE SCIENCE OF HUMAN COMMUNICATION, ed. Wilbur Schramm, pp. 18-19, N.Y.: Basic Books, Inc., 1963.
   see also: Festinger, Leon, A THEORY OF COGNITIVE DISSONANCE, N.Y.: Harper and Row, 1957.
21. Kelman, Herbert C., "Three Processes of Social Influence", ATTITUDES, eds. Marie Jahoda and Neil Warren, Baltimore, Md.: Penguin Books, 1966.
   NOTE 1: The meaning of "identification" in this section is not as strong as that of Freud, who uses it to indicate a more permanent acquisition of attitudes or behavior. Also, for Freud, identification could be with ideas, prohibitions, inanimate objects, for instance, as well as with people.
   NOTE 2: Borger and Seaborne state: "A motivated condition represents a particular sort of involvement of an organism with its environment, and in this sense reinforcements, being stimuli which are prominent in this involvement, have been referred to as 'significant' events. . . . The relationships that existed between other events, including responses . . . could, by being paired with reinforcement, come to be internalized." Borger, Robert and A. E. M. Seaborne, THE PSYCHOLOGY OF LEARNING, p. 64, Baltimore, Md.: Penguin Books, 1966.
22. Kelman, Herbert C., ATTITUDES, p. 155.
23. Kelman, Herbert C., ATTITUDES, p. 156.
24. *see also:* Hovland, Carl I., Janis and Kelley, COMMUNICATION AND PERSUASION, pp. 254-59; Borger, Robert and Seaborne, THE PSYCHOLOGY OF LEARNING.

3.

Group Behavior and Dynamics

OVERVIEW

The behavior and dynamics of a group include the participation and communication of the group members as they interact and affect one another in the situation which includes group emotion, group norms and goals, and the degree of cohesiveness of the group. Although participation is a form of interaction, these two together do not insure communication. Emotion can be a force for good or ill. It is difficult to think of participation and emotion separately, but in discussing the former, we include those aspects of emotion which are overt and directly involved in the problem-solving aspects of the discussion. In considering emotion, we will be more concerned with the emotions below the surface in the group, those not explicitly and directly stated during the interaction. The norms developed by the group operate as its standards for behavior, but also affect the group member when he is not present in the group. The interaction of these group properties or characteristics is a dynamic one in which each element affects and is affected by others.

PARTICIPATION: WHO, TO WHOM AND WHAT FOR?

Every time an individual makes a contribution to the discussion he is influenced, consciously or unconsciously, by his definition of the situation.[1] This includes the nature of his relationship to and with the group, his role or roles and status in the group, his estimate of the group opinion, plus that of any subgroup to which he belongs. In addition, he brings with him his own personality, and the cross-pressures of all his reference groups, attitudes and motivations.

The group member's definition of the situation may or may not be a very accurate one; what he actually says and how he says it may or may not be an accurate reflection of how he really thinks and feels; but an outside observer, watching and listening to his statement, would be able to classify or categorize it in relation to the problem-solving nature of the discussion, though he could not be sure of its interpretation or its ultimate effect on the various members of the group.

In 1950 one such observer, Robert F. Bales, endeavoring to find ways of measuring and studying the interaction of small problem-solving groups, devised a set of categories of observable individual contributions to discussions.[2] Bales was not trying to evaluate the fund of information going into the discussion, the quality of the ideas produced, or their value to the members, nor was he attempting to measure in any way the unexpressed emotions and thoughts of the speakers or listeners, but simply to characterize the actual statements themselves. Bales speaks of (a) problems of orientation; (b) problems of evaluation; and (c) problems of control. Under the last he lists, "asks for . . . and gives suggestions, directions (possible ways of action), implying autonomy for others". His classification has been used by many students of the subject.

As you examine the accompanying chart you will note that discussion usually starts with numbers 6 and 7 in the orientation or "a" area. These two categories consist of questions and responses which attempt to provide information, to understand the meaning of the information provided, and to establish the nature of the problem. Numbers 5 and 8 in the evaluation area further develop understanding through concretizing and attempts at balance and consistency. Numbers 4 and 9 in the control area continue the process of concretizing and balance and explore the possibilities of individual response, bringing the matter to the point of decision-making. With 3 and 10 we have moved over the line into the social-emotional area in Bales' terms. He sees the behaviors in the "a", "b" and "c" sections as possible of accomplishment in a fairly impersonal, unemotional, perhaps academic fashion. At no stage in these three areas would it be imperative that the group member take a public stand, revealing himself and his personal decision. With numbers 3 and 10, however, emotional factors will usually come strongly into play, as it is necessary to make a decision, presumably one which will carry with it some obligation to act. Of course, there may be many "little 3's" during the course of a discussion as members indicate agreement or disagreement with ideas, evaluations and minor proposals, and the emotional charge here may be unnoticeable. The outermost categories, "e-2" and "e-11", tension management, and "f-1" and "f-12", integration, are social-emotional contributions which can occur at any time during the discussion.

As we stated in talking of the phases of discussion, the progress is not through a rigid sequence, but the chart is valuable in focusing on the actual contributions which move the group through these phases, or fail to move, as the case may be. Sometimes it is helpful in thinking of individual participants and the sorts of behavior they usually demonstrate, both from the point of view of the task itself and of interpersonal relations in the group. Furthermore, as Bales suggests, the functions or behaviors in the task area are dynamically related to those in the social-emotional area: attempts to carry through the task tend to pull the group apart, making it necessary for social-emotional work to be done to glue it together again. Also work done in the social-emotional area weakens the group's efficiency for performing the task, making renewed stress on task activities necessary. Obviously, the "positive reactions" tend to help a group or further the discussion, while those in the "negative reactions" sector seem to slow down progress. However, it is equally obvious that this is an oversimplification, both because of the relation between the social-emotional area and because a group in constant agreement is either not thinking or not feeling, and thus not getting anywhere.

Forms of various kinds can be designed to provide for charting during a discussion, using the categories as here described. The purpose of the charting dictates to some extent the form of the chart. The most complete charts are chronological, and indicate the specific individual making each contribution, and the individual or group to whom it is made. Observers working with such forms can provide a group with feedback valuable in diagnosing group problems, role analysis, and the isolation of specific factors of interest.

Participation pattern. Another aspect of overt action is the participation pattern. In many discussion groups some members are silent, some speak a good deal, and others speak occasionally. Many things affect the participation pattern: characteristics of the individual members; relationships among members; the character

why is
participation
often unbalanced?

30

BALES' SET OF OBSERVATION CATEGORIES

SOCIAL-EMOTIONAL AREA:

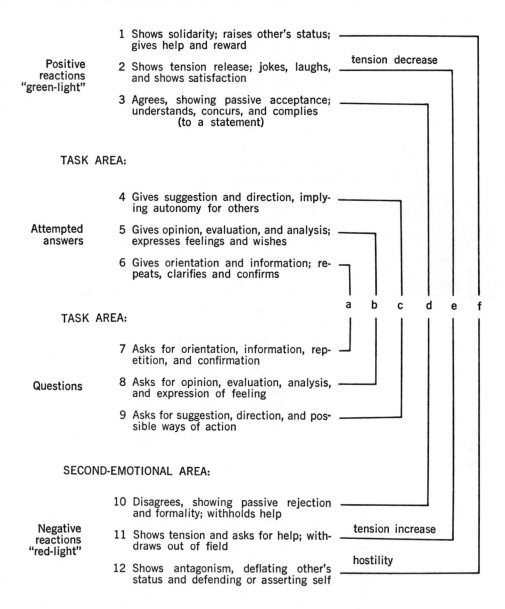

Positive
reactions
"green-light"

1 Shows solidarity; raises other's status; gives help and reward

2 Shows tension release; jokes, laughs, and shows satisfaction

3 Agrees, showing passive acceptance; understands, concurs, and complies
(to a statement)

tension decrease

TASK AREA:

Attempted
answers

4 Gives suggestion and direction, implying autonomy for others

5 Gives opinion, evaluation, and analysis; expresses feelings and wishes

6 Gives orientation and information; repeats, clarifies and confirms

a b c d e f

TASK AREA:

Questions

7 Asks for orientation, information, repetition, and confirmation

8 Asks for opinion, evaluation, analysis, and expression of feeling

9 Asks for suggestion, direction, and possible ways of action

SECOND-EMOTIONAL AREA:

Negative
reactions
"red-light"

10 Disagrees, showing passive rejection and formality; withholds help

11 Shows tension and asks for help; withdraws out of field

12 Shows antagonism, deflating other's status and defending or asserting self

tension increase

hostility

LEGEND: a. Problems of orientation (communication)
         b. Problems of evaluation
         c. Problems of control
         d. Problems of decision
         e. Problems of tension-management
         f. Problems of integration

Adapted with permission from Robert F. Bales, "A Set of Categories for the Analysis of Small Group Interaction," AMERICAN SOCIOLOGICAL REVIEW (1950), XV: 257–263.

and quality of the communication level; the nature of the leadership; and the size of the group. Elsewhere we will discuss ways in which more balanced participation may be achieved, but at this time we will look at some of the reasons why it is often unbalanced.

Haiman[4] lists eighteen reasons why group members do not participate in proportion to their ability to do so, and one leadership class of teachers, in ten minutes, came up with nineteen "causes of apathy"—only *one* of the possible reasons for non-participation. Haiman's list includes such things as "lack of skill in verbalizing ideas", personal habits of shyness or of detached observation, or a desire for deeper reflection on ideas before speaking about them.

Possible Causes of Apathy
1. Dominance of an individual speaker
2. Fear of expressing contrary opinion
3. Lack of interest in topic (material is not relevant or has been "talked out")
4. Lack of clarity as to role of "Leader" vs. "teacher"
5. Participant feels threatened by topic
6. Extremes of inferiority and superiority (complexes)
7. Tiredness on part of individual, or other physical problem
8. Feel material is "just an assignment"
9. Lack of encouragement to individual
10. Time element—too long or too short
11. Insufficient preparation before discussion
12. Lack of established and understood goals
13. Ongoing dialogue between two persons
14. In some situations, discussion is not "fashionable"
15. Poor leadership—Leader domination, poor questions, etc.
16. Size of group
17. Seating arrangement, time of day, other physical environmental difficulties
18. Artificiality (forced participation)
19. Presence of "experts" in the group

Many discussion groups have developed an unbalanced participation pattern because of their past history—they are used to a good deal of non-participation, believe they prefer it that way, and are highly resistant to change. Many groups actually have a built-in disbelief in the value of discussion, preferring the lecture method. Some members will tell the Leader at the beginning of a session, "I just come to listen, so don't call on me." Other members of the group will sometimes "protect" such a member, saying, "Mary doesn't like to talk—we understand, and don't mind it!" A poorly led group may develop a pattern in which one or two people carry on a dialogue with the Leader, and the rest of the group is a passive audience which occasionally expresses approval or disapproval of statements made by the "speakers".

An equally long list might give us only some of the reasons why people overparticipate, many of which would be the converse of the above and others, oddly enough, would be the same reasons. Some people overparticipate in a desire to help the Leader or the group, or to cover up for a silent friend. Others have a psychological need to dominate the situation, to gain recognition or to express their hostility. People who are very articulate and who think quickly on their feet are often oblivious of the length and number of their contributions, and people in the "talking professions", such as lawyers, salesmen and teachers, do a good deal of contributing simply through habit.

who to whom

Another characteristic of the participation pattern is "who talks to whom". Supposedly, in small group discussion, all contributions are made to all members of the group, but if you observe an ongoing discussion you will frequently find some people talking primarily to each other, ignoring the rest of the group. In an untrained group this is sometimes the situation, and group members may be quite unaware of it. A number of things contribute to this.

status

As might be expected, people who talk the most are talked *to* the most.[5] Another factor affecting the pattern is the way group members rank one another in their own minds. Some people are given a higher status than others, and it has been found that communications are more likely to be directed from equal to equal and from the higher-ranking members to the lower-ranking than from the lower-ranking to the higher-ranking. When the emphasis is on the task of the discussion, it will be found that there will be more interchange with high-ranking people, and when the interaction in the group shifts to the social-emotional area, there will be more interchanges among equals, both high- and low-ranking.[6]

The accompanying chart shows two discussions in progress, one dominated by the Leader, the other by one of the group members:

friends and enemies

People who like each other tend to talk to each other more, and people who know one another outside the group, even if they are not good friends, will tend to talk to one another more than each would talk to a stranger in the group. People who are "tuned

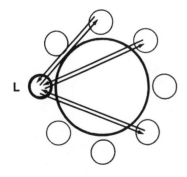

Leader dominated pattern

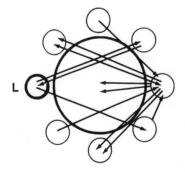

Single participant dominated pattern

DIAGRAMS OF UNBALANCED PARTICIPATION PATTERNS

cultural or
language
subgroups

shifting
participation in
disagreements

group size

in" on one another's "communication line" will tend to talk to one another, sometimes ignoring the group by using special language, slang, or concepts common to them, but not to other group members.

Disagreement in a group often will not only raise the total number of statements made, but in some cases can change the participation pattern directionally. For instance, it has been found that in situations of disagreement in a group in which the members have little emotional attachment to one another, the members holding the majority opinion will tend to direct most of their remarks to those holding the minority opinion, so long as the majority believe they can win over the minority to their point of view. When the majority feels there is no longer any chance for this, their statements to the minority opinion holders drop off so sharply that they are practically ostracized. As group size is increased, the number of contributions from more active members increases and contributions from less active members decrease further. This will happen with or without disagreement, but is intensified in the larger group.[7]

COMMUNICATION

We have talked about participation patterns as though all interchanges are equal in communication value. This is obviously not the case. Messages miss their mark, are lost, ignored, garbled, distorted and misunderstood. One definition of communication is ". . . the process by which an individual (the communicator) transmits stimuli (usually verbal) to modify the behavior of other individuals (the audience)."[8] The communication question is often phrased as *"who* says *what* to *whom* with *what effect."* It is sometimes amplified to include the channel of communication, in which case it reads, "who says what to whom by *what means* with what

effect." The participation pattern is one means of examining "who to whom", but tells us little about "what" and "what effect".

interaction involves communication

When we think of interaction in a group we are thinking of forms of communication. In the broadest sense, "what" is being communicated in interaction involves the environment, the materials of the presentation, the spoken words of the members, and the non-verbal communication present in the group. Each comment made by a member includes two types of information: (1) about what the words stand for, and (2) about the speaker or sender of the message. The *sender*, the *information*, and the *receiver* form a *communication system*. What actually is communicated may be something quite other than that intended. The speaker consciously wants to convey a message to the hearer, and he may also unconsciously want to convey another or somewhat different message. It is quite possible that neither of these messages is received by the intended audience. Some sort of communication exchange may have occurred, but *distortion* has damaged the information.

elementary parts of communication

distortion

inferences or assessments

In order to send his message, the group member makes inferences or assessments about the thoughts, feelings and attitudes of the person or persons to whom he is sending his message. Some of these assessments are accurate and some are not. As we try to understand each other, we try to improve the accuracy of our assessments, and thereby to phrase our message in terms which will better convey our messages. In the pure sense of the word, "communication" cannot be said to occur unless the "meanings received are equivalent to those which the initiator(s) of the message intended." [9]

messages as symbols

The information carried by a message is in the form of symbols, just as the messages we are sending you in this book are sets of symbols. Man observes an object or a phenomenon and assigns a symbol to it. He then communicates with others about this object by means of this symbol. Lundberg, Schrag and Larsen [10] use the Biblical account from GEN. 2:19 to illustrate the process: "So from the soil Yahweh God fashioned all the wild beasts and all the birds of heaven. These he brought to the man to see what he would call them; each one was to bear the name the man would give it." This small story can be instructive in considering communication problems. Sometimes what the sender needs to do is spread out his collection of thoughts about an object as fully and clearly as he can, and then see what his intended receiver would "call it".

encoding

The symbols most commonly used, of course, are words, but gestures and facial expressions are symbols also. The sender of the message translates or *encodes* his psychological states—his ideas, thoughts, feelings, etc.—into symbols. We all know from experience that this encoding may be unsuccessful. When we read something we ourselves have written, we sometimes realize it fails to convey our thoughts. How much more difficult it is for someone else to understand it. Accuracy in encoding is apparently as difficult as accuracy in *decoding*. Unless the *symbol-systems* of the sender and the receiver are the same, the communication is not apt to be suc-

decoding

shared
symbol-systems

receiver

decrease in shared
information

shared
information

feedback

direct feedback

cessful, regardless of other factors. The sharing of symbol-systems is a matter of degree; no two people have absolutely identical symbol-systems.

The receiver is not simply a passive recipient, but is an active part of this system; he may have been totally unaware of the sender, or he may be conscious that a message has been sent, but has not heard or seen it for various reasons, or he may have heard the words or seen the signal or gesture, but not understood the meaning intended. In addition, his own attitudes about either the information sent or the sender will influence the effect of the message on the receiver. For one reason or another he may inaccurately interpret or *decode* the message. After a message has been sent, there actually may be less shared information on the part of those involved in this transaction. A reduction in shared information is the result of the reception of misleading information, regardless of the intent of the sender.[11]

Information is "shared" when both parties understand the information contained in the message, understand it in the same way, and are both aware of this mutual understanding. This happens less often than we may think. Presumably, shared information is a goal of discussion,[12] and one of the ways of increasing it is *feedback*.

Feedback may be verbal or non-verbal, but it consists of another *message about the previous message*, this time sent by the original receiver to the original sender. This feedback might be a verbal or a non-verbal response such as a nod, or an action.

The accompanying diagram illustrates the sending of a single message and a single direct feedback act.

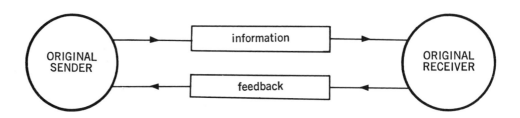

If the original sender listens to or observes carefully this *direct feedback* from the receiver he may be able to tell whether his original message was accurately received. If the first message sent was, "Please close the window", the feedback might consist in the original receiver closing the window. This would indicate good reception. If, however, the original message was, "Please close the window in the front of the room", and the receiver closed the window in the *back* of the room, the original sender may judge from this feedback that the message was probably distorted, possibly by faulty decoding on the part of the receiver.

We are all familiar with feedback in the operation of the thermostat on our heating systems. The thermostat makes our heating system a goal-seeking machine, or a servomechanism. The goal is a desired temperature for which the thermostat is set. The difference between the actual temperature and the goal temperature is made to affect the system so as to reduce this difference.

cybernetics
Norbert Wiener reminds us that we do not pay enough attention to these signals in our society, or do not plan adequately for them: "(The) control of a machine on the basis of its *actual* performance rather than its *expected* performance is known as *feedback*. . . . In (the animal and the machine), their *performed* action on the outer world, and not merely their *intended* action, is reported back to the central regulatory apparatus. This complex of behavior is ignored by the average man. . . . (U)ntil recently (the sociologist) has tended to overlook the extent to which (communications in society) are the cement which binds its fabric together." [13]

There is an increasing tendency for those working in several disciplines, including sociology, communications and education, to use the concepts of cybernetics in trying to think through the problems, theories and technology of their fields. Borger and Seaborne, after discussing the problems encountered in the stimulus-response theories of learning, state that cybernetics, ". . . which is concerned explicitly with problems of control in animals and machines, seems likely to provide a language which is more suitable for the analysis of human and animal behavior." [14]

The idea of acting, checking on the actual results of the action, and modifying future actions on the basis of what did happen, rather than what we intended, hardly seems new or startling. However, in the specific, planned fashion encouraged by cybernetics, there has been far too little of this. Also, when attempts were made, such as tests for achievement or the quiz or recitation method in the classroom, inadequate communication added to the problems of appropriate timing have made these means less helpful than anticipated. In the discussion situation, little attempt was made to analyze what was actually happening, and therefore planning was often done on the basis of inadequate information and unrealistic expectations. It is only recently that serious efforts have been made to find out what happens in specific attempts at communication. The discussion process will continue to benefit from these new avenues of investigation.

information
Communication is not really a success unless there is *new information* being sent. If you dial a number and get a recording which says, "I'm sorry, the number you have called is not in service", this is "new" information. But if you continue to listen, and the record continues to repeat itself, communication, in a real sense, has stopped. Attneave gives the following definition of information: "A statement or an observation is informative if it tells us something that we did not already know. If I hear someone say, 'Eskimos live in the far North, where it is cold', my modest store of information

about Eskimos is not increased. The statement may, however, give me some information about the person who makes it, or about the person to whom it is addressed. In any case, we can gain information only about matters in which we are to some degree ignorant, or uncertain: indeed, information may be defined as that which removes or reduces uncertainty." [15] We hasten to add, however, that few people would say that "I love you", repeated more than once, should be called a failure in communication!

Considering the difficulties involved, which we have just begun to touch on, it would seem that to communicate is just too difficult. However, Aristotle said, "A social instinct is implanted in all men by nature. . . . Nature, as we often say, makes nothing in vain, and man is the only animal whom she has endowed with the gift of speech." [16] And then there was Adam, naming the animals, and this while he still had only God to talk to! Increasing heterogeneity has probably made communication more difficult for us than it was for members of these earlier societies, but we are not likely to give up trying. As James W. Carey tells us, ". . . the act of communication, as O'Neil and Camus among other modern artists remind us, is the only source of joy and tragedy humans have. One can all too easily forget that the word 'communication' shares its roots with 'communion' and 'community', and it is the attempt to establish this communion that theories of communication, vulgar as they are in present form, attempt to capture." [17]

. . . and community

definition of the communication situation

We spoke earlier of the definition of the situation, and we can now refine some aspects of that definition. The *referent* is the subject of the message—whatever is being called to the receiver's attention. The following list of four *assessments* which the sender makes *about the receiver* of his message is based on that of Newcomb, Turner and Converse: [18]

1. What is the state of the receiver's information about the referent? Does he have more, less, or different information?
2. Does he have any positive or negative emotional feelings about the referent? Does he consider the referent to have desirable or undesirable properties? What is his attitude toward the referent?

3. How sound is his judgment apt to be in regard to the referent? Is he competent to make judgments about it?
4. How does the receiver feel about me, personally?

One of the factors contributing to the *level of communication* is the group climate. Others are the availability of information, communication skills, physical arrangements, group size, norms and procedures, group goals and group emotion, and all of these interact among themselves to create other effects. The level of communication is one of the products which demonstrates the process character of group discussions. The many factors involved in the dynamics of the group come into play, act upon one another, operate in a spiral or cyclical fashion and affect the communication level. In turn, the communication level acts upon some of these same factors, as well as affecting the productivity and effectiveness of the group. For instance, if some members of the group have a good deal more information available to them than other members, it might originally result in increased communication, but as the group members become more aware of this discrepancy of available information, they may become dissatisfied, and this dissatisfaction will adversely affect the group climate, lowering the communication level.

factors affecting communication level

GROUP EMOTION

In Chapter 2 we talked about the desires, wishes and feelings that individuals bring with them to the group and that affect their behavior in the group. It is obvious that the emotions of individual participants will sometimes be in opposition because of this, and that at no time will they melt together to become one emotion, or one "person" with exactly similar feelings toward every object. In reaction to an earlier tendency to lump members of a group together in an undifferentiated mass, some social psychologists spoke of the "group fallacy", negating, for instance, the notion that a group can have a "mind". In 1924 Floyd H. Allport wrote, "All theories which partake of the group fallacy have the unfortunate consequence of directing attention from the true locus of cause and effect, namely, the behavioral mechanism of the individual." Further, "there is no psychology of groups which is not essentially and entirely a psychology of individuals." [19]

the "group fallacy"

However, most students of groups today grant the reality of group phenomena. They recognize the necessity of studying the interplay of emotional forces which result in a complex and constantly shifting pattern, to which they give the name *group emotion*. It is quite true that all the emotions present in a group reside in the individuals making up that group, but the term refers to the fact that many of the emotions present result from interaction among the members and from a "group event" of some sort. The entrance of a newcomer into a closely knit group, the group's success in solving a difficult problem, can be seen by an observer as

. . . and group events

focusing the emotion of group members in such a fashion that the best way to describe the situation is in terms of a group emotion.

. . . and behavioral roles

An individual in the group can cast himself or be cast by the group in a particular *behavioral role,* so that the group has an emotional reaction toward him as "the person everyone loves", "the clown", or, by whatever term, "the scapegoat". Group feeling tends to polarize around the assigned role, and hence the person of the Leader rather quickly—seldom is a group emotionally unaware of its Leader. Individuals have varying personal emotional reactions

. . . and the Leader

to the Leader, but there is usually a group feeling toward him as well, which is intensified in any crisis situation. Group feeling toward him depends on many things, such as his personality, the group's history and its experiences with him, their degree of dependency on him, and its own mental picture or model of what a Leader should be.

A full range of emotions both negative and positive may be reflected in one way or another at various times in the group's life. T. M. Mills gives the following as elements of group emotion:

"1. the needs and drives which serve in the first place as causes of group formation;

2. feelings of satisfaction or frustration resulting from actual group experiences;

3. interpersonal attachments and animosities;

4. feelings of attachment to, or alienation from, the group as a whole." [20]

difficulties of assessing group emotion

Despite the fact that at some moments a particular group emotion seems readily identifiable, an adequate assessment is extremely difficult, since the greater part of group feeling is below the surface, appearing in naked form on rare occasions. Much detailed research has been done with sophisticated techniques, and yet that portion of emotion which appears above the surface in a group's activities is not always easy to interpret, and the larger body below is almost impossible to ascertain. Mills says, "In fact, few persons (if any) have been able both to trace the course of changes in group emotion in a given group, and clearly tell others how it is done." [21]

Despite difficulties of interpretation, the Leader at least should be aware of the existence of group emotion, and try to keep a light finger upon the pulse of his group. Group emotion has an affect on the capabilities and growth of a group, and some effort must be made to understand and sometimes to guide group emotion.

NORMS

Group norms result from the interaction of group members. The simplest definition of a norm is the shared acceptance of a value, an attitude, a standard or a rule. The interaction operating to initiate a rule may be as simple a step as the Leader asking the members of the group to be seated, and the group members then sitting down. The norms that may result from this simple interaction could include (1) the Leader is accepted as one who makes recommendations that the rest of the group will follow; (2) we sit down at our meetings; (3) we do things together, at the same time. Other norms may result from the *way* in which the Leader asked the members to be seated. If it were given as a command, and accepted by the group as such, this establishes a slightly different kind of acceptance by the group than "1" above; it becomes, "the Leader is the one we obey".

shared attitudes

The group, by the very fact that it has gathered, also has at least one other norm—they share a favorable attitude toward the reason for the meeting. *Shared attitudes* are those on which two or more people agree, and on which they have in some way communicated their agreement. Their presence at the meeting is a communication—they now know they share this favorable attitude toward this meeting. It is very likely that they are in agreement, are *consensual*, in respect to many other attitudes, but until they know more about one another they cannot be said to have other shared attitudes. Group norms come into existence through shared attitudes—certain things will be considered good, bad, appropriate, inappropriate, useful or not useful. Whether or not the group is aware of them, these norms will serve as their *rules*.

. . . or consensuality

. . . as rules formalized

Some of these rules may become *formalized*, and may even be written down in the form of procedures, or a constitution or by-laws. As long as these rules are accepted by the group and followed by them, they may properly be called norms. Rules formalized by some process, but to which the group pays no attention, are *not* norms. A group may sometimes feel that it would be wise for them to follow certain procedures at their meetings, and may even put them down on paper and circularize them among the membership, and yet really follow other norms, not formalized, which are their real rules. As a matter of fact, writing down the rules may indicate the group has doubts as to whether it really can or will follow them. Formalizing of rules indicates that there are some sort of sanctions attached which will be invoked. These sanctions may be no more than the group's approval or disapproval of the action; they are sanctions nonetheless. When sanctions are not invoked when a rule is broken, that rule does not constitute a group norm, at least in an unmodified form.

not formalized

There may be many norms, quite strictly followed by the group, which no one has ever mentioned and which group members would never think of if you asked them, "What are your rules?" Members of informal groups, when asked such a question, may often say, "We don't have any." However, all groups have norms, even if that norm could only be characterized as anarchy. Group members develop and accept norms because it is more comfortable to do so. Norms enable them to know what is expected of them, what to expect of others, and are helpful in accomplishing goals. It takes time to develop some of these norms, and during this stage of uncertainty about norms a group is unable to accomplish very much in the task area. The individual members are apt to be a bit tense, and their minds distracted from the task, by the need to find out "how I should behave".[22]

bad habits

Norms are supposedly established for the protection of the members, and to assist them in attaining their individual and group goals, but sometimes group norms develop which operate against these results—groups can develop bad habits which operate as norms. Sometimes members simply fail to establish certain necessary norms, or find that there are subgroups with differing norms present in the total group. Norms may serve the individual needs of one or two members, and fail to serve the rest of the group or the group needs.

development of norms as early goal

One of the first goals of any group is the development of useful and suitable norms, though a group does not always go about this task consciously. During the first meeting of your group there probably was some uncertainty about such things as "being called on" versus "speaking up whenever we want to". By now you have probably established some norms of participation, including dealing with the too-talkative and too-silent members. Even if this norm eventually becomes "a few members talk all the time and a few never talk", this would be your group norm for the participation pattern. Other norms may deal with such matters as "What do we do when a member arrives late and we are in the middle of our discussion?", and "Do we encourage or discourage highly personal revelations in our meetings?" Norms also cover how much the group expects the Leader to be responsible for discipline, and how much of this responsibility is assumed by the group as a whole. As group members follow a norm and see other members follow it, the norm

internalized norms

becomes *internalized* for them and thus *self-enforcing*. Internalized norms are difficult to change. Regardless of the original source of the internalized norms, and often regardless of their actual usefulness to the group, they exert considerable power over group members, and are therefore of importance both in the group itself and in the lives of the individual members.

group normativeness

A group's *normativeness* refers to this power of all the norms. A norm has two dimensions: (1) latitude—how much variation in conformity the group tolerates; (2) acceptability—the degree of approval or disapproval the group manifests in connection with conformity and non-conformity. For instance, if "not interrupting" is a group norm, latitude refers to such questions as "just what is considered interrupting?", "does it apply equally to all members?", "is everyone supposed to allow a silence after each contribution to be sure the speaker is finished?" Acceptability refers to the sanctions employed by the group: is an interrupter punished by being excluded by the group for a time? does he receive verbal criticism? cross looks? an averted gaze? is it simply ignored? is active approval manifested toward *non*-interrupters? As in child-rearing, high normativeness is found in groups in which the rules are fairly simple, clear and definite, and sanctions are consistently applied.

Many norms of discussion groups involve values and attitudes toward others as fellow human beings, particularly if the content of their discussions centers around such topics. Coming into the group with the thought of learning more about some such subject matter, members are already consensual in this general attitude, and develop and strengthen attitudes concerned with how life should be lived within the group situation. Since the tendency is for these norms to be internalized, the power of the group norms will continue to operate in many ways outside the group situation.

The degree to which these norms affect the perception, understanding, evaluation, decision-making and action of a member is dependent in part on the group's salience. *Salience* refers to the force or influence of a particular group upon an individual as it affects his conformity with the norms of that group. Salience is a characteristic which functions within the individual, though externally induced, and is usually only a consideration when he is actually apart from the group. Some aspects of a group may be more salient for an individual than others. We usually use the term to cover that degree of conscious or unconscious awareness of the group and its norms which is present to an individual in a situation in which those norms might be challenged in some way by opposing norms or ideas. For an individual who feels little attachment to a group, the group's salience for him would be low, regardless of

the presence of salient *cues* in the environment; and conversely, in the member for whom the group is important, the group's norms will more often be highly salient. Salience depends in part on cues in the environment—things which in some way remind him of the group, and the "reminding" need not always occur on a conscious level.

If a group member is exposed to strong recommendations countermanding group norms in a situation of low salience, his attitudes may veer away from the group norms to some extent. When group salience increases, in the same or a different situation, his attitudes most probably will turn back toward those he had in common with the group. As a matter of fact, it is sometimes the case that upon his return to his original, group-supported attitude, there will actually be a strengthening of this original attitude, possibly as a result of his feeling of concern or guilt at "betraying the group", i.e., operating in opposition to its norms. However, if a temporary attitude change has occurred, some residual elements of this opposing or contrary attitude are apt to be present after the increase in salience.

If, on the other hand, the group member receives conflicting information in a situation of high group salience, there is less likelihood of a change in attitude, but if there is a change, it is apt to be more lasting than in the previously described situation of low salience.[23]

A group's salience for any individual will naturally depend in part on his *valuation of group membership*. Among all the many groups of which any individual is a member, he values his mem-

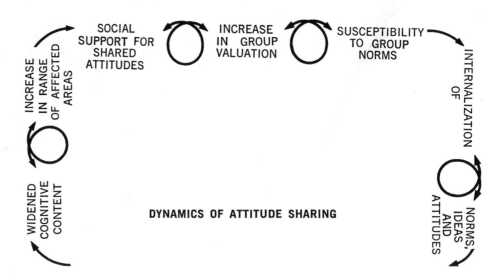

SOCIAL SUPPORT FOR SHARED ATTITUDES — INCREASE IN GROUP VALUATION — SUSCEPTIBILITY TO GROUP NORMS — INTERNALIZATION OF — INCREASE IN RANGE OF AFFECTED AREAS — WIDENED COGNITIVE CONTENT — NORMS, IDEAS AND ATTITUDES

DYNAMICS OF ATTITUDE SHARING

bership in some more than in others. In addition, it is quite possible for an individual to value a group of which he is not actually a member, but of which he aspires toward membership. He may emulate members of such groups and seek to make their values and norms his own. In speaking of attitudes we mentioned that some are more central to an individual than others, and hence more important to him. Salience may be thought of as a short-term centrality, and conversely, centrality may be thought of as a long-term, durable salience.

dynamics of attitude sharing

The dynamics of the development of shared attitudes include the assimilation of information and the discussion of feelings and attitudes related to ideas and opinions. This process goes through a number of stages. (See diagram.) (1) The cognitive content of such attitudes is increased or widened through a greater understanding of reasons supporting these attitudes. (2) The range of areas affected by these attitudes is increased. (3) Group members provide mutual social support for shared attitudes. (4) There is an increase in the group's attractiveness for the individual, i.e., an increase in his valuation of membership. (5) As group valuation increases, the individual becomes more susceptible to influence by other members of the group, and more resistant to influences contrary to group norms. (6) The foregoing factors lead to internalization of norms. According to at least one researcher, the relationship described in "5" is the only kind which will produce internalization.[24]
Members present in groups, but not genuinely attracted to them, may well give public acceptance to or compliance with the group's norms, but not private acceptance, or internalization.

dynamics of group attraction

In speaking of the individual in the group in Chapter 2, we said one of the reasons people enter groups is a desire to "maximize their shared values". This dynamic process of sharing attitudes and values is also a cyclical or spiraling process, in which sharing of attitudes leads to attractiveness of the group for the members, which in turn leads to a maximizing of their values, and increasing attractiveness, and so on.[25]

GROUP GOALS AND GROUP COHESIVENESS

cohesiveness

Group *cohesiveness* refers to that characteristic of groups whose members feel some emotional attachment to one another, and to the group, and demonstrate a feeling of "groupiness", a "we-feeling", and a certain solidarity. In a cohesive group the members work cooperatively; they can be characterized as having good morale. These factors affect the productivity of a group. The cohesive group understands and accepts its group goals, operates in a climate of trust and friendliness, is protective of its members, and is productive. As attitude sharing and attractiveness operate in a cyclical fashion within a group, so also do conformity to norms and cohesiveness.

individual goals and group effectiveness

The individual brings to the group his personal goals. There must be some satisfaction of these goals for him, or he will not contribute to the effectiveness of the group. On the other hand, if he constantly seeks his personal goals, without regard for the goals of the other members, he is the only one who will benefit, and even he will miss out on some of the benefits which the group might provide him. Both he and the group will be more effective and better satisfied if he sees his own goals as being advanced by the group goals. In recognizing the failure of the group's effectiveness and productivity, he himself will feel frustration. Though his own individual goals may to some extent be achieved, his stake as a part of the group will cause him dissatisfaction. Some suppression of behavior oriented toward individual goal achievement will be necessary. We may think of the individual's goals and the group goals as two overlapping circles. There will, of course, be some discrepancy, but the greater the degree of overlap the more productive and satisfying the group will be for the individual. It is in those areas where there is no overlap that conflict and group instability will occur.[26]

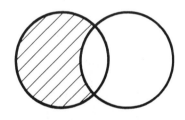

group goals

The group's goals, as seen by its members, the group's ability to satisfy the individual goals of its members, and the group's ability to achieve its goals are all factors affecting cohesiveness. The setting and achieving of successive goals or sets of goals is important in producing the cohesive group. Goals set, and not achieved, result in group frustration, loss of cohesiveness and member dissatisfaction. Here, too, is visible that dynamic interaction of group properties as they affect one another and together affect group effectiveness.

SHARING ATTITUDES & VALUES → ATTRACTIVENESS INCREASED → MAXIMIZING OF VALUES → ATTRACTIVENESS INCREASED

DYNAMICS OF GROUP ATTRACTION

FOR SOURCES AND FURTHER INFORMATION, CONSULT THE FOLLOWING WORKS:

1. Thomas, William I., and Florian Znaniecki, "The Definition of the Situation", READINGS IN SOCIAL PSYCHOLOGY, eds. Theodore M. Newcomb and Eugene L. Harley, et al., pp. 76-77, N.Y.: Henry Holt and Co., 1947. NOTE: Thomas' well-known statement is "situations defined as real are real in their consequences". Kurt Lewin's Field Theory also emphasizes the individual's perception of the events he experiences.

2. Bales, Robert F., "A Set of Categories for the Analysis of Small Group Interaction", AMERICAN SOCIOLOGICAL REVIEW, XV (1950), pp. 257-63. see also: Bales, Robert F. and Fred L. Strodtbeck, "Phases in Group Problem Solving", GROUP DYNAMICS: RESEARCH AND THEORY, eds. Dorwin Cartwright, and Alven Zander, pp. 389-98, N.Y.: Harper and Row, 1968; Bales, R. F., "How People Interact in Conferences", SCIENTIFIC AMERICAN, March, 1955, pp. 33ff.

3. Mills, Theodore M., THE SOCIOLOGY OF SMALL GROUPS, p. 31, Englewood Cliffs, N.J.: Prentice-Hall, Inc., 1967.

4. Haiman, Franklyn, GROUP LEADERSHIP AND DEMOCRATIC ACTION, Boston: Houghton Mifflin, 1951.

5. Bales, Robert F., Fred L. Strodtbeck and Theodore M. Mills, and Mary E. Roseborough, "Channels of Communication in Small Groups", AMERICAN SOCIOLOGICAL REVIEW, 16 (1951), p. 468.

6. Rieken, Henry W., and George C. Homans, "Psychological Aspects of Social Structure", HANDBOOK OF SOCIAL PSYCHOLOGY, ed. Gardner Lindzey, Vol. II, 786-832, Reading, Mass.: Addison-Wesley, 1954.

7. Festinger, Leon and John Thibaut, "Interpersonal Communication in Small Groups", JOURNAL ABNORMAL AND SOCIAL PSYCHOLOGY, 46, Jan., 1951, pp. 92-99. see also: Homans, G. C., SOCIAL BEHAVIOR, N.Y.: Harcourt, Brace & World, 1961.

8. Smith, B. L., H. D. Lasswell, and R. D. Casey, PROPOGANDA, COMMUNICATION AND PUBLIC OPINION, Princeton, N.J.: Princeton University Press, 1946. see also: Hovland, C. I., I. L. Janis, and H. H. Kelley, COMMUNICATION AND PERSUASION, London: Oxford University Press, 1953, p. 12.

9. Lundberg, George A., Clarence C. Schrag, and Otto N. Larsen, SOCIOLOGY, 3rd ed., p. 200, N.Y.: Harper and Row, 1963. NOTE: This is based on a definition by Joel Smith, R. C. Bealer and F. M. Sim in "Communication and the 'Consequences' of Communication", SOCIOLOGICAL INQUIRY, Winter, 1962, p. 12.

10. Lundberg, Schrag and Larsen, SOCIOLOGY, p. 29.

11. Brown, John, "Information Theory", NEW HORIZONS IN PSYCHOLOGY, ed. Brian M. Foss, p. 126, Baltimore, Md.: Penguin Books, 1966.

12. Newcomb, T. M., R. H. Turner and P. E. Converse, SOCIAL PSYCHOLOGY, N.Y.: Holt, 1965: ". . . equalization of information is not a goal of communication; it is only a relationship between the participants, usually not recognized by them, through which the motive satisfaction to which communication is instrumental can be attained" (p. 219).

13. Wiener, Norbert, THE HUMAN USE OF HUMAN BEINGS: CYBERNETICS AND SOCIETY, pp. 24, 27 (italics in original), Garden City, N.Y.: Doubleday Anchor, 1954.

14. Borger, Robert and A. E. M. Seaborne, THE PSYCHOLOGY OF LEARNING, p. 149, Baltimore, Md.: Penguin Books, 1966.

15. Attneave, F., APPLICATION OF INFORMATION THEORY TO PSYCHOLOGY, N.Y.: Holt, Rinehart and Winston, 1959.

16. Aristotle, POLITICS, Bk. I, 1, pp. 556, 557, in INTRODUCTION TO ARISTOTLE, ed. Richard McKeon, N.Y.: Modern Library, 1947.

17. Carey, James W., MCLUHAN: PRO AND CON, p. 305, ed. Raymond Rosenthal, Baltimore, Md.: Penguin Books, 1968.

18. Newcomb, Theodore M., R. H. Turner, and P. E. Converse, SOCIAL PSYCHOLOGY: THE STUDY OF HUMAN INTERACTION, pp. 200-1, N.Y.: Holt, 1965. see also: Gorden, R. L., "Attitude and the Definition of the Situation", AMERICAN SOCIOLOGICAL ASSOCIATION, V. 17, pp. 50-8 (1952), reprinted in ATTITUDES, eds. Marie Jahoda and Neil Warren, Baltimore, Md.: Penguin Books, 1966.

19. Allport, Floyd H., SOCIAL PSYCHOLOGY, pp. 9, 4, Boston: Houghton Mifflin, 1924.

20. Mills, Theodore M., THE SOCIOLOGY OF SMALL GROUPS, p. 71, Englewood Cliffs, N.J.: Prentice-Hall, Inc., 1967.

21. Mills, Theodore M., SOCIOLOGY OF SMALL GROUPS, p. 70.

22. Stogdill, Ralph M., INDIVIDUAL BEHAVIOR AND GROUP ACHIEVEMENT: A THEORY: THE EXPERIMENTAL EVIDENCE, pp. 207-11, Oxford University Press, 1959.

23. Hovland, C. I., I. L. Janis, and H. H. Kelley, COMMUNICATION AND PERSUASION, pp. 136-70, espec. 155-165, New Haven: Yale University Press, 1953. *see also:* Berelson, Bernard and Gary A. Steiner, HUMAN BEHAVIOR: AN INVENTORY OF SCIENTIFIC FINDINGS, p. 337, N.Y.: Harcourt Brace, 1964; Kelley, Harold H., and Thibaut, John W., "Experimental Studies of Group Problem Solving and Process", HANDBOOK OF SOCIAL PSYCHOLOGY, ed. Gardner Lindzey, Vol. II, p. 754, Reading, Mass.: Addison-Wesley, 1954.
see also, on "valuation of group membership", Lee, Alfred McClung, MULTIVALENT MAN, pp. 129-31, 140-41, N.Y.: George Braziller, 1966; Krech, D., R. S. Crutchfield and E. L. Ballachey, INDIVIDUAL IN SOCIETY, pp. 250-52, N.Y.: McGraw-Hill, 1962.
NOTE: Salience can also be defined as "the readiness of an individual to translate his previously expressed verbal attitude into overt action in relation to the attitude object", De Fleur, M. S. and F. R. Westie, "Verbal Attitudes and Overt Acts", in ATTITUDES, eds. Marie Jahoda and Neil Warren, p. 213, Baltimore, Md.: Penguin Books, 1966. This usage of the term is akin to that of some authors who use it almost as a synonym for "centrality" or "importance" of an attitude. For instance, Cooper and McGaugh speak of it as one of six measurable attributes of attitudes, and equate it with "importance", also indicating that it may, in truth, be inseparable from one of the other five attributes, namely "strength". Cooper, Joseph B., and James L. McGaugh, INTEGRATING PRINCIPLES OF SOCIAL PSYCHOLOGY, pp. 245-48, Cambridge, Mass.: Schenkman Publishing Co., 1963.

24. Festinger, L., "An Analysis of Compliant Behavior", GROUP RELATIONS AT THE CROSSROADS, eds., M. Sherif and M. O. Wilson, N.Y.: Harper, 1953.

25. Mills, Theodore M., SOCIOLOGY OF SMALL GROUPS, p. 79, Englewood Cliffs, N.J.: Prentice-Hall, Inc., 1967. *see also:* Newcomb, Theodore M., R. H. Turner, and P. E. Converse, SOCIAL PSYCHOLOGY: THE STUDY OF HUMAN INTERACTION, p. 227, N.Y.: Holt, 1965.

26. Issue Committee, THE LEADER'S DIGEST, Adult Education Association of the U.S.A., Vol. I, pp. 17-19, Chicago, Ill.: Adult Education Association, 1952-53.
NOTE: Concerning "group emotion", see also: Mills, Theodore M., SOCIOLOGY OF SMALL GROUPS, p. 71; Redl, F., "Group Emotion and Leadership", SMALL GROUPS: STUDIES IN SOCIAL INTERACTION, eds. Paul Hare, Edgar F. Borgatta and Robert F. Bales, pp. 79, 80, N.Y.: Knopf, 1955; Bion, W. R., EXPERIENCES IN GROUPS, AND OTHER PAPERS, pp. 29-34; 77-86, N.Y.: Basic Books, 1959.
NOTE: Concerning "functions" and "roles", some writers have subsumed the idea of "leadership functions" under the concept of "role". See, for instance, Benne, K. D. and P. Sheats, "Functional Roles of Group Members", JOURNAL OF SOCIAL ISSUES, 4, pp. 41-49 (1948); Bonner, Hubert, GROUP DYNAMICS: PRINCIPLES AND APPLICATIONS, N.Y.: Ronald Press Co., 1959.

4.

Group Organization and Democratic Leadership

OVERVIEW

Group operations are affected by the *type* of the group, the *leadership*, the degree of *autonomy* enjoyed or exercised by the group, by the *size* of the group and by its *formal and informal organization*. It is important for the learning group that it be small and that it have some degree of autonomy. The public structure of a learning-discussion group is fairly simple, but its private structure may be more complex. We advocate democratic leadership, as opposed to what is called autocratic or laissez faire types, and explain what we mean by *democratic leadership*.

48

GROUP CLASSIFICATION

Groups may be classified in many ways, and their public structure varies considerably with the type. The following outline is based on the *activities* of groups. Many groups incorporate a variety of activities at one time or another in their history. In thinking about groups, their operation, successes and failures, it is sometimes useful to examine them in the light of some such system of classification.

TABLE OF GROUP CLASSIFICATION

Circumstances:
   Closed (no audience)—sometimes called "Private"
   Public (audience)
   Mixed (sometimes meeting with, sometimes without an audience)
Communication:
   Advocacy (one-way)
   Discussion
Purpose:
   Decision-making, without implementation or direct action by
      members of group making decision
   Decision-making, with implementation of action by group
   Mixed—decision-making, enlightenment
   Enlightenment, cathartic
   Enlightenment, learning—may be "cerebral", "gut", or "mixed"
Membership:
   Peers (equality presumed)
   Authority and group (inequality presumed)—with or without
      active audience response
   Mixed

Groups may also be classified on the basis of the partisanship expressed by the Leader. Such a classification could be described on a continuum, ranging from the completely impartial parliamentary chairman through the impartial guide of a learning discussion group, and the relatively impartial moderator to the completely partial or partisan Leader found in some small committees, conferences and round tables.

AUTONOMY

Groups vary in their degree of autonomy. Some groups are quite autonomous, their goals, activities and their very existence being totally dependent on the choice of their members. Many groups have a lesser degree of autonomy, being dependent upon a parent or sponsoring organization. This parent organization may allow considerable independence, perhaps simply providing the physical

and parent organization

space at certain stipulated times, or may control the actions of the group through considerable direction, identifying the Leader, perhaps stipulating the existence of other members of the public organization, specifying the goals, methods, procedures and materials to be used. The parent organization or institution has, at least, overall goals which are supposedly reflected in some way in the more limited goals of its subgroups such as a discussion group. Sometimes the only external controls are (1) geographical—all coming from the same community, a form of control of membership, and (2) a previously stated purpose of "discussion", imposed prior to the first meeting, probably by the person or persons issuing the invitation and providing the physical arrangements. Those who come into the group are usually aware to some extent of the goals of the parent organization, and presumably are not directly opposed to them, so they may be said to share, at least to a limited extent, in these goals, and also in what they understand to be the goals of the discussion group.

and goals (margin)

Most learning-discussion groups are limited in autonomy, being an assigned part of a parent organization and having stated long-range goals, personnel and possibly some procedures. However, within its existing structure, even such groups demonstrate individual differences, and develop a history, which in turn affects the operations of the group. There are usually many short-range goals and procedural details over which the group itself has decision-making control. Examples of such learning-discussion groups might be: individual classes in schools and universities, study groups in organizations and churches, seminars and training groups in business and industry.

and learning-discussion groups (margin)

GROUP SIZE

We have mentioned the importance of the "small" as opposed to the large group for discussion. If we think of a group of twenty people engaged in a two-hour discussion, and then think of a group of eight people in the same situation, it is easy to foresee a large difference in the number of communications that each member will send out. It has been found that the larger the size of the group, the more members there are who contribute little or nothing, not only in terms of absolute numbers, but even in terms of proportion. Frequency of communication is important to involvement of the individual member and to group cohesiveness.[1]

and participation pattern (margin)

In a range in group size from five to twenty members, the larger group will demonstrate an increasing degree of separation and differentiation between the assigned Leader and the group members. The larger group will need and tolerate a greater degree of direction or domination by the Leader and by a greater number of formalized norms. The larger group will provide a less satisfying experience for its members because: (1) the participation pattern will be unbalanced, with increased participation by more vocal

disadvantages of the large group (margin)

members and decreased participation by the less vocal; (2) group climate is less friendly and more impersonal, and (3) more frequent formation of subgroups will occur. The group product suffers as group size increases, because exploration in depth is inhibited by the unbalanced participation pattern and increased difficulty in pursuing understanding and resolving differences.[2] For a decision-making or action-group such as a committee, five members has been found to be the most satisfying number, but for the average learning discussion-group, twelve to fifteen members seems to be the best size, with the possibility of deliberate subgrouping at times.

GROUP ORGANIZATION

public structure   The *public structure* of the discussion group model we have been considering has a simple organization and the assigned public roles are limited to the *Leader* and group *member* or *participant*, each constituting a single role, regardless of whether there are one

or two assigned Leaders, and regardless of the number of participants. We also mentioned the possibility of another assigned role, such as secretary. This role arrangement and its relationships constitute the public structure or formal organization of the group, at least during the time that it is functioning as a discussion group.

private structure

There is another kind of structure or organization, variously called the *private structure*, silent organization or hidden organization, which may be viewed in several ways. The private structure is composed of sets and relationships of assigned or assumed private roles, both behavioral and non-behavioral, including the hidden power structure. We spoke in Chapter 3 of behavioral roles as describing the way the group regards the person, such as "the clown", and "the person everyone loves". Sometimes the roles are *functional* in nature, such as "the one who always volunteers to do the dull jobs", "the one you can count on to have the door key", "the one who pours oil on troubled waters", or "the one who always has a good idea when the discussion gets stuck".

functional roles, or leadership functions

dysfunctional roles

Sometimes these roles or behaviors are *dysfunctional* and can be disruptive, e.g., "the one who always loses his temper", "the one who never prepares the assignment", "the one whose remarks are always irrelevant", or "the one who is always on his soapbox". Sometimes assigned roles have little relevance to ongoing behavior, and are such as "the newest member", or "the oldest member"—roles which often affect behavior, but are not behavioral in origin. This "silent organization" sometimes wields more influence on the discussion than the officially established roles. Some of these roles obviously derive from the task area of the group's activities, some from the social-emotional, and some originate in accidental factors.

assigned non-behavioral roles

It is neither possible nor desirable to think of "erasing" this hidden organization or of creating a situation in which each member always plays exactly the same role or roles. Role creation is a product of group interaction, building on the natural proclivities of the individuals. Each individual may fill more than one role at a time and also may change roles from time to time. Sometimes roles become institutionalized, not in the sense of becoming part of the formal, public structure, but simply because the group pins a mental label on the individual, or the individual does this to himself, and both he and the group come to accept it as fixed. Such rigidity in behavioral roles is not helpful to the group—it is best if the *functional roles, or sets of functions,* become *dispersed* throughout the group in such a way that each member can on occasion "have the good idea", "pour oil on troubled waters", and so forth. Everyone will be guilty at times of dysfunctional behavior, but it is certainly better if the group does not "count on" some particular member to be the disruptive force. We always hope that the one who "always loses his temper" will grow to have less need to do so, and that everyone will love everyone, and not just "the one".

institutionaliza-tion of behavioral roles

The private structure, however, should be tempered and used

hidden power structure

by the group in such a way that it promotes rather than hinders the group's pursuit of its goals. The norms and procedures of the group, the leadership and the group climate all can serve to coordinate these role relationships. It is necessary that this be done, as otherwise the power of the private structure, or the hidden power structure, can exercise a harmful kind of control, and much potential for good in the group can be lost.

... and status

Status in a group in terms of lower-ranking and higher-ranking members creates a form of role which has some peculiar characteristics. We mentioned in speaking of participation patterns the tendency of status to affect "who talks to whom". Status also affects adherence to norms, in that it is often found that low-status members may tend to be much stricter with themselves in regard to group norms than high-status members. The low-status member may well be trying to improve his status in the group by this means.[3] The converse does not always hold true, however. Sometimes the high-status member is the one who conforms most closely to the group norms.[4] His popularity may be due to the group's admiration of his conformity, and also one who has achieved high status in a group may feel that his popularity depends on his conformity, even if such is not the case.[5] In addition to the conforming high-status member, however, we have the high-status member who, in a sense, is pampered by the group—allowed to break the rules because of the group's admiration of him. This can be seen in groups which happily tolerate their eccentric member, their pet clown, provided these people have the group's admiration for some other factor, such as occupying the "oldest member" role, or status in the community outside the group. It can also be seen in a Visiting Authority on which the group may confer so much status that they deliberately try to keep rules and other norms hidden from him to allow him free play.

... and group norms

Visiting Authority

high-status member as agent for growth

The other side of the coin is the high-status member who serves the group as innovator, goal-enlarger, or in other ways as an agent for growth. A high-status member is in a better position to try to change norms which he believes are limiting or otherwise harming the group in some way. His status enables him to more easily win adherence to a new point of view or change in direction, both in the accomplishment of the group task and in its norms and goals.[6]

LEADERSHIP

The term "leader" is applied to many different assigned and behavioral roles in our society. If you ask someone, "Who is a leader in your community?", your respondent may name three or four people; if you ask, "Who is the political leader?", you may get a different name. We also speak of "labor leaders", the "Boy Scout Leader", the local "gang leader", "the real leader" of a group of friends who meet socially. All these terms convey different kinds of activities and behaviors and even what are often called "types" of people. What is the common term in all these roles? Considering the varying functions of each individual in these roles, we probably can say only that the term conveys the idea of *some sort of special relationships* with groups of people *and* some special *responsibility* in connection with the activities of groups. This very vague definition can also be applied to a "group discussion Leader", but we can be a bit more specific, having narrowed the field. Also, since we are not talking about a plant management team decision-making discussion, or a therapy group, we can narrow it still further to a "learning group discussion Leader". Within this group situation, it is customary to speak of three types of leadership: autocratic, democratic and laissez faire.

These terms derive from an early experiment in the field of group leadership conducted by Kurt Lewin, Ronald Lippitt and Ralph White in 1939.[7] Much valuable information came from this work, and many of the concepts of leadership that evolved have been in common use ever since. Unfortunately, some of these terms were misinterpreted, and considerable misunderstanding has arisen by applying insights gained under very specific experimental conditions to other situations in which they were inappropriate. Lewin and his co-workers defined their terms very carefully, specified very clearly the nature of the groups' tasks, and the composition of the groups, but their equally carefully defined and evaluated results have been pressed into use in quite different situations, and their terms descriptive of the leadership characteristics have been handled at times in such a way that they have been distorted to "dictator" (bad), "irresponsible Leader" (bad), and "democratic Leader" (good), with no shades of difference in between.

One result has been a tendency to burden Leaders with a situation in which they are damned if they do and damned if they don't; they feel guilty if they intervene in their group's activities in any way, because then they believe they are being a dictator, or they feel guilty if they do not take over when a group needs help, because this makes them "irresponsible". Thelen says there are certain stereotypes about "democracy" which interfere with useful thinking about group leadership. One is that there is only one way to be a democratic Leader. As Thelen says, "leadership should be appropriate to the situation".[8]

The extremes of autocratic or authoritarian leadership and of laissez faire leadership result in a poor substitute for discussion as we desire it to be. Autocratic leadership largely eliminates reflective, critical thinking, substituting the pre-determined ideas and values of the Leader who sees his role as that of the one who *knows* and who must drive the other group members down *his* path to *his* conclusions. He may be subtle or brutal in his coercion, but the results are much the same. The values of discussion are lost, and the lecture method would be a more humane procedure for his purpose.

On the other hand, the laissez faire Leader sees his role as scarcely distinguishable from that of any other group member. He

Leader, defined

types of leadership

autocratic

laissez faire

assumes that leadership functions will automatically be evenly distributed in the group, and that he has no special responsibilities. The Leader who attempts to operate in this fashion can usually expect that if the group survives and becomes productive, it will be because one or two real or actual Leaders have taken over his job. The success or failure of the group then depends on the qualities of these emergent Leaders.

and emergent leadership

The one who "emerges" may well be an authoritarian Leader, or a power struggle between two potential Leaders may ensue, breaking the group into two opposing camps. In a self-determining experimental group, such as a sensitivity group, the observation of this process has value as a learning experience, but the end result may be the dissolution of the group before the accomplishment of any other goals, or the reduction of the group to a mechanism for the fulfillment of the goals of the emergent Leader. Such an experience for a learning-discussion group, formed for the purpose of the accomplishment of other goals, is a time-wasting and sometimes destructive process, in terms of its stated goals. It constitutes an abdication of responsibility on the part of the appointed Leader or the parent group, despite its possible advantages as a special kind of learning experience for some particular individuals in the group. We are inclined to agree with Howell and Smith who speak of the pursuit of leaderless discussion as "pursuit of an illusion".[9]

styles of democratic leadership

Many people in group work consider the democratic Leader as the one who emerges from the group spontaneously, because of unique abilities to help the group in its progress, and the recognition of his leadership by the group. They oppose this concept of the "Leader" to that of a "head"; that is, the head is someone appointed by higher authority to the position, rather than being democratically selected from within the group. They consider the activity of a head to be "domination" rather than leadership if he is so appointed. However, as Gibb points out, being appointed a head does not rule out leadership. He goes on to say that many so appointed "are recognized by their subordinates as making very positive contributions to group progress, and are therefore accorded willing co-operation and, through it, leadership status." [10] Very often, what is talked of as "emergent leadership" refers to the concept of "leadership functions" as we use it in this book. Viewed in this way, the emergent Leader is that individual who at that particular moment in a discussion or in the life of a group provides the leadership function needed by the group, without changing the public structure of the group in any way.

leadership functions

The democratic Leader has sometimes meant a Leader who

parliamentarian

moderator

democratic
leadership in
learning
discussion groups

responsibilities

... and functions

... and growth

protection of
the minority

has his group decide everything by vote, which means that the majority rules, the minority is unprotected, and the contribution the Leader might make in guiding the group to possibly more fruitful discussion is lost. Such leadership frequently is employed in action groups, either with or without parliamentary procedure. Another common concept of democratic leadership is that of the moderator of a discussion, who usually makes an initial statement to start the ball rolling, and then devotes his time primarily to traffic regulation—he tries to achieve some balance in both participation and variety of opinions expressed, summarizes at intervals to keep everyone up to date, and sometimes is responsible for reorienting the discussion when he feels enough has been said on a particular topic. He may give a summary at the end, outlining the various viewpoints expressed, and the conclusions the group reached. These functions have their place in certain types of learning groups, particularly in public performances. They are very seldom appropriate for the sort of learning group in which we are primarily interested.

All the evidence seems to indicate that the flexible democratic Leader best serves the group from the point of view of the growth of the individual group member and the group, the cohesiveness of the group, and the accomplishment of the group goals. Some of the factors which affect the degree of directiveness needed are the task involved, the goal desired, the time allotted, the age, experience and training of the group. The helpful democratic Leader sees his role as *fulfilling those functions which are necessary* for the group in achieving its goals, while remembering the importance of individual and group growth and all the factors relevant to the accomplishment of these aims. His actual behavior will vary with the total situation, and depend in great part on the ability of the group to share in the leadership functions. Democratic leadership is less a "third path" than an area on a continuum, partaking of some features of both autocratic and laissez faire leadership when needed, but avoiding the extremes of both. The Leader has a role or a set of functions. It is obviously neither necessary nor desirable that he personally fulfill all the leadership functions described in Chapter 1. He should strive to assist group members in their efforts to fulfill these functions, and so long as he remains the appointed head, he carries a special responsibility toward group goals and group growth.[11]

One of his functions is the protection of the minority. Without the assistance of a Leader, the group risks domination by a dictator arising within the group, or at least of majority rule. A minority which might make valuable contributions to the group is overpowered by the social pressures of the majority. Allowing the expression of minority opinions does not damage the quality of the group product, as it is very unlikely that the minority opinion can convince the majority unless there is truth or value in their statements. This sometimes places the responsibility upon the Leader of making difficult value judgments about certain contributions made by members. His strong desire for group satisfaction and the benefits accruing to the group by virtue of high cohesiveness and conformity to norms must not blind him to the fact that he must not sacrifice the superior individual to the group, or stifle a minority opinion which may have considerable value. He may find that his greater temptation is to give acceptance to the minority opinion when it happens to coincide with his own, and to be oblivious to its possible value, or even its existence, when he is in disagreement with it.

And yet, how can he trust his own judgment as to the "superior individual", or the lone opinion of "considerable value"? He must help all of the group members to rely on their own judgment, even when they are in disagreement with the rest of the group. The basic idea of encouraging *individual decisions*, as opposed to "groupthink", is a valuable assistance, and the group should be encouraged to hold fast to this principle, even at the cost of lowered cohesiveness. Maier and Solem may be overly optimistic in their view that "when it is wrong, the minority cannot convince the majority", but this is usually the case, and the alternative of "group-decision" creates far more problems than it solves.[12] The well-trained Leader distinguishes between allowing a group to be harangued by an opinionated speaker, and informed by a speaker with an opinion.

In May, 1969, LIFE published a report on a poll concerned with high school education. The extensive and detailed survey was made by Louis Harris and Associates, Inc., and Bayard Hooper, senior editor at LIFE, reported on some aspects of the findings as follows: "A recurring theme in the . . . Poll . . . is that the good teacher is one who makes class discussion the center of his teaching and encourages the students to probe, to challenge, to explore, to speak their minds. But this can be a perilous course for a teacher to follow, for to replace a structured course with open-ended inquiry requires more intellectual self-confidence than many teachers possess. It may also bring him into conflict with a tidy-minded school administration whose own preoccupations are with grade transcripts, achievement tests, college prep requirements and the maintenance of order in the hallways and lavatories. To cease acting as a dispenser of measured doses of knowledge is to risk head-on confrontation, too, with the community's traditional concept of education." [13]

In 1959, Esther Lloyd-Jones, as head of the Department of Guidance and Student Personnel Administration at Teachers College, Columbia University, wrote, "Commissions of thoughtful educators, some Foundation spokesmen and a few educational prophets are stating ever more positively that simply lecturing at large groups of students in college is not necessarily the best way to educate them. A rising tide of opinion holds that college students must take more responsibility for self-education, must become more critical, must show more intellectual initiative and should become more intellectually excited. Often this thinking relates to the problem of financing the education of the increasing numbers of college students, but usually states squarely that the taking even of copious lecture notes, doing required reading, writing required papers and regurgitating on examinations will not stimulate many students to take initiative, to become critical and creative, and to be self-educating." [14] She goes on to recommend the use of the small-group discussion method.

The typical seminar in an institution of higher learning does contain an "instructor" of some kind, but it is becoming increasingly the case that he differentiates between his role as a lecturer and as a leader of a seminar, having found it more productive to do so. There are also many seminars held throughout the country in which the seminar leader is not an instructor in any sense of the term, but a fellow-learner who sometimes participates in the discussion, and sometimes does not.

Haiman points out the special factor which poses difficulties for the teacher who practices democratic leadership. The teacher is, by definition, the one who knows more about the subject than the group. He is the expert and his "essential function is to enlighten the group". How can he, as an authority, head a group which operates on the principle that each member is equally valuable and has an equal voice in decision-making? Haiman cites Alfred M. Cooper's opinion that no one can be a democratic Leader unless he is convinced that the group as a whole possesses more knowledge than he. The function of the teacher is not, per se, a "democratic" function. Furthermore, the Overstreets have said, with some truth, "Those who have had the hardest time to become good discussion leaders were those who have the cards stacked against them by their previous training—ex-teachers and ex-ministers." [15] Despite these problems, we advise the educator to use democratic leadership as his method for discussion groups, wherever possible and appropriate.

resistance to democratic leadership

. . . by group

Despite the advantages to the group and the Leader of democratic leadership, it is frequently resisted by both. The group resists it primarily because it is simply not their model of how a group and a Leader should operate. Many people, due to previous experience in home, school and work situations, are used to autocratic leadership, and therefore expect it. They feel more comfortable in familiar situations in which they know the "roles and the rules", and are resistant to change.[16] They actually feel threatened at times by such a shift of responsibility from the Leader to the group members. Furthermore, "once burned, twice shy" applies to some group members who have participated in group situations in which the format was seemingly democratic, but before the session or sessions were ended, the "right" answers were delivered by the Leader or his appointed member, and these participants were shown up in some way as having been "wrong".

Some members of a learning group feel cheated, having come to a group where they expected to be "informed by an expert", and are ill at ease in a situation in which they are expected to think through a problem and make their own decisions. Some people are motivated in a learning situation by the expectation of rewards, and approval by the authority figure in the group offers some a far greater sense of reward than the approval of his peers. It may take time for such people to find learning self-rewarding.

In adult learning groups some participants view a discussion experience largely as an "entertainment". Normally responsible, decision-making individuals, they look upon such a group as a vacation from responsibility, and resent the work involved in doing their own decision-making in this situation. As T. M. Mills says, "groups tend in their actions to fulfill the prophecy contained in their models",[17] and if most of the members of a group lean strongly toward the model of the authoritarian Leader, they will be very resistant to change. This is particularly true in the case of an "old" group faced with a "new" Leader, or their old Leader with some new ideas. Groups do tend to attract like-minded members, and sometimes to lose the non-conformist members. Those who remain tend to become more like-minded. Their attitudes, behavior, and other characteristics tend to create a personality for the group as a whole, so it may be characterized by such terms as "tractable", "extremely individualistic", "quarrelsome", or "authoritarian". The term sometimes used for this group personality or performance is *syntality*. If the group syntality has hardened into an authoritarian model, a Leader seeking to develop a more democratic group personality will meet rebuff. However, even those who advocate fitting one's behavior as a Leader to the syntality of a group offer the Leader the encouragement that groups can change with training. Uris points out that syntality is not as firmly anchored as individual personality or character, so that a Leader wishing to be democratic may have to start out as more authoritarian than he would desire, but can develop his group to the point where it can better accept democratic leadership.[18]

syntality

resistance to democratic leadership by Leader

Leaders, too, sometimes resist the democratic approach. They as well as their groups may operate from a model of authoritarian or laissez faire leadership, and find it difficult to develop a new and equally satisfying model. A Leader's resistance to the democratic approach may result from a variety of causes. Frequently it is a lack of conviction that another way is worth a trial. Sometimes it is due to laziness, fear of responsibility or incompetence; sometimes the autocratic Leader fears the loss of pleasure he derives from the exercise of power. In the former case he should seek to develop competence, or relinquish the job to others. In the latter, he should recognize that pleasures differ, and much satisfaction comes to the Leader who not only can feel pride in the growth of a group under his guidance, but will also find that as the group becomes stronger and more independent, he also grows.

discussion as a teaching method

No single method should be considered the only approach to learning or teaching, but discussion should be considered a method to be used whenever possible. As Zelko said in 1957, "This is an age of communication. There is no substitute for the discussion process in bringing about our objective of understanding through communication."[19] Few contemporary writers on education fail to stress the need for discussion, those in most areas of adult education tend to think of it as *the* method, and such men as John S. Morgan of the General Electric Company and James M. Black of the American Association of Industrial Management believe it is absolutely necessary for planning, informing, problem-solving and training.[20] Although method and detail differ, democratic leadership is the preferred style.

role clarification

When the instructor is also the discussion Leader, both group and leader face the problem of differentiating these roles and situations. If, as Leader, the teacher continues to actively participate in the discussion, contributing his ideas and judgments, the group will retreat from actual discussion, since the lecture-recitation classroom is being reproduced. Also, when the Leader alternates roles in this way, he may encounter difficulties in his instructional role, finding it difficult to exercise effective control or to give the necessary weight to his statements. On the other hand, the group may feel dissatisfaction if they believe the teacher-as-Leader is withholding helpful information and "knows something they don't know".[21]

Leader responsibility

Regardless of the reality of the situation, any group is apt to think of its Leader as a "teacher" until it is trained to do otherwise. Our culture has so habituated us. In working toward the resolution of these problems, the Leader should accept the group and the individual member where he is, and train the members to accept responsibility to go where he thinks they should. To this degree the Leader is "autocratic". In view of his special responsibilities toward group goals and group growth, if he has decided that the weight of evidence indicates the advantages to the group of democratic leadership, he determines this as a group goal, he decides at least some of the initial procedures for reaching that goal, and he seeks to assist the group in following the path he has chosen. When the Leader encourages the sharing of leadership functions he is not relinquishing his leadership. T. M. Mills says, "The same is true in the teacher-student relationship when the student acquires the teacher's methods of thinking, without becoming the teacher" or necessarily adopting all of the teacher's opinions.[22]

. . . and leadership functions

Problems arise in a group in which the leadership functions are either inadequately or inappropriately filled. Sometimes group members become frozen in a particular function, performing that function in and out of season and even jealously guarding their right to be its exclusive provider. In other groups a few members may try to handle almost all functions, regardless of their competence or taste for the job. Even if they are capable of such multidimensional activities, their unwillingness to relinquish these functions inhibits the growth of other members. Group members grow through increasing their skills and their repertoire of functions, and the responsible, growing group encourages such development. Leadership responsibility for group growth is largely carried out through assisting and encouraging individual experimentation in new functions.[23]

FOR SOURCES AND FURTHER INFORMATION, CONSULT THE FOLLOWING WORKS:

1. Bales, Robert, Fred L. Strodtbeck, Theodore M. Mills, and Mary E. Roseborough, "Channels of Communication in Small Groups", AMERICAN SOCIOLOGICAL REVIEW, 16, 461-68 (1951).
   see also: Newcomb, T. M., R. H. Turner, and P. E. Converse, SOCIAL PSYCHOLOGY: THE STUDY OF HUMAN INTERACTION, p. 364, N.Y.: Holt, 1965.
2. Berelson, Bernard and Gary A. Steiner, HUMAN BEHAVIOR: AN INVENTORY OF SCIENTIFIC FINDINGS, p. 358, N.Y.: Harcourt Brace, 1964.
3. Hovland, C. I., I. L. Janis and H. H. Kelley, COMMUNICATION AND PERSUASION, p. 152, London: Oxford University Press, 1953.
   see also: Berelson and Steiner, HUMAN BEHAVIOR, p. 340; Argyle, Michael, THE SCIENTIFIC STUDY OF SOCIAL BEHAVIOR, Methuen, p. 155, 1957; Johnstone, John, and Elihu Katz, "Youth and Popular Music: A Study in the Sociology of Taste", AMERICAN JOURNAL OF SOCIOLOGY, 62, p. 563 (1957).
4. Hovland et al., COMMUNICATION AND PERSUASION, p. 152;
   see also: Newcomb, T. M., PERSONALITY AND SOCIAL CHANGE, N.Y.: Dryden Press, 1943; Schachter, S., "Deviation, Rejection and Communication", JOURNAL OF ABNORMAL AND SOCIAL PSYCHOLOGY, 46, 190-207 (1951).
5. Kelley, H. H. and E. H. Volkart, "The Resistance to Change of Group-anchored Attitudes", AMERICAN SOCIOLOGICAL REVIEW, 17, 453-65 (1952).
6. Merton, R. K., "Patterns of Influence: A Study of Interpersonal Influence and of Communications Behavior in a Local Community", in COMMUNICATIONS RESEARCH, 1948-1949, pp. 180-219, eds. P. F. Lazarsfeld and F. N. Stanton, N.Y.: Harper, 1949.
7. Lippitt, Ronald and Ralph K. White, "An Experimental Study of Leadership and Group Life", in READINGS IN SOCIAL PSYCHOLOGY, rev. ed. pp. 340-55, eds. Theodore M. Newcomb and Eugene L. Hartley et al., N.Y.: Henry Holt and Co., 1952, or see a fuller treatment in Lippitt, R., "An Experimental Study of the Effect of Democratic and Authoritarian Group Atmosphere", UNIVERSITY OF IOWA STUDIES IN CHILD WELFARE (194) XVI, 43-195.
8. Thelen, H. A., DYNAMICS OF GROUPS AT WORK, p. 314, Chicago: Phoenix, University of Chicago Press, 1963.
9. Howell, William S., and Donald K. Smith, DISCUSSION, p. 247, N.Y.: Macmillan, 1956.
   see also: Zelko, Harold P., SUCCESSFUL CONFERENCE AND DISCUSSION TECHNIQUES, pp. 98-9, N.Y.: McGraw-Hill, 1957.
10. Gibb, Cecil A., "The Principles and Traits of Leadership", JOURNAL OF ABNORMAL AND SOCIAL PSYCHOLOGY, 42, p. 273 (1947).
    NOTE: Gibb maintains that we should distinguish leadership, headship, and domination.
11. Mills, Theodore M., THE SOCIOLOGY OF SMALL GROUPS, p. 92, et passim, Englewood Cliffs, N.J.: Prentice-Hall, Inc., 1967.
12. Maier, N. R. F., and A. R. Solem, "The Contributions of a Discussion Leader to the Quality of Group Thinking: The Effective Use of Minority Opinions", HUMAN RELATIONS, 5, 288 (1952).
13. Hooper, Bayard, "The Task Is To Learn What Learning Is For", LIFE, May 16, p. 39 (1969).
14. Hoffmann, Randall W., and Robert Plutchik. SMALL-GROUP DISCUSSION IN ORIENTATION AND TEACHING, foreword by Esther Lloyd-Jones, p. vii, N.Y.: G. P. Putnam's Sons, 1959.
15. Haiman, Franklyn, GROUP LEADERSHIP AND DEMOCRATIC ACTION, pp. 70-72, Boston: Houghton, Mifflin, 1951.
16. Mill, T. M., SOCIOLOGY OF SMALL GROUPS, p. 10.
    see also: Korten, David C., "Situational Determinants of Leadership Structure", in GROUP DYNAMICS, RESEARCH AND THEORY (3rd ed.), pp. 351ff, eds. Dorwin Cartwright and Alvin Zander, N.Y.: Harper and Row, 1968.
17. Mills, T. M., SOCIOLOGY OF SMALL GROUPS, p. 14.
18. NOTE: The term "syntality" is not used in the same way by all people in group work. It was apparently introduced in 1948 by R. B. Cattell in "Concepts and Methods in the Measurement of Group Syntality", PSYCHOLOGICAL REVIEW, 55, 48-63 (1948); Lee, Alfred McClung, MULTIVALENT MAN, pp. 168, 398, N.Y.: Geo. Braziller, 1966; Uris, Auren, TECHNIQUES OF LEADERSHIP, pp. 53-67 et passim, N.Y.: McGraw-Hill, 1953; Cooper, Joseph B., and James L. McGaugh, INTEGRATING PRINCIPLES OF SOCIAL PSYCHOLOGY, p. 227, Cambridge, Mass.: Schenkman Publishing Co., Inc., 1963.
19. Zelko, Harold P., SUCCESSFUL CON-

FERENCE AND DISCUSSION TECH-NIQUES, p. 6, N.Y.: McGraw-Hill Books, Co., Inc., 1957.

20. Morgan, John S., PRACTICAL GUIDE TO CONFERENCE LEADERSHIP, pp. vii-viii, 4-8, N.Y.: McGraw-Hill Book Co., 1966.

21. Mills, T. M., SOCIOLOGY OF SMALL GROUPS, p. 65.
    see also: Heise, G. A., and Miller, "Problem Solving by Small Groups Using Various Communication Nets", JOURNAL OF ABNORMAL AND SOCIAL PSYCHOLOGY, XLVI, 327-36 (1951), reprinted in SMALL GROUPS, eds. Hare, Borgatta and Bales, pp. 353-67; Leavitt, Harold J., "Some Effects of Certain Communication Patterns on Group Performance", JOURNAL OF ABNORMAL AND SOCIAL PSYCHOLOGY, XLVI, 38-50 (1951); Cohen, A. M. and Warren G. Bennis, "Predicting Organization in Changed Communication Networks", JOURNAL OF PSYCHOLOGY, LIV, 391-416 (1962).

22. Mills, T. M., SOCIOLOGY OF SMALL GROUPS, p. 92.

23. LEADER'S DIGEST, Issue Committee, "What Roles Does Your Group Need?", Vol. I, 49-50 (1952).
    NOTE: Concerning "functions" and "roles", some writers have subsumed the idea of "leadership functions" under the concept of "role". See, for instance, Benne, K. D., and P. Sheats, "Functional Roles of Group Members", JOURNAL OF SOCIAL ISSUES, 4, pp. 41-9 (1948); Bonner, Hubert, GROUP DYNAMICS: PRINCIPLES AND APPLICATIONS, N.Y.: Ronald Press, 1959.

5.
The Leader as Trainer:
The Group as Decision System

OVERVIEW

It is fairly obvious that the Leader of a group is responsible for two jobs, leading *and training* his group. Fortunately, the job is not so overwhelming as may at first appear. The good Leader does considerable training without conscious effort, and the well-led group is usually unaware of its first steps in training. A new group has its first lessons in *sharing leadership functions* simply by participating in a well-led discussion, and thus beginning its own construction of a *model* of "what discussion should be". The Leader uses his own model in helping the group and its members grow, in improving the quality of their discussions, and in finding ways to solve group problems of operation. In the beginning, the Leader concentrates primarily on his own *attitudes,* the group *climate,* and the *progress of the discussion.* As time goes on, he encourages his group to accept more responsibilities and perhaps to take some time from their regular discussions for consideration of their behavior and operations as a group. The group will tend to imitate the Leader's attitudes in the early stages of group life, and will later take a real interest in the growth and progress of the group. As a *system* with some *responsibility for its own maintenance and growth,* the group requires some means of self-inspection which may be provided in various ways by *feedback.*

LEADER AS TRAINER

Leader begins training with first session

participant attributes

A. exploration

The Leader trains his group members to be good participants, and thereby begins the necessary training in leadership functions. He trains the group both by example and by deliberately encouraging the development of appropriate attitudes and skills. This requires time and patience. The attributes of the successful group member are: (A) *the ability and desire to explore in depth the problems under consideration.* He is willing to (1) give thoughtful attention to all revelant contributions; he is open-minded, willing and able to change his mind, and is not too busy with a single phase of the discussion to try to work creatively with other phases; (2) he is able to see relationships, similarities and distinctions, to (3) identify sources of disagreement, linguistic tangles, and to distinguish between genuine differences of opinion and differences arising from extrinsic conflict. He assists in (4) protecting minority views by demonstrating a willingness to give them serious consideration and encouraging their expression. (5) He contributes his ideas when he believes this will be helpful to the group, or when it will help him through direct feedback from the group. (B) *Adequate*

B. communication

communication skills: Such a group member has learned to (1) listen and to make every effort to understand what others are saying; he hears and tries to grasp the meaning or intention of other speakers, he asks for repetition or clarification when necessary. He will also be (2) observant to such non-verbal cues as those indicating agreement, disagreement, concern or distress. He is able to (3) absorb the input of the discussion, from whatever source; he zeroes in on matters of importance, can read written materials with comprehension, see and understand films, drama, etc., can grasp the principal points of a spoken communication, see things from a variety of perspectives, and is mentally and emotionally aware. He is able to (4) contribute to the discussion in a clear, concise way. (C) *An*

C. human concern

attitude of human concern. In addition to the two foregoing groups of primarily problem-solving functions and the attitudes associated with them, he has an attitude of human concern for the group members as individuals and for himself as an individual. He seldom finds it necessary to indulge in dysfunctional behaviors. He assists in the maintenance of the group through helping to (1) sustain a healthy group climate. He demonstrates his (2) friendly and cooperative attitude toward his fellow group members, and is able to assist the group in (3) handling emotion in a healthy and creative way. He does not shirk the responsibility of (4) decision-making, and recognizes and (5) facilitates the moments of such responsibility in others.

The accompanying charts show how these participant attributes provide the group with the leadership functions. The only leadership function not entirely accounted for is "providing feedback" under "Demonstrating Human Concern", VIIg. Once the group has decided upon suitable forms of feedback, the provision of such delayed feedback may then become a participant attribute, partaking of a number of the attitudes and skills already charted.

So long as he remains the titular head, the Leader retains overall responsibility for the health and welfare of the group—the obligation to see that its needs are met, regardless of which members of the group perform the necessary functions. He knows there is no group which cannot improve. The final stage of his responsibility would be to work himself out of the job, and he should do this, but only when the benefit to the entire group will be greater than if he were to remain in his position. There frequently are conflicting obligations which require him to leave his group without any such certainty. In order to help his group achieve its goals, including the goal of group growth and individual growth, the Leader must step back and look at the group's norms, procedures and operations. He must give consideration to the content and to the process, to the task area and to the social-emotional or maintenance area.

DISCUSSION GROUP AS DECISION SYSTEM

In order to think productively about all these many aspects of his group and the relationships of these aspects to one another, the Leader develops and "fleshes out" his model. His model may range from a loose collection of ideas and principles concerning "what groups are like" or "what groups should be like" to a formalized, detailed construct. Such a model may be patterned along the lines of a variety of systems.

Any group which has as a part of its activities periods of discussion may be thought of as a *data-processing-decision system*, made up of individual communicators who both send and receive messages, process them, make individual decisions and share in the making of group decisions. The data of this system include facts, opinions, concepts and emotions, feelings and beliefs; its decisions are often not clear-cut; its processing includes some non-identifiable elements and the analogy frequently falters. However, the decision-system model can be useful in diagnosing group problems, identifying strengths and weaknesses and planning for future activity. It must be considered strictly as a diagnostic and planning tool, and

A. EXPLORING PROBLEM

LEADERSHIP FUNCTIONS

I. INITIATING (primarily Task)
a. guidance of transitions
b. getting something started

II. INFORMATION INPUT (primarily Task)
a. stimulating group thinking
b. clarifying
c. providing resources
d. linking

III. EVALUATING (Task)
a. testing validity
b. reality testing
c. recognizing contradictions
d. determining opinion

IV. REGULATING (Task & Maintenance)
a. setting, maintaining goals, agenda
b. keeping on track
c. clock-watching
d. summarizing

V. CLIMATE-MAKING (primarily Maintenance)
a. listening with understanding
b. treating contributions with respect
c. tension relief
d. supporting & encouraging
e. handling over-aggressive
f. encouraging expression of personal feelings
g. harmonizing & integrating emotion
h. performing chores

VI. DECISION-MAKING (primarily Task)
a. resolving controversy (intrinsic)
b. recognizing, allowing for conflict
c. seeking consensus where needed
d. assisting individual decision-making

VII. TRAINING
a. helping balance Task & Maintenance
b. structuring situations for understanding
c. helping group promote good climate
d. aiding planning for problem-solving
e. aiding planning for dynamics diagnosis
f. seeing problems as group problems
g. providing feedback
h. encouraging experimentation-role, etc.

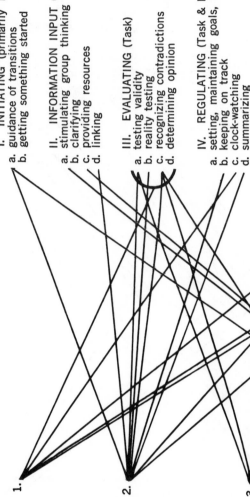

PARTICIPANT ATTRIBUTES

give thoughtful attention to all
relevant contributions
(III - all; IV c; VI b, d; VII a, d)

see relationships, similarities
and distinctions
(I a; II d; III a, b, c; IV b, d; VII b)

identify sources of disagreement
(III a, d; VI a, b; VII d, d, b; V a, b)

protect minority view
(III d; V a, b; VII b)

contribute information, ideas
(I b; II a, c; VII d, e)

PARTICIPANT ATTRIBUTES DEVELOP INTO LEADERSHIP FUNCTIONS

B. COMMUNICATION SKILLS

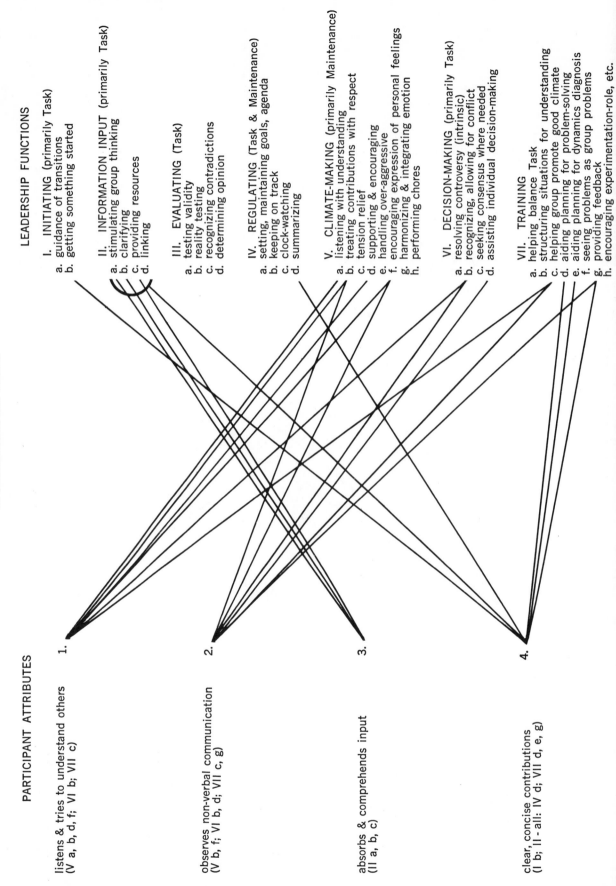

LEADERSHIP FUNCTIONS

I. INITIATING (primarily Task)
a. guidance of transitions
b. getting something started

II. INFORMATION INPUT (primarily Task)
a. stimulating group thinking
b. clarifying
c. providing resources
d. linking

III. EVALUATING (Task)
a. testing validity
b. reality testing
c. recognizing contradictions
d. determining opinion

IV. REGULATING (Task & Maintenance)
a. setting, maintaining goals, agenda
b. keeping on track
c. clock-watching
d. summarizing

V. CLIMATE-MAKING (primarily Maintenance)
a. listening with understanding
b. treating contributions with respect
c. tension relief
d. supporting & encouraging
e. handling over-aggressive
f. encouraging expression of personal feelings
g. harmonizing & integrating emotion
h. performing chores

VI. DECISION-MAKING (primarily Task)
a. resolving controversy (intrinsic)
b. recognizing, allowing for conflict
c. seeking consensus where needed
d. assisting individual decision-making

VII. TRAINING
a. helping balance Task
b. structuring situations for understanding
c. helping group promote good climate
d. aiding planning for problem-solving
e. aiding planning for dynamics diagnosis
f. seeing problems as group problems
g. providing feedback
h. encouraging experimentation-role, etc.

PARTICIPANT ATTRIBUTES

listens & tries to understand others
(V a, b, d, f; VI b; VII c)

observes non-verbal communication
(V b, f; VI b, d; VII c, g)

absorbs & comprehends input
(II a, b, c)

clear, concise contributions
(I b; II - all; IV d; VII d, e, g)

PARTICIPANT ATTRIBUTES DEVELOP INTO LEADERSHIP FUNCTIONS

C. DEMONSTRATING HUMAN CONCERN

LEADERSHIP FUNCTIONS

I. INITIATING (primarily Task)
a. guidance of transitions
b. getting something started

II. INFORMATION INPUT (primarily Task)
a. stimulating group thinking
b. clarifying
c. providing resources
d. linking

III. EVALUATING (Task)
a. testing validity
b. reality testing
c. recognizing contradictions
d. determining opinion

IV. REGULATING (Task & Maintenance)
a. setting, maintaining goals, agenda
b. keeping on track
c. clock-watching
d. summarizing

V. CLIMATE-MAKING (primarily Maintenance)
a. listening with understanding
b. treating contributions with respect
c. tension relief
d. supporting & encouraging
e. handling over-aggressive
f. encouraging expression of personal feelings
g. harmonizing & integrating emotion
h. performing chores

VI. DECISION-MAKING (primarily Task)
a. resolving controversy (intrinsic)
b. recognizing, allowing for conflict
c. seeking consensus where needed
d. assisting individual decision-making

VII. TRAINING
a. helping balance Task & Maintenance
b. structuring situations for understanding
c. helping group promote good climate
d. aiding planning for problem-solving
e. aiding planning for dynamic diagnosis
f. seeing problems as group problems
g. providing feedback
h. encouraging experimentation-role, etc.

PARTICIPANT ATTRIBUTES

sustain healthy climate
(IV a; V - all; VI b, c, d; VII c)

friendly, cooperative attitude
(IV a; V b, d, e, h)

assist in handling emotion
(V - all; VII a, c, f, h)

accepts responsibility in
decision-making
(IV c; VI - all)

facilitating decision-making
in others
(VI - all; VII b, h; I b; IV c)

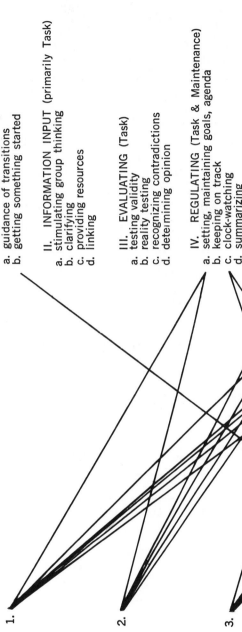

should not be developed as a rigid frame within which group members are to be limited and confined.

Systems concerned solely with data processing operations, without the element of decision-making, may be viewed as pure *information systems*. In such a system information is simply changed in form, stored, and reproduced when desired. Included in the information elements are *input*, or data received from outside the system, *memory*, which consists of information stored within the system, and *feedback*, which contributes information about the actual activities of previous operations of the system, fed back into the system. In such a system information may be rearranged, but no decisions are made which transform data into plans of action.

Decision-making represents a transformation of the information through weighing input, feedback and memory in the light of the *control* element, and putting forth a decision. The control element is made up of plans, policies and so forth which guide the operation of the whole system. The accompanying diagram shows the relationships of these elements, and indicates the corresponding elements of group operations.

SCHEMATIC REPRESENTATION OF A SYSTEM AND ITS ELEMENTS

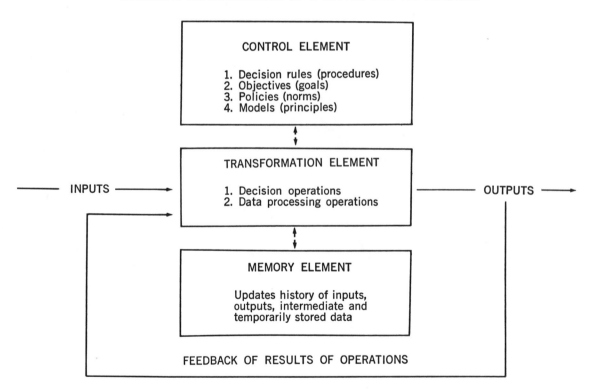

(adapted from Richards and Greenlaw)

Richards, Max D., and Greenlaw, Paul S., MANAGEMENT DECISION MAKING, Richard D. Irwin, Inc., Homewood III., 1966, p. 77

discussion group as data-processing-decision system

The discussion group contains the elements of such a system. It has inputs of information both from the presentation and from the individual participants who bring information into the group. It has control elements in the form of its norms, goals, procedures and the principles of the parent organization. It has a memory system which contains its history, including past discussions and the information stored in the group members. It also has feedback, a necessary part of a decision system.

feedback

In Chapter 3 we talked about increased shared information through direct feedback or immediate feedback within the discussion process, in terms of individual communicators. A similar feedback process operates within the group as a whole. Successful groups use some method of feedback. Group members may be unfamiliar with the term in this situation, but usually have some grasp of the concept. In this use of the word, feedback simply means *information concerning the reaction to the work of the group.* Groups are constantly in the process of evaluation as they seek their goals. Only very simple and immediate goals are achievable without this means of checking, evaluating, adjusting and reorient-

goal-seeking without feedback

ing. Simple goal-seeking without feedback might be illustrated this way:

PRESENT FUNCTION

FUTURE POSITION

group → goal

**goal-seeking
with feedback**

Usually there is some systematic provision for feedback. Starting with an overall goal, the group would take a first action step. This would be followed by a step of fact-finding directed toward the evaluation of its new situation. On the basis of the data obtained, the group would reassess and possibly modify its overall goal and use the knowledge acquired in deciding its next step. What follows again consists of a cycle of action, fact-finding, reevaluation of the overall goal and decision on subsequent action. The fact-finding is, or provides, the necessary feedback. This mode of operation can be illustrated as follows:

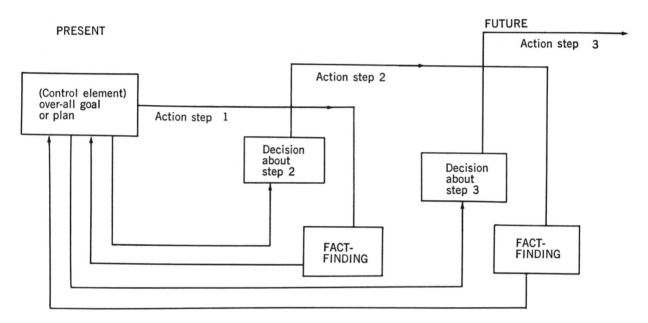

**immediate and
delayed feedback**

Most discussion groups have two kinds of feedback: (1) *immediate feedback* within the discussion process, concerned primarily with the *content* of the discussion, when communications are responded to, resulting in immediate alterations in the course of the discussion; (2) *delayed feedback*, concerned primarily but not exclusively with *process*, which delivers information via observers, group members, or by the entire group, to be reprocessed by discussion.

**process and
content**

In general, *process* may be defined as ". . . a sequence of related events leading to a relatively specific and predictable consequence." [1] Within the discussion, process factors include all those actions performed by group individuals or by the group as a whole. They can be most readily differentiated from "*content*" by thinking of the latter as that which could be conveyed in a disembodied form, as by transcribing the input and output of the discussion as though produced by a single individual. *Content* contains the information, the ideas of the discussion, *process* the interaction which produced them. The content is the "consequence" of the "events" of the process.

decisions

Within the total field of the discussion process, information is analyzed, compared with stored information and reworked. As the discussion progresses, decisions on "meaning", for instance, may be made by all or part of the group and, at the close of each discussion, the output includes those individual decisions made by the members. We are now ready to amplify our original picture of the system to include other elements of the discussion process, as the accompanying chart demonstrates.

when there are
problems in the
system

As with any such system, things can go awry. There is a tendency to think of "emotion" as the ogre of discussion—the cause of all the problems. Such diagrams as these may appear to further

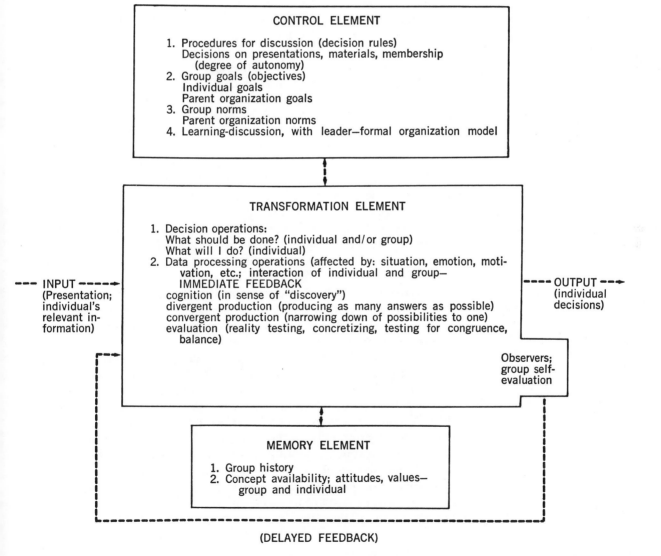

SCHEMATIC REPRESENTATION OF A DISCUSSION GROUP AS A
DATA-PROCESSING-DECISION SYSTEM

CONTROL ELEMENT

1. Procedures for discussion (decision rules)
   Decisions on presentations, materials, membership
     (degree of autonomy)
2. Group goals (objectives)
   Individual goals
   Parent organization goals
3. Group norms
   Parent organization norms
4. Learning-discussion, with leader—formal organization model

TRANSFORMATION ELEMENT

1. Decision operations:
   What should be done? (individual and/or group)
   What will I do? (individual)
2. Data processing operations (affected by: situation, emotion, motivation, etc.; interaction of individual and group—
   IMMEDIATE FEEDBACK
   cognition (in sense of "discovery")
   divergent production (producing as many answers as possible)
   convergent production (narrowing down of possibilities to one)
   evaluation (reality testing, concretizing, testing for congruence, balance)

INPUT
(Presentation;
individual's
relevant in-
formation)

OUTPUT
(individual
decisions)

Observers;
group self-
evaluation

MEMORY ELEMENT

1. Group history
2. Concept availability; attitudes, values—
     group and individual

(DELAYED FEEDBACK)

such a view, since they seem to convey the ideal of a mechanized, coldly intellectual process. This is incorrect. Both emotion and cognitive processes are necessary ingredients; both can be a negative or a positive force in a group. We often classify input as "fact" or "emotion", placing "fact" in the task area, and "emotion" in the maintenance area. In discussions among human beings of human problems, emotion is part of the facts, and affects decision and action; therefore some of the emotion present in group discussion properly belongs to the task of the group. Despite the hazard of the mechanized chart, when discussion is unproductive, when communication falters or breaks down, it is sometimes helpful to try to classify and perhaps diagram the elements in seeking possible causes and remedies. To classify all "negative" emotions as "impeding" or "distorting" is an oversimplification—"negative" emotion can sometimes move a group forward productively.

Bion's terms   Bion, who did some early work with therapy groups, named the productive area of interaction in the group "work". He described interchanges in the work area as goal oriented and reflective, and characterized by group members listening to each other. Because of the nature of his groups, much of this "work" was with emotions. On the other hand, that interaction characterized by non-listening, disorder and strong personal feeling he called "emotionality", and gave four categories describing typical behaviors. These categories are useful and identifiable in most groups, whether therapy groups or not, and represent a variety of forms of retreat from the problems at hand. His categories are: (1) dependency; the group demonstrates an inability or unwillingness to try to solve its problem, and places reliance on an outside source, e.g., "the Leader"; (2) pairing; two members seek avoidance of confrontation with problem by mutual dependence; (3) fight, and (4) flight.[2] Because the terms "work" and "emotionality" are thus contrasted, there has been some tendency for people concerned with groups to overextend the content of these concepts, and believe that any and all emotion is antithetical to work or productivity and harmful to group success.

emotion and extremes   An overreaction to such downgrading of emotion has led some to believe that only groups characterized by the vigorous expression of constant and untrammeled emotion have any value at all. At the other extreme are those who might wish a discussion group could operate with the efficiency of an electronic data processing system, but this is rather like a supermarket manager who knows he could run his market very efficiently if he could just figure out how to get rid of the customers. A discussion group is for the customers. Efficiency in mechanical systems is achieved by elimination of extraneous factors and interferences, and man is not, nor would we have him be, a robot—we want him as he is, with all his "extraneous factors" and despite his "interference". At the same time, a learning-discussion group is neither established for, nor equipped to deal with, discussion centered solely on the feeling level, without an agenda or the material of a presentation. We are here concerned

74

with discussion groups established for the purpose of learning and problem-solving in some subject other than that of the group interaction of and by itself. Such groups should recognize that neither extreme represents a desirable norm.

inspect all points of the system

A discussion group can suffer a failure in the system because of any number of factors, and the Leader seeking ways to help his group improve should give thoughtful consideration to all points in the system, rather than presume that runaway emotion or any other single factor is inevitably the problem. A very common problem is inadequate inputs of information. Other problems may arise from the control elements—procedures, norms, goals or the model itself may suffer from inadequate planning. Lack of continuity due to absenteeism or high turnover in group membership affects the group memory. The Leader may decide, or the group may decide, that some assessment of their progress is desirable, or some attempt to discover weak points is needed. This is usually approached by delayed feedback.

DELAYED FEEDBACK

Delayed feedback consists of reports of observations on any aspect of the group's functioning fed back to the group. It results in "discussion about the discussion" through which a group can improve its quality by an examination of its processes and products.

informal process feedback during discussion

Some group members become aware of and interested in process on a quite informal basis. Without labeling their behavior "feedback" or "participation observation", they include a brief mention of such observations during their contributions to the discussion. Someone in the group may say, for instance, "We two have been doing all the talking—why don't the rest of you get in this discussion?", or "Harry, all you ever do is ask questions—we'd like to know your answers sometimes." Task-oriented members may say, "I don't think we have enough information on this point to make a discussion of it worthwhile", or "I think we have to go back to an earlier point in this discussion and try to define these terms." Many groups seldom go beyond this informal stage in which aspects of what we are calling "delayed feedback" are incorporated *within* the discussion. Any extensive or thorough attempt to develop delayed feedback skills among group members requires skill, knowledge and tact on the part of the Leader.

formal feedback procedures

More formal methods of feedback can be set up through the use of *content observers* to observe specific task operations and *process observers* to report on process operations apart from content. An observer absents himself from active participation in order to devote his time to close observation of the group, and tries to hand on his findings in a usable form. Discussion of such findings by the group may result in a decision to modify some aspects of the group operations.

Feedback, as provided by observers or by group self-inspection on a formal basis, has become increasingly important in group work, as those studying groups realize the importance to group growth of awareness of process and its interaction with and effect on content. Successful utilization of feedback by a data-processing-decision system normally requires: (1) records of previous decisions and their results; (2) processing of the recorded data in usable form; (3) appropriate timing; (4) if necessary, a means of moving some information to a position of priority, as being more urgent for immediate consideration. A learning-discussion group planning to use feedback in its work of group growth should recognize that since the above conditions cannot be fully met, the analogy with such a system is inadequate, and therefore totally analogous results are not to be expected.

some feedback too costly
An action group, such as a civic committee or a school board, would probably have written records to fulfill the first criterion, and in a learning-discussion group the group memory has a store of some decisions and results, though in a less reliable form. However, the second criterion of "usable form" must consider the individual members as human beings first and foremost. In the business world, the element of cost is always a necessary consideration in determining the extent of feedback, and some feedback may be far too costly by the time the recording, tabulating and methods of presentation to the system are all given due consideration. In a discussion group, the cost may be in time spent and, if improperly handled, in hurt feelings and in less rather than more effective work toward the group goals. A discussion group might have less trouble with Number "4" than a mechanical system, once its own priorities were established. However, Number "3", "appropriate timing" of feedback, is not always easy to determine.

For instance, if a discussion group should decide that one of its problems is unbalanced participation, it might think the best way to correct this would be to have a process observer interrupt the group regularly whenever participation showed imbalance. A single, or even two participation observers, using chart forms of some type, could determine such things as the number of times each individual spoke and the total length of time used by each speaker, and might interrupt the discussion whenever imbalance was noted. This could be totally disruptive of the content of the discussion. If, in an effort to obviate this difficulty, one or two content observers were appointed to evaluate the quality of the contributions and the progress of the content of the discussion, it might be possible for the process observers to check with the content observers to determine whether the imbalance was sufficient to outweigh the possible quality factors of the discussion. This conference for evaluation by the observers would take them away from their observation of the discussion, so there would be a gap in their records. At the same time, this conference might so delay their report to the group that the discussion would have progressed to quite a different state, both in process and in content. It would represent the kind of "out of phase" problem encountered in some industrial situations, and the result would be equally unhelpful. If, on the other hand, it was decided that such reporting not be done by interruption, but delayed until the close of the meeting, its value for that meeting would be lost, and the information given the group might come at a time when they were in a poor state for its acceptance, especially because of its rather judgmental character, and the report might be forgotten or incorrectly remembered by the time of the next session. If the report were not given until the start of the next session, group members' memories might be inaccurate, even if the observers' written records were correct, and dissatisfaction with the observers and/or the group itself might be the result, eventuating in a poor climate and a subsequently unproductive discussion. Such possible problems as these must be considered in planning the type and timing of feedback.

process observers

In addition to participation observation, process observers may work with various kinds of scales and charts for such things as climate, fulfillment and distribution of leadership functions, and various means of interaction process analysis, using chart forms such as those based on Bales' interaction categories, Amidon and Flanders' interaction analysis system,[3] or the Instroteach system.[4]

content evaluation

As we noted in our discussion of Bales' Observation Categories, process observations omit a number of things and concentrate on the problem-solving process and observable behavior. One of the things omitted is content—*what* ideas are actually brought forth, an evaluation of their usefulness and quality for the needs of the group. In an attempt to match the serviceability of Bales' work on process, some methods of registering and measuring the content of certain kinds of discussions have been advised, such as Mills' Sign Process Analysis,[5] but the use of such tools requires considerable training and skill. An even more complex system, requiring the use of a computer, is The General Inquirer.[6] These sophisticated tools are at present beyond the reach of the usual learning-discussion group, though useful, simplified versions may be developed in the future.

non-verbal communication and unexpressed emotion

It is not a wise procedure for a discussion group to appoint an observer to watch for "unexpressed emotion". His reporting to the group after the discussion would inevitably have a judgmental character and his interpretations of what he saw, heard or felt are very subjective and may easily be incorrect. Furthermore, such emotions are often fleeting and frequently forgotten by the participant by the end of the discussion. Such a report, even if accurate, might do more harm than good. What might appear to an observer as an "emotional reaction to member X's contribution" might, in fact, be a "bit of undigested cheese", or a painful memory of a personal experience totally unrelated to that contribution, or even to the group. It is well to keep in mind that even game theorists are forced to assume "rational players". Since common sense tells us that people do not always behave rationally, sociologists and psychologists have questioned those working with game theory as to why findings concerning irrationality in human behavior have not been incorporated in their principles. Game theorists have replied that such knowledge is not sufficiently precise to be useful! [7]

Despite these precautionary words concerning the hazards of formalized attempts at observation of emotion, sensitive Leaders and other group members do pick up signals missed by others, and properly so. Some of the "unexpressed" thoughts, feelings and judgments are present in kinesic signs, and the Leader who cultivates a tactful and empathetic approach to the group will assist in developing this approach in others. By learning to watch for non-verbal reactions and responses the Leader will learn when to avoid and when to approach a group member, and while avoiding both paternalism and brutality will offer protection and challenge as needed. Erving Goffman says, "Even in 'unfocused interaction', although an individual can stop talking, he cannot stop communicating through body idiom; he must say either the right thing or the wrong thing. He cannot say nothing. Paradoxically, the way in which he can give the least possible amount of information about himself—although this is still appreciable—is to fit in and act as persons of his kind are expected to act." [8]

. . . and Leader responsibility

The minimum the Leader should require of himself is an effort to see by facial expressions, gestures, or general body movements when members seem to be registering a desire to speak, agreement or disagreement, boredom, irritation, puzzlement or distress. His response should be an effort to involve these members and facilitate the resolution of the problem through his questions. As the group grows and becomes more aware of and concerned about its members, participants will assume much of this responsibility, patterning their responses on those demonstrated by the Leader. Through the selection of suitable techniques such as subgrouping or role-playing, particularly with the use of the alter ego, the Leader may help the group bring to light and deal with some of the problems of unexpressed emotion.

GROUP DEVELOPMENT

informal group self-evaluation

Many groups begin early to try a limited amount of self-examination and evaluation with the aim of improving group processes. This can be done very simply by spending a few minutes at the end of the discussion proper talking about how it "went" in the light of the group's established norms, procedures and goals. Even new groups profit from such an informal conversation, and the Leader is wise not to be too directive in handling such evaluation sessions, though he should be careful not to allow them to become name-calling affairs. Informal conversations about the quality of the *content* of some of their discussions is a procedure often of benefit to both Leader and other group members.

With the encouragement of the Leader, a group may be helped to keep these observations as objective and positive as possible, and the time spent on "helping our group grow" can be somewhat expanded. A group meeting for a series of sessions may decide to take ten or fifteen minutes at the end of every other session for such a group inspection discussion. If the group becomes aware of such problems as imbalanced participation, the Leader may suggest the possibility of asking one of the members to make a participation chart. Such a chart, consisting of lines of communication or checks indicating "who speaks to whom", can be shown the group by the observer without comment, thus retaining maximum objectivity, and the group may discuss it from the point of view of their own satisfaction or dissatisfaction with what it shows.

written evaluations   Written comments or questionnaires are often used, but are of little value unless their contents are fed back to the entire group. Such a procedure may form the basis for very useful discussion by the group. New groups often feel more comfortable if the written material is handed in to the Leader anonymously, collated, and returned to the group for consideration. As the group matures, members will often voluntarily acknowledge ownership of various comments and be quite willing to expand their remarks in the group. They will usually grow to do without the written material. Again, the Leader must be careful to convey to the group his understanding that any problem is a *group* problem rather than that of a problem participant. As a rule, "getting rid of Mary" is not solving the group problem. If Mary talks too much, the other side of the coin is obviously that other members talk too little.

Some groups may wish to work seriously on growth or improvement while planning to remain together as a group and without the members desiring to move into the role of the Leader as titular head. Such a group may develop what might be called diagnostic functions, or the abilities necessary to spot problems in the group operations, identify their causes, and seek their solutions. When a group decides to work in formal sessions of this type, with the goal of greater effectiveness as a group, they constitute a special form of *training group*, and the members then spend a designated part of their time together in pursuit of improvement through discussions-about-the-discussions, and in various exercises chosen or designed to ameliorate specific problems. Such sessions may take a variety of forms. The term "T-group" has been applied to the basic laboratory unit of a wide range of types of training in human relations or sensitivity training. People who intend to continue working together as a group and whose primary interest is improvement of the operations of that group and their own activities and effectiveness in that group will usually find their needs are better met by a kind of training which uses an agenda, is group-centered and sociologically oriented. Such training is sometimes called applied human relations training or training for organization development.[9]

Some group members undertake sensitivity training for personal growth, in addition to or instead of the sort of training mentioned above. This type of sensitivity training is more person-oriented and less group-oriented, and seeks to uncover and give expression to hidden emotion in the group, both positive and negative, and various kinds of blocking which hamper individual response and growth. It is not possible to sharply distinguish differences among the many types of sensitivity training. Max Birnbaum, director of Boston University Human Relations Laboratory, has roughly categorized two general types: (1) "those training experiences . . . designed to improve an individual's capacity to work effectively as a manager or member of a group for educational or re-educational purposes, and (2) those that are designed to stimulate the individual's personal growth and . . . might be labeled para-therapy, in the sense that it is parallel to therapy, rather than therapy itself." [10]

The latter group of training experiences has considerable value for many people, but such training should not be undertaken without professional guidance, and should usually involve some sort of screening of group members, as the experience can be harmful. It should not be thought that training such as is presented in a leadership course such as this, or participation in a sensitivity training course is adequate preparation for assuming the responsibilities of a sensitivity trainer. Sensitivity training can be a useful adjunct to training in leadership for group discussions, but one is not a substitute for the other.

A group which finds itself in difficulties may occasionally benefit from the services of an outside observer, acting as a "group doctor". For this to be helpful, it is necessary that the group recognize a felt need, trust the outsider, and demonstrate a genuine desire for change. Such an outsider would join the group for a short-term period, recognizing that his function was an advisory one and that he must avoid making the group dependent upon him. Such a person would have to be sensitive, tactful, skillful and, usually, knowledgeable about group behavior in the type of group which he is attempting to assist. He should make clear to the group that he could not recognize or cure all its ills, but could make only a few observations on a limited number of aspects of the group's operations.[11]

prevention vs. cure

Group leaders accept considerable responsibility in guiding groups through evaluative procedures, formal feedback, or training in process observation. It is best to make every effort from the beginning to guide a group in the development of a healthy climate, suitable norms and procedures and successful discussions in accord with the group goals. The Leader may thus forestall the more serious group problems which might necessitate radical treatment involving extensive diagnosis and retraining. Groups formed for the purpose of improving their members' participative skills have every right to spend all their time in such procedures, but groups with other goals should use the simplest and least time-consuming methods for feedback. Learning groups frequently have a pre-determined and relatively short life-span. The Leader of such groups should not feel he has failed the group if he has not developed observation functions in the group. Although a Leader has a proper and natural interest in process and a desire to develop new Leaders, he must avoid letting the tail wag the dog. Groups, like people, can become hypochondriacs or develop other neurotic symptoms if their Leaders lose sight of primary avowed group goals.

TRAINING LEADERS

advantages of feedback in development leadership

Formal feedback procedures should be carefully planned and undertaken only when the group is in accord on their possible value and the methods to be used. Otherwise participation may be inhibited, resentment aroused, and the group climate damaged. The problems are not, however, insuperable and the advantages can be great. In groups in which there is a serious interest in and need for developing those who can step into the executive, or the titular head role, some procedures of this sort should be instituted. It is not advisable to try to develop Leaders by inflicting such activities as observation on a group without their active cooperation. Leaders who see potential leadership ability in the group may be tempted to force matters by arbitrarily asking these individuals to perform such functions without consulting the group. In such a situation, these activities will be much less fruitful and may arouse resentment which will distort the learning experience of the potential trainees and harm the discussion and hence the value of the total situation for all group members.

A group which has enjoyed successful discussions and developed cohesiveness can often become interested in moving on to such new activities, when their purpose and advantages are explained. New procedures can be introduced slowly and on a small scale, and the group will usually find them very interesting. If, however, their introduction is allowed to interfere seriously with the group goals as the group understands these to be, and real dissatisfaction is encountered, it is better to develop a separate group made up entirely of those who are interested in going on into leadership roles. It is possible that time will not permit them to continue simultaneously with their original group. Such training takes time, but the need for trained leadership is great, and the advantages inherent in the training are so considerable that the diversion of some group members for this purpose is well worthwhile. It must be remembered, however, that the group from which some of its able members are removed will suffer in cohesiveness and productivity. It takes time for the wound of excision to heal.

content observation

In leadership training it is wise to deal to some extent with the observation and evaluation of content. The content observer tries to make some judgment on the quality of the contributions, including the questions, judging by the criteria of the importance of the problem under question, the depth of exploration, the richness or value of the ideas developed, the effort made to develop responsive understanding and the correspondence of the discussion with the selected goals. Such judgments are inevitably subjective, but in the hands of a knowledgeable observer they can be of considerable service to a leadership training group.

A method of observing, recording and evaluating data relevant to at least some aspects of content is provided by portions of the Instroteach scales mentioned above. Both the Instroteach and Amidon and Flanders' methods are concerned with the observation of overall teaching activities, but a large proportion of the categories analyzed are related to the activities of a discussion group.

Leadership training groups frequently suffer from the necessity of moving members too rapidly through the various stages of development. Ideally, candidates for training would have had considerable experience in a well-led group using somewhat the same methods before being forced to the individual and group self-examination necessary in training. The need to examine the discussion process from many angles creates a situation in which there is little opportunity for consolidation in one role before another role is forced upon the trainee. Frequently the result is an initial period of exhiliration, followed by confusion or frustration. The trainee experiences some of the same difficulties he would if he were asked to run up a steep hill and down again, but was forced to stop and explain the action of each nerve and muscle after each step, and also to explain the plans for all possible future steps before moving on. However, the pieces eventually begin to fall into place and a leveling out stage ends in confidence restored.

FOR SOURCES AND FURTHER INFORMATION, CONSULT THE FOLLOWING WORKS:

1. Lundberg, George A., Clarence C. Schrag and Otto N. Larsen, SOCIOLOGY, 3rd ed., p. 91, N.Y.: Harper and Row, 1963.
2. Bion, W. R., EXPERIENCES IN GROUPS, London: Tavistock Pub., 1961.
3. Amidon, Edmund J., and Ned A. Flanders, THE ROLE OF THE TEACHER IN THE CLASSROOM, rev. ed., Minneapolis: Assoc. for Productive Teaching, 1967.
4. Deever, R. Merwin, et al., THE EVALUATION OF TEACHING EFFECTIVENESS IN THE CHURCH: The INSTROTEACH Board, 1970.
   NOTE: "INSTROTEACH is a counterpart of the Instrument for the Observation of Teaching Activities (IOTA) which was developed in California by Dr. Lucien Kinney et al. . . . (and) which has been used extensively in workshop programs for public school personnel, especially in California and Arizona."
5. Mills, Theodore M., GROUP TRANSFORMATION, Englewood Cliffs, N.J.: Prentice-Hall, pp. 19-41, 1964.
6. Stone, Philip J., Dexter C. Dunphy et al., THE GENERAL INQUIRER: A COMPUTER APPROACH TO CONTENT ANALYSIS, Cambridge, Mass.: MIT Press, 1966.
7. Luce, R. Duncan, and Howard Raiffa, GAMES AND DECISIONS: INTRODUCTION AND CRITICAL SURVEY, p. 5, N.Y.: John Wiley & Sons, 1957.
   see also: "Trust, Trustworthiness and the F-Scale" ("The Study of Conflict of Interest through Games"), JOURNAL OF ABNORMAL AND SOCIAL PSYCHOLOGY, 61, 138-140 (1960).
8. Goffman, Erving, BEHAVIOR IN PUBLIC PLACES, N.Y.: Free Press, 1963.
9. Birnbaum, Max, "Sense about Sensitivity Training", SAT. REVIEW OF LIT., Nov. 15, 1969, pp. 82ff.
   NOTE: Examples of some techniques and exercises are provided in Matthew B. Miles, LEARNING TO WORK IN GROUPS, N.Y.: Teachers' College Press, Columbia Univ., 1959.
10. Birnbaum, "Sense about Sensitivity Training", SAT. REV. OF LIT., Nov. 15, 1969.
    see also: Bradford, Leland P., Jack R. Gibb and Kenneth D. Benne, T-GROUP THEORY AND LABORATORY METHOD, N.Y.: John Wiley & Sons, Inc., 1964; Shein, Edgar H. and Warren G. Bennis, PERSONAL AND ORGANIZATIONAL CHANGE THROUGH GROUP METHODS: THE LABORATORY APPROACH, N.Y.: John Wiley & Sons, Inc., 1965.
11. Bennis, Warren G., Kenneth D. Benne and Robert Chin, THE PLANNING OF CHANGE, 2nd ed., N.Y.: Holt, Rinehart & Winston, Inc., 1969.

6.
Sources of Problems

OVERVIEW

Groups behave productively or unproductively, in terms of
the task and the social-emotional areas. A Leader is often tempted
to think of unproductive behavior as being the fault of one or
more "problem participants", but it is usually more accurate as
well as more fruitful for the group and more helpful to the individual to think of these problems as "*group problems*". Problems
may arise because of *conflicting models* salient to the group members, because of specific *conflict* in the *social-emotional area,* or
because of *difficulties* in the *task area* or the *group-Leader relationships*. The Leader should familiarize himself with the possible

sources of these problems, learn to distinguish among them to some extent, and seek ways to help his group resolve their difficulties. The findings of Group Dynamics can be of assistance.

DISTURBED PARTICIPANTS

The exception to this is the presence in the group of someone who is extremely neurotic or emotionally disturbed. The mentally or emotionally ill can in truth be very disruptive to a learning-discussion group, and it is no real kindness to keep them as members. They need help the group is not equipped to provide, and the group may spend all its energies on such a person, destroying any possibility of reaching its goals, and without providing any real assistance to such individuals. The learning-discussion group, as considered in this text, is not and cannot be a therapy group, though for "normal" individuals much that goes on can be therapeutic in nature. It is true that the line between the normal and the not normal is fine indeed, but it is sometimes necessary for a Leader to take the responsibility of drawing this line for the sake of those who have accepted his leadership. It should not be done hastily or without consultation, but sometimes it must be done.

MODELS

Since "discussion group" means many different things, one common cause of discomfort in the early life of a group derives from the variety of expectations held by group members. There is the element common to many models, of a discussion in which the Leader will somehow provide the "right answer". Alternatively, there is the model in which the Leader provides no guidance at all. Many members have experienced activities designated as discussion which vary widely from the concept presented here. They have developed one or more models of discussion groups.

One common model is the "book review", a discussion which ensues following a presentation by the Leader of his own ideas on the subject under discussion, or a description by him of material gathered from one or more sources. In such discussions, the Leader speaks first, often at some length. Regardless of his subsequent attitudes and behavior, he has made himself very much the center of attention and reinforced his image in the minds of the rest of the group as the "expert" or "authority". After such a performance, group members tend to direct the majority of their remarks to him, and also to either seek to shape their thinking in accord with their understanding of his views, or to debate or argue with him. The idea of a shared search for understanding is very difficult to approach under such circumstances. In the classroom situation, where the group members are students used to receiving information from the teacher, the latter will have to find new forms of presentation and new approaches to the educative process to help students break out of their old mold as recipients of "poured on" ideas, and will have to be particularly careful to talk as little as possible at the beginning of a discussion session.

A similar situation exists if a guest speaker is brought in and remains during the discussion period. Such a resource person must be helped to understand his role, or the entire discussion will consist of questions to the speaker, or an interchange between the guest and the regular teacher. Sometimes such a situation is best handled by having a short question and answer period immediately following the lecture, after which the guest leaves. A speaker accustomed to the type of learning discussion here advocated may remain and serve a useful function in much the same way that printed materials, films or tapes provide a means of checking the accuracy of the members' memory of what was actually presented. Some speakers are interested in remaining without making any comments, on the grounds that they are seeking information as to whether their talk was presented in such a way as to be accurately perceived by the listeners. The same situation applies, of course, to panel presentations or debates or similar presentations.

In the classroom, the most common model is the quiz. In a quiz, the Leader is the expert who asks only those questions to which he *does* know the answer, and indicates in one way or another whether their responses are to his liking or not. Experience has obviously made many students deeply suspicious of activities billed as "discussions"; they anticipate a thinly veiled quiz type activity.

Two other models, closely related, are also common. One is what is sometimes called the "purple passages" approach, frequently used when a book or other written material forms the presentation, but also apt to occur with other media. In such discussions, with the encouragement or at least the acquiescence of the leader, group members read or gloss sections of the presentation which appealed to them in some way, or gave them new insights. Such an approach often leads to a sort of public meditation session, harmless but seldom very productive. The well-trained and well-prepared Leader can use such an activity as a jumping off point, if he so desires. It presents a number of problems which lead to member dissatisfaction, and often results in a discussion centering on minor points, omitting the most important areas for exploration. It can be fruitful with a small experienced group working either with very familiar material or with a very brief presentation of a small amount of fresh, innovative ideas. The second, and related model, is the friendly, personal chat, or what might be termed a bull session or a rap session. It may derive either from a presentation or from a topic offered for discussion without a presentation. This offers the same problems and opportunities as the purple passage approach. Particularly in the topic discussion there are the additional problems of the self-appointed expert and the lack of a common ground. Such a discussion is best used in a group of peers discussing matters within their own speciality. Even here the

Leader will have to be on his toes to see that problems are worked through and that real discussion ensues, rather than simply the presentation of several viewpoints.

TV has provided many people with a discussion model of the entertainment variety, in which a leader or moderator assembles a group of people, often controversial in their ideas, and proceeds to draw them out, frequently baiting them or offering his own ideas in rebuttal. True discussion is not a spectator sport, and is seldom enjoyable to the looker-on unless he is an experienced leader or participant interested in the process as an object of study, rather than the content of the discussion. The things which provide pleasure for the audience are often the same things which damage the value of the discussion for the participants. Short demonstration discussions are sometimes used to interest groups in the method of discussion, but their value is questionable. Participants are usually overly aware of being on display and feel hampered and ill at ease, and the audience is usually rather confused and dissatisfied. The physical arrangements often present a very real problem in themselves, particularly if the audience outnumbers the participants. In such a situation closed circuit TV offers help with the physical problem, but introduces the cameraman as "editor", and for the group unused to being filmed or taped it introduces some of the same problems of discomfort as a live audience.

Many of these models are familiar to members of a new group, and although most people find the kind of discussion we present a fascinating experience, it takes time for them to develop their new model. They may feel dissatisfied because of a lack of security, resentful of the discipline or discouraged by the amount of work involved. Until they settle in and become comfortable with the method, they may react in ways not only unsuitable for discussion but even foreign to their own norms. A new Leader with a new group may be unduly discouraged by the first few sessions unless he recognizes that change, even remarkable in its depth, will occur in the behavior of the group and its individual members as they learn the rules and roles.

SOCIAL-EMOTIONAL AREA

In about 1580, in an essay called, "That To Philosophize Is To Learn To Die", Montaigne wrote: ". . . whatever role man undertakes to play, he always plays his own at the same time." [1] For every man, there are times when "his own role" is of predominating importance. When needs are strong and unmet, behavior will result which is dysfunctional in terms of the group task, and which may cause storms in the group climate. The pursuit of the satisfaction of individual needs at the expense of group needs is often referred to as work on the hidden agenda. [2]

frustration and aggression

Our motivated behavior does not always lead to success, and when we fail, or believe we might fail, we often resort to defense mechanisms. Aggression is such a common reaction to frustration, and seems to be behind so much other behavior, that some psychologists believe it is always present in frustrating situations.[3] It may show itself in critical or even insulting remarks, in a generalized hostility, and if remarked upon, may turn to a blaming of others for the situation.

scapegoating

Aggression in the group may be directed against an individual thought to be creating interference with the group's progress toward its goal. If the irritating member is in a favorable position in the group because of status or an appealing personality, or is a group favorite for some other reason, the aggression may be displaced onto a scapegoat, either in or outside of the group. Under certain conditions, a high status person may be the target of increased aggression.[4] Aggression can be turned against oneself, also, and may result in some members refusing to speak, even when they have something they really wish to say. A frustrated group may become involved in telling jokes, making irrelevant humorous remarks, or general regression to rather childish behavior. Groups also become involved in rationalization when their discussion is not going well. The room is thought to be too hot, the meeting too soon after a holiday, or the presentation too boring.

group regression

rationalization

power struggle

One of the most frequent problems to be found in a group is a struggle for power or domination. One or more members may do all the talking, either on rare or frequent occasions, or by brief but frequent statements or questions seek to turn the discussion in another direction. They may also interrupt frequently, or in their statements give the impression that theirs is the only possible correct answer. They may indicate a general disapproval of procedures, subject matter, or their fellow members, but they will usually do this in a positive, rather than a negative fashion, often making suggestions for a "better way".

need for recognition

A related problem is that of the need for recognition. All of us have this need, but at times some need recognition more than others, and feel they are receiving less. Such a need may be manifested by a wide variety of behaviors, ranging from sulkiness to aggressive attack, from overtalkativeness to the occasional insertion of wild irrelevancies or unsuitable jokes. Extreme physical restlessness, late arrival or early departure, overenthusiasm or expressed contempt for the subject matter—all may be ways of seeking increased recognition.

axe-grinding

Axe-grinding can be mildly or seriously deflecting to the purpose of the discussion. We all have axes to grind, but the whir of the turning grindstone may become a constant whine, and neither the preacher nor the preached-to benefits when every discussion, no matter what the intended topic, becomes a platform for the advocacy of vegetarianism, the single-tax or the problem of water pollution.

blocking

What is sometimes called "blocking" or "interference" seeks to turn the group's activities from whatever is in progress, and can take the form of asking for frequent definitions or clarifications, frequent retreading of previous discussions, irrelevancies, refusals

to try to cope with direct questions, and an inability to hear accurately or remember correctly what others have said. Its causes can be as numerous as its overt results.

withdrawal

In a group which has been working together for some time, withdrawal can slow a group's progress as much as attempted domination. A member who persists in silence, who seems inattentive, disinterested, who keeps his nose in a book or writes copious notes, who makes clipped, overacademic replies, turns his chair away from the group, averts his gaze or starts to wear dark glasses —all can cause consternation in a well-knit group. There are times when a group member feels unwell, is overly tired, or is all wrapped up in a personal problem. It is not always the case that withdrawal behavior is related to the group situation. Despite a realization of this, however, group members will tend to manifest some disturbance when one of their group behaves in this fashion.

reaction formation and reactive love

Groups or group members may indulge in reaction formation. Reactive love can be a frequent problem in groups discussing racial or ethnic intolerance or religious bigotry. There is apt to be a strong moral feeling against such attitudes, coupled with various degrees of prejudice. This conflict in motivation causes discomfort. A prejudiced person may speak with irrational overpraising of the people against whom he is prejudiced. Hall says of this praise, in contrast to real admiration, "Reactive love protests too much; it is overdone, extravagant, showy and affected. It is counterfeit, and its falseness, like the overacting of the player-queen in *Hamlet*, is usually easily detected." [5]

subgroups Group productivity may be hindered by subgroup behavior. Subgroups, like roles, may be divided into behavioral and assigned. Behavioral subgroups arise quickly within all groups, and consist of two general types: (1) factions, and (2) liking and disliking groupings, frequently called "sociometric" groupings. We are speaking here, of course, of spontaneous subgroups. The first can be of a long-lasting type, in which case it can be destructive, particularly if the subgroups are truly in opposition to the group goals and norms. On the other hand, factions can quickly arise and subside and may consist of nothing more than those who happen to share an opinion which differs from the majority. Sociometric groups of two or more members who like and admire or dislike and disapprove of one another are to be found in all groups. These feelings may be weak or strong, unconscious or conscious. They may consist simply of two friends who happened to enter the group together and are slightly more aware of statements originating from within their subgroup than from other group members. Or they may be strangers who rapidly develop a two-way or even a one-way antipathy or liking for one another's views. As a rule, sociometric groupings do not cause difficulties, but occasionally they may become large enough or sufficiently emotion-laden to split a group.

newcomers One or more newcomers in a group operate as a subgroup. When several newcomers enter a group there is resistance to as-

similation on both sides. The larger the proportion of new members entering at about the same time, the greater the resistance. Two or more newcomers in an "old" group may remain a subgroup for quite a long time, thinking in terms of "we" and "they". When groups combine this phenomenon is readily observable, and if there has been an appreciable difference in the norms of the two groups, or the type of leadership, the group may find itself not a "group" but a confrontation of two factions.

problems from outside   A group may face certain other problems over which it has no initial control—attack by hostile forces or other sudden emergencies, or the loss of a group member. These damage or at least threaten the autonomy or area of freedom of a group, or its climate. Paul Torrance has investigated such "stressors" and finds that the immediate reaction is often increased cohesiveness on the part of the group, with temporary improvement in productivity. However, such things as these, as well as other problems we have indicated in this chapter, can cause the "death" of a group. Torrance lists as mediating factors in conditions of stress: duration, intensity, and leadership and interpersonal behavior.[6] Over the first two a group may have no immediate control, but leadership and the area of interpersonal relations should respond to training efforts.

GROUP-LEADER RELATIONS

Truman's sign, "The buck stops here", gave concise expression to a law of executive responsibility. Many believe that one of the functions of the titular head is to absorb the complaints and dissatisfactions of other members and the hostility of the outside world.[7] In a learning-discussion group, we believe such a stance should be moderated, but it is certainly true that the Leader will often be the first point of attack and the first line of defense. It is often difficult to strike a balance. Paternalism, martyrdom, and the abandonment of responsibility are equally unsuitable responses for the Leader, who must try to examine his own feelings and goals and the reality of the external situation. He must be able to do this without the need to be defensive. He should consider this neither unjust persecution, nor trivia to be ignored, but accept it as an indication of possible problems to which he should give thoughtful consideration.

"Get the Leader!"   The Leader is an ideal scapegoat for the group, representing as he does someone who is "other" than the group, and yet present and obviously affecting its operation, and someone who often represents the parent organization to the group. The group may feel that the parent organization makes unjust demands on the individual members, and recognizes that the Leader as the "authority"—a role in which he is inevitably cast—is their point of contact. The outside world tends to identify the Leader with the group and to hold him responsible for its activities. To set aside these facts at times of stress is to ignore some of the realities of the situation.

dysfunctional Leader responses	The Leader who becomes aware of such attitudes on the part of his group tends to overreact. He may accept the group's verdict, consider himself guilty of the group's failure, and attempt to placate the group with apologies and blandishments. The group will in turn feel that their diagnosis of their problem was a correct one, and without turning their attention to the solution of their real problem waste further energies on comforting their Leader—after all, he is "theirs". If, on the other hand, the Leader feels affronted by the group attack, he may attack them in unrighteous anger and by punitive attitudes, remarks and actions spur them on to further unproductive behavior. If they are sufficiently fearful of him, the members may select one of their own for attack, while still harboring considerable resentment against the Leader.[8]
group attitudes toward authority	A group will sometimes demonstrate reactive love toward a Leader, unconsciously blaming their lack of success on him, but feeling guilty because he represents an authority to them. They will hasten to reassure him that the group's failure is not his fault, thus concealing their hostility. The entire group may behave in this way, or such behavior may be confined to a faction who react in totally inappropriate ways because of their previous experience with other authority figures. They may seek to win his approval, or they may fear and distrust him. Allport explains this as being motivated by needs which no longer exist, and resulting from what may have been experiences in early childhood.[9]
visiting "authorities"	Such behavior may be seen in the presence of visitors to a group who carry status with the group or in the community. Any stranger who enters a group and does not participate, whose behavior is not adequately explained, and who sits and watches the group in action can disturb the group, who tend to regard him as a peculiar kind of authority, or at least a "spy" for some unknown authority. An authority figure can totally dominate a normally democratic group by even minimal participation. If both group and visitor are prepared for the experience, forewarned of the possible negative effects, and encouraged to try to meet as equals, some of these difficulties may be lessened.
the authority in the group	Group members are expected to bring to their group experience their own knowledge and background. If a group includes, for instance, a lawyer or a physician, it is perfectly reasonable that in a question of law or of medicine the group would expect to hear some more knowledgeable technical statement from such individuals. It would be foolish to exclude such information when it is pertinent to the problem under discussion. A difficulty arises when such individuals are accorded deference in all fields because of their special knowledge in one. There is also the occasional problem which arises when the Leader asks a question to which only the specialist in the group can address himself, or when the group becomes interested in the technical ramifications of a particular question to the exclusion of other material in the presentation or in the common knowledge of the group.

In such cases it may be wise to schedule a lecture or another presentation if the group is obviously interested in further input on the subject. The object of the presentation is to provide common material so that all members of the group can make useful contributions. If the questions under discussion are addressed to the group as a whole and are based on the presentation or on common knowledge, the "authority" should find them of interest and should enjoy hearing how other group members understand the problem and its possible solutions. A Leader may find that it is not the "authority" who wishes to dominate the discussion, but the group which insists on deferring to his opinion and seeks definitive answers from him. Basically, the group may be trying to dodge the pain of thinking.

protection in frustration

An underlying reason for a great deal of this non-productive or dysfunctional behavior is that demands are made on us, by others or even by ourselves, which we cannot fulfill. We want to do so, are motivated toward a goal, but are frustrated at some point, and to protect ourselves from anxiety and discomfort we grasp at these "irrational" means of protection. This is not done consciously or deliberately. The Leader cannot always identify the causes, either in the group or in himself, but neither can he close his eyes to the results. He is neither obligated nor equipped to deal with serious and deep-rooted personal problems, but he must help the group members find the best ways to operate in order to achieve their individual and group goals within the context of the group situation.

TASK AREA

The group problems we have been discussing so far have been primarily in the social-emotional area. Other problems arise in the task or problem-solving area. In his list of stressors, Torrance lists a number which are concerned with the task area: "failure of group mission or objectives; unrealistic goals . . . difficult tasks; frequent repetition of events . . . lack of group-task structure . . . rigid group-task structure . . . (and) inadequate training for individual and group tasks." [10]

In examining the goals and procedures of the group, the Leader can help the group identify such problems and seek their resolution. When listed, they seem immediately obvious, and yet many groups founder because of such failures in planning.

There are identifiable difficulties within the "group-task structure" and the "training for tasks". We have discussed specific types of communication difficulties, but open-mindedness, clear thinking and the differentiation between conflict and controversy are important to group productivity and, in some cases, go beyond what we specified as "communication problems".

open-mindedness

A middle range of open-mindedness is desirable in the members of a group. The totally open-minded participant would have no values of his own, and no special interests. He would immediately agree with every statement made, disregard contradictions, and have no special ideas or values which he might wish to introduce. To be totally closed-minded he would have to lack all ability to cooperate, and share no values with other members of the group. Neither of these extremes is likely to appear or remain in a group. Many people widen their view on many topics within the group experience, or add to the number of areas in which they have a middle range. A good group climate helps members to be able to do this.

clear thinking

If a group contains a large number of members who lack ability or training in systematically thinking through a problem, or who resent a systematic approach to problem-solving, the group may make slow progress. If a group contains only a few such members, the temptation to neglect their well-being or ignore their potential presents a challenge to the Leader and other group members. On the other hand, some Leaders may find themselves too inflexible in their approaches to problem-solving, believing that there is one way, and only one way, to approach the process, and may be intolerant of those with a more intuitive approach or those who feel hampered or irritated by a too formal logical pattern.

The Leader must anticipate that problems such as these will be found in most groups. Slow, patient and cheerful training will help any group make progress toward both greater flexibility and more logical thinking, and expand its repertoire of approaches to problem-solving. Neither "logic" nor "flexibility" however should be thought of as ends in themselves—they are tools which the group uses to achieve its purposes, and tools which group members will find useful in other situations as well. The Leader must remember that his own goals for a learning-discussion group give priority to the growth of the individual members rather than to the "elegant solution".

CONFLICT AND CONTROVERSY

Some Leaders seem to feel a discussion session has failed unless there is a "good fight". Others feel equally distressed by any forceful expression of differences within a group. We first wish to distinguish between "conflict" and "controversy" by speaking of the former as primarily emotional and the latter as primarily intellectual. Elements of emotion naturally enter into intellectual controversy and the cognitive functions are not absent from emotional controversy; also, a conflict in a group can become a controversy, and vice versa. However, the group members will usually feel the difference as that of emotional conflict versus intellectual controversy. We speak of *controversy* in those cases in which a difference of opinion arises from the material of the presentation and its exploration. Controversy is a normal, healthy and even necessary part of discussion—if everyone thought exactly alike throughout a discussion, there would be little point in discussing. Controversy is sometimes spoken of as "intrinsic conflict", and can often be

controversy

resolved by further exploration within the subject matter. It may be the result of differing symbol-systems, different ways of reasoning, or reasoning from different sets of facts. Controversy is perhaps more apt to arise concerning concepts, while conflict is more apt to occur when attitudes are involved.

conflict   *Conflict,* on the other hand, is largely imported into the group's discussion, being based on emotional charges of various kinds which each individual brings with him. It is sometimes called "extrinsic conflict". When group members become angry it is because they consider an attack upon their ideas as a personal attack—sometimes they are right! When someone voices an opinion or belief and finds it strongly challenged, this may constitute an attack on an attitude which is very central for him. This may be a real threat to much that he holds dear, and to allow himself to believe this differing opinion could be a shattering experience. He may not recognize this at first, but as the discussion continues it may become increasingly obvious to him, and therefore increasingly dangerous. What is operative here is the fact that a cherished value with which he arrived is being damaged or destroyed.

This threatens his self-image. Under such circumstances he will cling to irrationalities, deny contradictions, and perhaps strike out verbally at the one he finds so threatening. He may well find his opponent's own soft spot and in turn wound him. This is, indeed, conflict—based on something outside the group, on past experiences, but creating a present experience of considerable discomfort.

True conflict is, indeed, an uncomfortable business, but it is not always harmful. The group and the Leader will usually want to avoid conflict, but for a cohesive group there are times when it represents growth.

GROUP DYNAMICS: FORCES: FIELD: FINDINGS: FRIEND

As the Leader strives to help his group he tries to increase his knowledge of group operations. Since 1930 there has been much research in the operations of small groups. Many disciplines and many areas of life have been involved. Because of the variety of groups and problems studied, and because the theories, methods and terminology have been drawn from many fields, there is a confusing array of literature, disparity in terminology and considerable disagreement as to the purposes and values of some of the work. Even the term "group dynamics" is used in a variety of ways, sometimes pejoratively. Malcolm and Hulda Knowles give four uses of the term. First, "it is used to describe something that is happening in all groups at all times, whether anyone is aware of it or not". It refers to "the complex *forces* that are acting upon every group . . . the interaction of these forces and their resultant effects." Second, it is also used to designate a *field of study,* and as such "employs the tools and personnel of several disciplines of the social sciences." A third use is in reference to the "body of basic knowledge about group behavior . . . the *findings* of group dynamics." A fourth use is descriptive of the "applied knowledge or technology, which attempts to translate the findings . . . into practical principles and methods." [11] It is this last use which we have designated as *friend,* and yet it is this last use which some have regarded as foe.[12]

The charge is sometimes leveled against group dynamics that its purpose is manipulation, not in its meaning of "to handle skillfully" or to "work by hand", but in the sense of "to manage or use unscrupulously or to alter fraudulently". Studies in group dynamics aim at understanding what goes on in a group, and the applied knowledge seeks to assist groups in accomplishing their goals. It is quite true that if your goal is to "manage unscrupulously" or "alter fraudulently" the members of a group entrusted to you, such knowledge could be of assistance, at least temporarily. However, there are other ways of accomplishing such aims. It is far more likely that, without a knowledge of at least some of the findings of group dynamics, a Leader might, quite unintentionally, accomplish undesirable manipulation. A knowledge of chemistry

is useful both to the poisoner and to the physician, and one who dabbles in chemistry untaught may cause unfortunate results.

Karl Stern, in speaking of the current trend toward a dehumanized society, says that the official psychology would "have to be a psychology of *I* and *it, I* and *they,* Pavlovian mechanic sets, cybernetics or communication models, discrimination cages, graphs and formulas, personality tests, group dynamics and so on. This is the only kind of psychology which enables us to run people." [13] His caution to us is valuable and his concern is shared by many. However, in the case of findings from the above fields, it would be foolish to refuse insights offered because of attendant dangers.[14] Many of the research findings referred to in this book come from those working in group dynamics.

Lifton, studying "Thought Reform" in the "revolutionary colleges" of Communist China, found that their programs demonstrated a knowledge of group dynamics as well as of individual psychology. However, this use showed some striking features. The seemingly "open" discussion and the seemingly "neutral" discussion Leader rapidly became something quite different. The discussion of the doctrines of the party was temporarily put aside until an inquisitorial approach resulted in increasingly detailed and progressively more public "confessions" in which the group member denounced his past beliefs and activities and also and most particularly his father "as a symbol of the exploiting classes, and as an individual". The Leader was a strong partisan in the discussions, encouraging constant criticism by other group members of the individual who was at that point the center of attention. The individual was subjected to a situation of total environmental control, constant observation, suppression of individuality and spontaneity, encouragement of mutual hostilities and emotional appeals. The continuing of the responses induced by this program is heavily dependent upon the support of and demand by the general national environment, without which the program would be ineffective.[15]

The obvious conclusions, reached by Lifton, Brown [16] and others, are that even though such a program is reasonably successful in effecting change in Communist China, and even here it has not been totally successful,[17] a similar attempt in the U.S., based on such procedures, would ultimately fail without the necessary ingredients of the past history, non-individualistic societal pattern, and national support; and furthermore, the well-intentioned and well-informed Leader would neither be able to use, nor desirous of using, his knowledge of psychology and group dynamics in this fashion.

group discussion in business and industry

Democratic group discussion as now advocated and sometimes practiced in business and industry is at times justly criticized as being merely another way to make you do what management wants, only more cheerfully. Group-decision and group-action are an essential outcome in business and industry, rather than the personal, individual decision and action sought in the learning-discussion group. Furthermore, the options or range of choice must obviously be strictly circumscribed in the industrial situation, whereas in a learning discussion there are no sanctions applied to limit choice, other than the group social pressure. In the strictly voluntary group, the accepting of such pressures is dependent upon individual choice. In the ordinary learning situation the economic sanctions do not apply in the same ways. Even in business and industry considerably more genuine democratic discussion is now taking place, as management realizes the benefit to the company in developing initiative and making use of the interest and creative thinking available in many levels of its total work force.[18]

leadership and knowledge of theory

As is so often the case, the trouble has developed or the threat has been felt in the misuse of knowledge, the misapplication of theories, neutral in themselves, and the attempt to put into practice theories insufficiently developed or incomplete in terms of relevant factors. As Kurt Lewin said, "Nothing is so practical as a good theory", or as others have said, "There's no such thing as a good theory which won't work." It is also true that some theories are not neutral in themselves. It is the obligation of those who accept leadership, and thereby the power to influence others, to investigate the theories upon which their practice is based, and the premises upon which these theories are built.

FOR SOURCES AND FURTHER INFORMATION, CONSULT THE FOLLOWING WORKS:

1. COMPLETE WORKS OF MONTAIGNE, trans. by Donald M. Frame, Stanford University Press, 1958.
2. National Training Laboratories, GROUP DEVELOPMENT, NTL, Washington, D.C., 1961.
3. Dolland, John, *et al.*, FRUSTRATION AND AGGRESSION, New Haven: Yale University Press, 1961.
4. Wiggins, James A., Forrest Dill and Richard D. Schwartz, "On Status-Liability", GROUP DYNAMICS, eds. Dorwin Cartwright and Alven Zander, 3rd ed., pp. 538-45, N.Y.: Harper and Row, 1968.
5. Hall, Calvin S., A PRIMER OF FREUDIAN PSYCHOLOGY, p. 92, N.Y.: New American Library of American Literature, Inc., 1955.
6. Torrance, E. Paul, "A Theory of Leadership and Interpersonal Behavior under Stress", LEADERSHIP AND INTERPERSONAL BEHAVIOR, eds. Luigi Petrullo and Bernard M. Bass, pp. 100-17, N.Y.: Holt, Rinehart and Winston, 1961.
7. Schutz, William C., "The Ego, FIRO Theory and the Leader as Completer (Based on Ego Psychology)", LEADERSHIP AND INTERPERSONAL BEHAVIOR, eds. Luigi Petrullo and Bernard M. Bass, p. 62, N.Y.: Holt, Rinehart and Winston, Inc., 1961.
8. Thelen, Herbert A., DYNAMICS OF GROUPS AT WORK, pp. 297ff., Chicago: University of Chicago Press, 1954.
9. Allport, Gordon W., PERSONALITY, pp. 191ff., N.Y.: Henry Holt & Co., 1937.
10. Torrance, E. Paul, "A Theory of Leadership . . . under Stress", pp. 100-17.
11. Knowles, Malcolm and Hulda, INTRODUCTION TO GROUP DYNAMICS, pp. 11-14 (italics added), N.Y.: Association Press, 1959.
   see also: Bennis, W. G., Kenneth D. Benne and Robert Chin, THE PLANNING OF CHANGE, 2nd ed., pp. 58-9, N.Y.: Holt, Rinehart & Winston, 1961; Cartwright, Dorwin, and Alven Zander, GROUP DYNAMICS (Research and Theory), 3rd ed., "Issues and Basic Assumptions", pp. 22ff., and "Origins of Group Dynamics", espec. pp. 4-5, N.Y.: Harper & Row, 1968.
12. Bonner, Hubert, GROUP DYNAMICS, Ronald, 1969.
   NOTE: Although Bonner is obviously not denying the value of the findings in this field, he does raise some important issues. See comments and quotations, pp. 508-15.
13. Stern, Karl, THE THIRD REVOLUTION, p. 194, N.Y.: Image, 1954.
14. Kelman, Herbert C., "Manipulation of Human Behavior: An Ethical Dilemma for the Social Scientist", THE PLANNING OF CHANGE, eds. W. G. Bennis, K. D. Benne and R. Chin, pp. 582-95, N.Y.: Holt, Rinehart and Winston, Inc., 1969; Benne, Kenneth D., "Some Ethical Problems in Group and Organization Consultation", THE PLANNING OF CHANGE, eds. Bennis, Benne and Chin, pp. 595-604; Jourard, Sidney M., DISCLOSING MAN TO HIMSELF; Becker, Ernest, THE STRUCTURE OF EVIL, N.Y.: George Braziller, 1968; Berger, Peter, INVITATION TO SOCIOLOGY, N.Y.: Doubleday-Anchor, 1963; Kelman, Herbert C., Kenneth D. Benne and Alvin Gouldner, "Some Value Dilemmas of the Change Agent, THE PLANNING OF CHANGE, Bennis, Benne and Chin, pp. 582ff.
15. Lifton, R. J., "Thought Reform of Chinese Intellectuals", ATTITUDES, eds. Marie Jahoda and Neil Warren, pp. 196-209, Baltimore, Md.: Penguin Books, 1966. It will be noted that there are similarities between these procedures and some of those followed by Synanon and derivative groups. The general failure of less radical approaches to the rehabilitation of addicts probably provides an acceptable rationale for these measures.
16. Brown, J. A. C., TECHNIQUES OF PERSUASION, pp. 268-93, Baltimore, Md.: Penguin Books, 1963.
   NOTE: This material is derived in part from Robert J. Lifton's "Thought Reforms: A Psychiatric Study of 'Brainwashing' in China", in THOUGHT REFORM AND THE PSYCHOLOGY OF TOTALISM; Gollance and E. Hunter, BRAINWASHING IN RED CHINA, N.Y.: Vanguard Press.
17. See recent issues of the weekly, PEKING REVIEW, published in English in Peking, China, and available by mail in the U.S.
18. Cartwright, Dorwin, and Alven Zander, eds., GROUP DYNAMICS, 3rd ed., p. 336, N.Y.: Harper and Row, 1968.
   see also: Argyris, Chris, PERSONALITY AND ORGANIZATION, pp. 128, 189-90, and references to the work of Rensis Likert, N.Y.: Harper & Row, 1957.

see also: Jourard, Sidney M., DISCLOSING MAN TO HIMSELF, pp. 9, 10, 21-3, Princeton, N.J.: D. Van Nostrand Co., Inc., 1968.

7.

The Value of Group Discussion in Education

OVERVIEW

Discussion is a tested method of education. In many fields it offers a number of advantages over such methods as the lecture, recitation, quiz and independent study for attitudinal change and the internalization and retention of information. It offers additional benefits in motivation, communication skills and human relations training, and training in participative problem-solving and decision-making. It provides a satisfactory means for continuing education for adults past the current usual age of schooling.

100

EDUCATION

How do people learn? *Why* do people learn? What is the best way to *help* people learn? Many schools of thought have developed answers to these questions, but despite the long history of the search, there are still disagreements and no total answers. When we try to help others learn, we often fail, and when we investigate instances of success we have difficulty evaluating the reasons and analyzing the factors which have produced the success. We have talked about the motivation of the individual learner, certainly always a factor, but even here there are many differences of opinion. The motivated individual does not always learn, and the person who enters the learning situation without motivation sometimes does learn. Some people learn under what would seem the most adverse conditions, and vice versa.

Studies in comparative education show us that rather different goals and premises underlie educational systems in such countries as England, France, Denmark, East Germany and the U.S.[1] These goals and premises are made manifest in the curricula, methods and procedures as well as in the climate of the schools in these countries. And yet the products of these different systems become somewhat similar functioning units in comparable modern technological societies. No one of these approaches is inevitably good or bad for all whom the systems serve. It is not always reasonable to suppose that a particular educational approach will produce the same results when exported. Neither is it reasonable to suppose that a particular technique or set of techniques will work equally well with all individuals or with all groups in any one country. The learning-discussion group, per se, will certainly not solve all the problems of education. There are some individuals and groups for whom it would have minimal value most of the time, and there are others for whom it would have only occasional value. There are some circumstances and some subjects in which it would prove time-wasting and even harmful. There are times when the individual working alone will achieve far more; there are times when demonstration, supervised performance, exhortation, silent viewing or meditation or various kinds of non-verbal activity are of far greater benefit.

There is a recognized need for experimenting in methods of education. Arthur A. Lumsdaine, writing in support of teaching machines and programmed instruction, makes a number of points which are also valid in supporting the use of such methods as discussion. He says that in education ". . . defects occur in ordinary text and lecture material but they pass undetected because there is not sufficient point-by-point feedback from the student to the instructor." He also says, "When students listen to a lecture, for example, the instructor is not requiring them to respond in any readily observable way. If he calls for recitation, any one student is responding only a small fraction of the time. And there is no assurance that the other students got the point. . . . During the usual lecture there are many lapses of attention even on the part of good students. Most students have no way to know until too late whether they are learning what the lecturer intends. These difficulties can be multiplied many times when the instructor is removed from the learner even farther by teaching over radio or television or by a presentation on film." [2]

Surely the rather tired joke about the lecture method being the quickest way to get material from the professor's mind to the student's notebook without having it pass through the student's mind tells us something. Walk through the corridors of most educational institutions at whatever level and you will find the most pervasive sound is usually that of the voices of the instructors. *They* are participating, *they* are active—hopefully, *they* are learning. Many times their students are not.

discussion not an educational frill

The question of immediate concern to us is the value of group discussion as an educational tool. There is still a tendency on the part of many educators to think of discussions in terms of a "reward"—if the class has performed a difficult task satisfactorily, they may look forward to "having a discussion", or if "the work" is completed by a certain deadline, there will be "time" for a discussion. The problem with this attitude is that the teacher thinks of discussion as play or recreation, somehow of less value than the foregoing "work". His expectations are conveyed to his students, and their mutual performance reflects this expectation. Discussion should be "re-creational" in the finest sense of the word, but it is also work, and often very arduous. The very real effort involved should be stimulating, but it can be rather exhausting. After good discussion there is need for relaxation and "play".

The evidence is certainly overwhelmingly in favor of any learning procedure which actively involves the learner in the process, and to that degree group discussion would seem a helpful method. However, there are obviously other means of eliciting active participation, and many educational principles and procedures have been developed to this end. Group discussion, however, offers a certain number of specific advantages.

1. INCREASED INTERNALIZATION THROUGH IMPROVISATION. The form of participation is such that the material learned becomes more *meaningful* to the learner because he must constantly rephrase the information in his own terms. Many studies on improvisation versus "mere repetition" have demonstrated the greater degree of internalization resulting from improvisation.[3] There is apparently considerably more involved than simply an increased familiarity with a new vocabulary. Maria Bos, working with children of six to thirteen years, found that in discussion the necessity of communication resulted in a constant process of clarification as individuals explained and re-explained their statements, often discovering their own areas of vagueness or distortion, and thus resulting in greater clarity in the minds of the group members and probably in the mind of the original contributor.[4]

2. INCREASED INTERNALIZATION THROUGH SITU-
ATING IN CONTEXT. A "fact", out of context, can be almost
meaningless. A learner must have the freedom to investigate the
matrix in which this fact is embedded. Discussion offers the learner
the opportunity to question and probe until he sees his new fact
in a meaningful context. Other methods of instruction must presume
what will be meaningful for large numbers of learners and present
their facts in such a context, hoping that murkiness and uncertainty will be cleared up by the individual recipient. Discussion
thrusts the learner immediately into the process, and makes him
the active seeker and inquirer.

3. GREATER CHANGE IN BELIEFS, PREFERENCES,
ATTITUDES. Studies indicate that the discussion method produces
greater changes in beliefs, preferences and attitudes than the more
passive types of exposure.[5] Much education is concerned with
materials which, for understanding and acceptance, require the
individual to readjust his valuing in some way. In fact, some educators hold that all education involves attitudinal change, and thus
at least some restructuring of the value system. Certainly in such
fields as social studies, the behavioral sciences, philosophy, religion and the arts, education means constant attitudinal readjustment.
As the group increases in importance to the individual member,
it takes on the character of a reference group for him and he is
more influenced by communications advanced within that group.[6]
One of the most important determiners of the acceptability of the
information depends on what is often called the "prestige effect".
The attitude of the listener toward the communicator greatly influences the former's acceptance of the message. It might seem that
this fact would act as an argument in favor of the authoritative
teacher as communicator, rather than the group. The question nat-

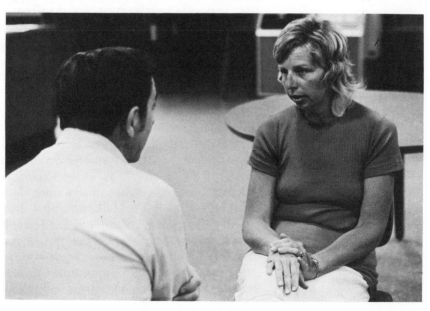

urally arises, "Will group members actually be influenced by statements made by their peers?" Yes, they will, because in addition to the reinforcing and internalization created by their own participation in the group discussion, there is a long-range tendency to dissociate the source and the information, especially when the communication contained "arguments and evidence which could be evaluated on their own merits and are likely to be recalled without bringing the source to mind." [7]

4. ACCEPTANCE OF CONCLUSIONS. In the group discussion situation motivation is provided for acceptance of the conclusions, as distinguished from merely learning the content. It is possible to "accept" information and simply store it in a fairly watertight compartment where it has little effect on attitudes and behavior.[8] It is interesting that some studies demonstrated that the amount of opinion change through active participation depends on the amount of improvisation, and that too much stress on verbal conformity, such as giving prizes, may actually interfere with acceptance or real opinion change.[9]

5. RESOLUTION OF DISSONANCE AND IMBALANCE. Group discussion provides a suitable situation for the resolution of dissonance and imbalance. The cohesive group provides the necessary comfortable situation in which an individual is free to work out problems of dissonance and internal conflict.[10] The individual working on a seeming contradiction is more apt to be willing to expose his problem in such a setting and to be able to accept the help of his friends in resolving his dilemma.

6. INCREASED RATE OF LEARNING. There seems to be a direct relation between the rate of learning verbal material and overt verbalization.[11] Material is learned more rapidly when the learner talks about it at some length during the learning period.

7. RETENTION. Also, retention is increased by the discussion process,[12] and there is greater persistence of opinion change.[13]

8. SATISFACTORY QUALITY OF WHAT IS LEARNED. The probability is that the quality of the content of what is learned will be satisfactory. Research shows that "discussion groups are more likely to accept sound suggestions than to reject them; more likely to reject bad ones than to accept them." Furthermore, those who reach the "right" answers through discussion "tend to hold them more tenaciously than do individuals who have 'wrong' answers".[14] Norman R. F. Maier found "that when a minority individual has an incorrect answer he fails to persuade the majority, but when he has the correct answer he often can persuade the majority to accept his answer. . . . These experiments . . . show that groups holding problem-solving discussions led by leaders who merely encouraged others to talk obtained better solutions than groups holding discussions without a leader. The cause of the difference obtained was found to be the presence of a discussion leader. A discussion leader gives persons with views that differ from those of the strong majority an opportunity to express themselves. However, these minority views carry an influence only when they are sup-

ported by external realities. Ungrounded opinions of persons in the minority had little influence in either type of discussion." [15]

A quality presentation and skillful questioning are additional factors aiding a group to reach "good" conclusions. It is always possible for an expert, lecturing to a group, to present a large amount of sound information. However, to say this is not at all the same thing as to say that his hearers have learned a large amount of sound information, even in the sense of acquiring a large number of unassimilated, discrete units. Although "the function of the group is often in large part the summation of individual efforts in a strict arithmetical sense . . . the group has also a censoring function: it alters suggestions in accord with whatever interests or criticism may appear in the minds of those who hear each suggestion offered." [16] A group is apt to abandon a "false lead" more rapidly than the individual who first happens on it in attempting to think through a problem. [17]

9. MOTIVATION AND REINFORCEMENT. The group provides motivation and reinforcement for learning. In actual fact, of course, a great deal of every individual's learning is done in what might be called a group situation, or even a group discussion situation, from the parent-child relationship through the classroom to the management-employee relationships. Even monologic advocacy involves communication between individuals. However, the kind of group discussion we have been working with involves the development of openness, warmth and trust—of group cohesiveness—and is also designed for successful productive work. Therefore such a group offers additional special advantages as a learning environment. The learner, identifying himself with the group, derives satisfaction from participating in its activities. Positive and negative reinforcement are provided by the group itself as it rewards, or gives him satisfaction, for his efforts toward the accomplishment of the group goals, and withholds satisfaction for behavior which lessens achievement. [18]

10. LESSENS FEAR OF FAILURE. The cohesive group reduces the tension of the self-fulfilling prophecy of failure, and hence promotes success. The tension of expected failure is eliminated or reduced, and the positive gains in knowledge are self-rewarding. Group cohesiveness spreads the good feeling of success when the group as a whole has moved forward. Even the slower or more passive group members are encouraged by the process, and their attitude is more apt to be one of expectation of future success than anticipation of continued and deepening failure, as is so often the case in the more individualistic competitive situation. [19]

11. PROVIDES EDUCATIONALLY EFFECTIVE INTERPERSONAL RELATIONS. We mentioned the fact that there is general agreement on the importance of participation, of involvement of the learner in the process of education. There is coming to be an equal stress on the importance of the quality of interpersonal relations. Ralph Garry says, "Research increasingly supports the principle that the learning that occurs in any classroom is func-

tionally related to the kind of personal relationship existing between a teacher and her pupils and between pupils. One's basic needs for self-esteem, recognition, and acceptance find their satisfaction in this matrix of interpersonal relationships. Compared with the forces of self-acceptance, teacher-acceptance, and group-acceptance, the specific incentive conditions created by the teacher are of secondary importance." [20] Apathy, disinterest and boredom are seldom problems in an effective discussion group.

Although as a teacher of science, J. J. Schwab is primarily concerned with discussion in the classroom as the preferred method to impart skills in inquiry, he believes discussion "affords a situation in which the teacher can establish more effective interpersonal relations and use them much more frequently with many more students in a given learning period than most teaching methods permit." [21]

12. IMPROVED COMMUNICATION AND HUMAN RELATIONS SKILLS. This has been called "The Age of Communication" and "The Age of the Dialogue". If we think in terms of man as a symbol-handling creature it is probable that all ages have been ages of communication, but simply because so many functions previously performed by man are now performed by machines there is an increase in time available for communication. Also, since many tasks formerly performed by men working more or less independently are now performed by interrelated groups of men and machines there is an increase in the need for communication. In government, business and industry, management spends most of its time communicating, and the greatly expanded education sector of society is based on communication. Communication skills are improved in learning discussions—skills of observation, reading, listening, speaking. Regardless of the particular material or subject studied in such a discussion group, its members are becoming better communicators.

Furthermore, the experience in the group provides the members with some training in human relations skills. The training in listening to others, in grasping other people's views and experiencing the effects of group interaction promote empathy, sensitivity to others, self-acceptance and helpful ways of working with others.

13. ENCOURAGES COOPERATION AND COMMUNITY. We also consider the stress on cooperativeness, rather than competition, a valuable feature of our learning discussion group. Unlike many group learning situations wherein competition is valued and hence encouraged, our discussions seek the growth and learning of all the members—not the success of some at the expense of others, but for the benefit of all with the assistance of all. Differences in ability and experience are not eliminated, but the stress is on each member helping every other member to reach the understanding which is their mutual search. Instead of making a "secret" of some insight in order to score points against or above some other member, the individual tries to share what he has gained, and share it in a way comprehensible to the others.

14. TRAINS MEMBERS FOR EFFECTIVE PARTICIPA-TION IN SOCIETAL GROUPS. The obvious spin-off value of train-ing in participative decision-making has long-range effects on the members of such groups. At home, on the job, in organizational activities, in participation as citizens at whatever level in a demo-cratic society, most people spend a good deal of time trying to solve problems and make decisions in formal or informal discussion situations. Surely, education should assume that it is one of its functions to aid individuals in improving their abilities to partici-pate in these vital activities.

15. PREPARATION FOR CONTINUING EDUCATION. Allied to the need for improved communication, the whole matter of the purposes of education is important in our consideration of dis-cussion in education. The "knowledge explosion" has finally suc-ceeded in convincing us that it is impossible for anyone to know all about everything, or even for most people to know all about any-thing. The food-gatherers became food-growers, and the fact-gather-ers are becoming fact-generators. Bits and pieces of information do not constitute an education, and the educated man is no longer the possessor of encyclopedic knowledge. As Borger and Seaborne [12] have said, "the growing tendency toward early specialization is met—not too successfully—by an increase in the time allotted to formal education; the argument seems to be that since there is more information available a student must take more time to assimilate it, before he can be let loose on the real world". They go on to say that they believe this involves a fallacy because today's information and specialized techniques may rapidly become obsolete, thereby fur-nishing the student with more baggage to be unloaded before he can acquire the knowledge he needs for any particular moment.

Borger and Seaborne state as the "proper objective of formal education . . . to enable people to learn and adapt more easily without the aid of such formal guidance; to extract from those situations in which they will find themselves what is to be known. . . . (W)e must concentrate on enabling every single individual, within the limits of his intellectual capacity, to deal with new situations, enabling him on the one hand to absorb, without guidance, new, already formulated knowledge presented in books or other symbolic forms, and on the other to create new knowledge for himself." They believe that "whatever opportunities for learning are provided during people's working lives, these will not achieve their aim unless the first educational experience constitutes an explicit and deliberate preparation for taking advantage of them." They recommend that from the primary school, increased emphasis be placed on *"learning by the child* rather than on *instruction by the teacher"* (emphasis in original). The discussion group member of whatever age learns to make discriminations, evaluate reasoning, pursue information and make decisions. This stimulates his ability and desire for independent study.

The student certainly perceives a difference between the instructor who knows what you need to know and will teach it to you!, and the discussion Leader who demonstrates his need to learn and his interest and pleasure in learning. The latter presents to the student a model of the adult who has accepted and accepted happily the idea of continuing education as an important and necessary part of life. Noam Chomsky was asked, "How can teachers help create an atmosphere of creativity?" He answered, "I really don't think there are ways of teaching this, that there are any principles to be established that people can follow. Teachers must first experience for themselves the pleasure of discovery and creation. They must simply show by example how it's done and try to bring others into joining with them in these experiences. Even at the university level, some of the most creative and exciting teaching I've done has been in areas that I really don't know at all. I've tried to teach in fields I was just barely acquainted with and to use the opportunity to learn something about these fields with students, some of whom bring abilities and knowledge that I don't have. As far as possible, we can explore the area and its problems together." His interviewer continued, "Can that work in lower schools too?", and Chomsky went on, "I think it can be done at every level in different ways, depending upon the personalities and experiences of the people involved." [23]

The discussion method, emphasizing learning rather than teaching, slowly develops in the individual the ability to learn to ask the right questions, the necessary questions, which is the beginning of independent learning. Before decisions are made, information must be available, and before information is sought, there must be the recognition of the gaps which need filling. When "answers" are provided before questions arise and are formulated, the information is less well integrated by the learner, and furthermore the process tends to stifle the spirit of inquiry, the analysis of the problem, the possibilities of other, quite different questions, the possibility of creativity, and the development of criteria for reliable answers. The discussion member learns to be dissatisfied with superficial answers, to seek understanding in depth, to hold himself in readiness to explore new ideas, not to turn away from a strange notion before he has explored its possibilities, not to feel that "changing his mind" is a threatening experience to be avoided by holding rigidly to old opinions, leaving new evidence uninvestigated.

The discussion method certainly does not obviate the need to seek information from knowledgeable sources, and the group member should learn to value and seek out resource people and to develop criteria for reliability of information. He will learn to seek verification for his opinions and if his search produces disconfirming evidence his experience in the group will provide support for the sometimes painful development of new and more meaningful opinions. He is thus developing his own agenda for learning.

Many innovative educational tools and techniques are available, such as teaching machines or programmed texts, audio-visuals such as films, closed circuit TV, and tapes for language labs, and many methods based on Dewey's principle of "learning by doing". These will be improved, and yet more will be developed and will provide better ways of conveying information. However, the reception of information does not in itself constitute education. Furthermore, it is hard to imagine a society from which discussion would be absent. There has been an increase in recent years of various kinds of discussion with the aim of finding, creating and strengthening "community". There seems to be a feeling abroad in the land that if people would just sit down and talk to each other, all would be well. It used to be expressed as "reason together", and although the pendulum seems to have swung to the other end of "feel together", the hope still prevails. Discussion is used as a means to learning, problem-solving, decision-making, improved human relations, and as a path to relationships of love. It deserves greater use in many areas of education.

DISCUSSION IN ADULT EDUCATION

the need

In this era of accelerating change and the "knowledge explosion", one fact has clearly emerged—the need for continuing education. More than the accumulation of facts, the child needs to acquire the skills of learning, the motivation for continued learning, and an ever increasing flexibility and adaptability. The young person starting out in his first job must recognize that ten years from now he will probably be doing a very different job, or be carrying on his present work in a very different way, and the older worker must realize that unless he continues to grow, his job and the world around him will leave him behind. The citizen needs to know more about his community, his country and his world, and everyone must accept the fact that a strange future will find him bewildered and lost unless he himself helps to mold it. Happily, increasing leisure will provide at least the time necessary for that learning, but time alone is not enough. Every field of human endeavor and every academic discipline has an obligation to find ways to aid those beyond the age of usual schooling to continue their education.

There was a time when the phrase "adult education" properly belonged to the realm of entertainment, amusement or hobbies. This time is past. It is, of course, perfectly reasonable and desirable for an adult with time on his hands to spend some of that time acquiring the ability to play a new game, learn a new craft for pleasure only, or improve his skills in some sport or other hobby. However, the broad field of adult education can no longer be viewed in this way. The time is coming when in all probability the qualifying term "adult" will vanish, since part of everyone's life, at every age, must be spent in education. Certainly it no longer occurs to those firms in business and industry or those professional groups which require of their members in-service training or additional academic work to label these activities "adult education". The term used, when there is one, is more often "continuing education", but this will become a redundancy. Marshall McLuhan has said, perhaps only a trifle extravagantly, "Under electric technology the entire business of man becomes learning and knowing. In terms of what we still consider an 'economy' (the Greek word for a household), this means that all forms of employment become 'paid learning', and all forms of wealth result from the movement of information." [24]

complicating
factors

Recognizing the need has given rise to other questions, however. One poses the problems of increasing dehumanization and alienation. With the current necessity for the increased size of educational institutions and for a faster pace of learning in many fields, and the dilution of the time available on the part of the teaching staffs, many young people feel that the educational process attacks, pummels and abuses them more than it aids and nurtures them. They are further discouraged when they see their elders apparently equally at the mercy of large, so-called "anonymous" corporations which move them about like pawns on a chessboard or process them through a system which fails to discriminate between them and other non-human bits. Somehow the human values and the value of the human individual have been strained out and disposed of as unnecessary. The addition of large numbers of adults to the already overburdened educational institutions may increase the dimensions of this problem. The adult learner is no less likely to object to educational practices which he sees as "alienating" or "dehumanizing"—after all, it was he who taught the young these words!

The eruption of communes of young people, the proliferation of small new religious groups, often bizarre in comparison to mainstream religions, the growth of the underground church, the popularity and continuing life of the sensitivity and encounter group, are all linked in some way with the search for "community", being undertaken within many areas of the establishment. New life styles are sought in an attempt to maintain a sense of the human and of the relatedness of man to man. Although the actual number of people involved in these movements is still a small percentage of the population, they express needs and longings common to a much larger number, and expressed by the majority through many small dissatisfactions and disillusionments. Any new educational procedures developed to help meet the need for increased dissemination of knowledge must take account of these lacks and stresses in our society.

can older people learn?

The question of whether older people can learn has received considerably more attention since the need arose within industry to retrain employees. Although some work had been done in the area of how adults learn and the relation of age to learning during the twenties and thirties, there was a great increase in the number of studies made and works published during the fifties and sixties both in the United States and in Europe. The early part of the century had seen a few studies in China and Japan as well as in Germany and the United States which culminated in the first major work in the field by the American psychologist E. L. Thorndike, ADULT LEARNING, published in 1928. These early studies established that adults could learn over a wide age span; that there was a greater loss of ability to learn when the material presented for learning was "nonsense" rather than "meaningful" material; and that those with a higher level of formal education suffered less loss of ability to learn. Subsequent studies have offered much information on specific problems and suitable methods in the education of adults, but have not substantially changed Thorndike's basic findings as noted here.

In an experimental degree program for adults at Brooklyn College, Graduate Record Examination scores were compared with college sophomores and seniors in a sample of colleges and universities. The adults, whose average age was 42, achieved superior scores in the social sciences and humanities, though somewhat inferior scores in the natural sciences.[25]

It has been shown that those with high intelligence tend to level out or even drop, as measured by standard IQ tests. At the same time even these mildly negative findings should be considered in the light of the fact that older subjects are penalized by factors of speed, pacing and nervousness. Faced with a testing situation after years away from such activities, conscious of the folklore which says, "you can't teach an old dog new tricks", aware of the fact that they do react a bit more slowly—extreme nervousness is often present. Also, in both the testing and the learning situation the older person is more comfortable and performs better when he sets his own pace. There is also evidence that intelligence may be preserved by use.[26]

Faced with new and complex material, the older student tends to have a slower rate of discrimination and comprehension, particularly when exposure is brief and the pace is controlled by others.[27] Kidd says he is apt to suffer more anxiety about poor success."[28] Whether his anxiety is "more" than that of children and young persons might well be doubted by some. John Holt, in WHY CHILDREN FAIL, stresses the very harmful effects of what he sees as the general prevalence of fear and anxiety in the elementary school classroom. These problems can be largely overcome by appropriate educational methods.

The Duke Center for the Study of Aging and Human Development, headed by Dr. Ewald W. Busse, has found that "older people can retain and recall information practically as well as young people do, if they are given the time. They can also learn with about half as much energy. A built-in mechanism apparently makes them conserve strength." There are now over 18.5 million Americans over 65, and one prediction puts the total at 33 million by the year 2000. Research in the field of aging has been neglected in the past, but a number of research centers and agencies are now trying to find ways to prevent abnormal or premature aging, and to help solve some of the sociological and psychological problems of those whom our government calls the "older Americans". Busse speaks of the "terrible waste of skills" of intelligent, aging persons, who must be helped to "cut back into society."[29]

Two known factors affect retention of learning in the older student. Activity following learning affects long-term memory to a greater degree as age increases, and the interference of prior learning of long standing can naturally make "unlearning" more difficult. Various means, such as learning sessions long enough to allow for consolidation and sessions free from distraction, programs designed to avoid or rapidly detect and correct early errors, meaningful problems and materials, and methods which encourage active participation and use, rather than passive reception of information and recapitulation, can overcome most of these problems. Early studies seldom considered the teaching methods involved, and therefore sometimes seemed to demonstrate considerable inferiority of the older learner.

Physical factors are too often ignored, also. Physical losses will naturally impair learning unless adequate compensation is made. Impairment of vision and hearing are not insuperable barriers, but merely factors to be properly considered, if distraction from the learning situation is to be avoided. The educator who re-members to provide a comfortable, distraction-free environment, creates a feeling of self-confidence in a non-threatening situation, and encourages self-pacing and participation, need not worry that the content of his course should be reduced for the older students. He must, however, give considerable attention to his methods.

If, as we have stated, most adults *can* learn, the question remains as to whether they *will*. This is, again, a question of motivation. As Paul Bergevin says, adult education programs must keep in mind that "most adults are not scholars and they aren't interested in becoming scholars. . . . Children have to attend school; adults don't, usually, and most of them won't unless they can see some advantage in it." [30] On the other hand, Malcolm S. Knowles says, "(m)y hunch is that those whose style of life has been one of high involvement will continue to be involved, and that those who have never been deeply involved will continue to be uninvolved. But I think we have to leave them the option. I believe that I'll have to go along with Abraham Maslow in assuming that the highest human need is for self-actualization, and that we work at it until we die; and with Harry Stack Sullivan, that the deepest human need is for self-esteem, and that each of us has an obligation to help each other achieve and maintain it." [31]

There is some evidence to indicate that unless an "interest" is established before the age of 25, it is unlikely that it will be pursued with any enthusiasm in later years.[32] In terms of long-range planning, this would seem to indicate the desirability of encouraging the development of a broad spectrum of interests in the early years. There is still much hope, however, even for those whose interests have been limited. TV has widened the world of many adults—its results have not been *all* bad! Furthermore, once an adult begins any educational program, if he finds the experience rewarding, he is apt to continue, slowly expanding his diet by moving into fields allied to his first sphere of interest. For instance, Kidd points out that "Interest in religion seems to follow two curves —one that rises sharply in childhood to slope off when other intense interests come along to compete in the late teens and early twenties, followed by another pronounced shift in the later years. The attitude toward religion is often accompanied by an interest in reading about or studies about religion, philosophy and human relations on the part of the older adults." [33]

Carl Rogers has said, "I have come to feel that the only learning which significantly influences behavior is self-discovered, self-appropriated learning. Such self-discovered learning, truth that has been personally appropriated and assimilated in experience, cannot be directly communicated to another." [34] If this applies to all learning, it is certainly of central importance in working with adults. M. F. Clough in EDUCATING OLDER PEOPLE has observed, "The most favorable conditions are when students can reflect on what they are doing and feel sufficiently free to regard their supervisors as consultants, not as judges." [35]

These and similar insights have been important in leading educators to use discussion as a preferred method in working with adults. Bergevin says that in the discussion group context individuals are "trained to participate actively in the learning experience. ... One objective of this kind of systematic learning is to become a disciplined learner by being accepted and disciplined by your fellow-learners and by helping to discipline your fellow-learners. Adults trained to learn in this way know the importance of expressing their feelings and beliefs to their fellow-learners, and they are expected to assume responsibility for what they say. Moreover, they learn to listen to others with the same understanding they expect to receive." [36]

Once involved in a learning discussion group experience in a subject which is of interest to them, the experience itself will provide the motivation to continue learning.

FOR SOURCES AND FURTHER INFORMATION, CONSULT THE FOLLOWING WORKS:

1. King, Edmund J., OTHER SCHOOLS AND OURS, rev. ed., N.Y.: Holt, Rinehart and Winston, Inc., 1963; Grant, Nigel, SOCIETY, SCHOOLS AND PROGRESS IN EASTERN EUROPE, Elmsford, N.Y.: Pergamon Press, 1969.
2. Lumsdaine, Arthur A., "Teaching Machines and Programmed Instruction", SCIENCE OF HUMAN COMMUNICATION, ed. Wilbur Schramm, pp. 139-40, N.Y.: Basic Books, 1963.
3. Hovland, Carl I., Irving L. Janis and Harold H. Kelley, COMMUNICATION AND PERSUASION, pp. 233-37, New Haven: Yale University Press, 1953.
   see also: B. T. King and I. L. Janis, "Comparison of the Effectiveness of Improvised vs. Non-improvised Role-playing in Producing Opinion Changes", HUMAN RELATIONS, 9, pp. 177-86 (1956).
4. Bos, Maria, "Experimental Study of Productive Collaboration", ACTA PSYCHOLOGY, 3 (1937), pp. 315-426, discussed by T. M. Newcomb, R. H. Turner and P. E. Converse, SOCIAL PSYCHOLOGY, pp. 470-71, N.Y.: Holt, 1965.
5. Eisenson, John J., Jeffery Auer, and John V. Irwin, THE PSYCHOLOGY OF COMMUNICATION, p. 267, N.Y.: Appleton-Century-Crofts, 1963.
   see also: Fish, Kenneth L., CONFLICT AND DISSENT IN THE HIGH SCHOOL, Ch. 10, N.Y.: Bruce, 1970; Allport, Gordon, NATURE OF PREJUDICE, Ch. 29 and 30, Reading, Mass.: Addison-Wesley, 1954.
6. Siegel, Alberta E. and Sidney, "Focus on Change", ATTITUDES, eds. Marie Jahoda and Neil Warren, p. 195, Baltimore, Md.: Penguin Books, 1966.
   see also: Hovland, Janis, and H. H. Kelley, COMMUNICATION AND PERSUASION, pp. 167-68; Berelson, Bernard and Gary A. Steiner, HUMAN BEHAVIOR: AN INVENTORY OF SCIENTIFIC FINDINGS, pp. 331, 334, N.Y.: Harcourt Brace, 1965.
7. Hovland, C. I., I. L. Janis and H. H. Kelley, "A Summary of Experimental Studies of Opinion Change", ATTITUDES, eds. Jahoda and Warren, pp. 148-49.
8. Hovland, Janis and H. H. Kelley, COMMUNICATION AND PERSUASION, pp. 218ff., 244.
   see also: Berelson and Steiner, HUMAN BEHAVIOR, p. 354.
9. Hovland, Janis and Kelley, "A Summary of Experimental Studies of Opinion Change", ATTITUDES, eds. Jahoda and Warren, p. 148.
   NOTE: This article summarizes a good deal of material from Hovland et al., COMMUNICATION AND PERSUASION.
10. Hovland, Janis and Kelley, COMMUNICATION AND PERSUASION, pp. 383-84.
11. Hovland, Janis and Kelley, COMMUNICATION AND PERSUASION, p. 217.
12. Borger, Robert and A. E. M. Seaborne, THE PSYCHOLOGY OF LEARNING, p. 158, Baltimore, Md.: Penguin Books, 1966.
    see also: Hovland, Janis and Kelley, COMMUNICATION AND PERSUASION, p. 253 and refs., pp. 250, 263-64.

13. Hovland, Janis and Kelley, COMMUNI-CATION AND PERSUASION, Ch. 8; pp. 30, 35, 37, 39-40, 139.
14. Eisenson, John Auer and J. V. Irwin, THE PSYCHOLOGY OF COMMUNICA-TION, p. 268.
15. Maier, Norman R. F., PRINCIPLES OF HUMAN RELATIONS: APPLICATIONS TO MANAGEMENT, p. 325, N.Y.: John Wiley & Sons, 1952.
16. Murphy, Gardner, and L. B. Murphy and Theodore M. Newcomb, EXPERI-MENTAL PSYCHOLOGY, p. 734, N.Y.: Harper and Bros., 1937.
17. Shaw, Marjorie E., "A Comparison of Individuals and Small Groups in the Rational Solution of Complex Prob-lems", AMERICAN JOURNAL OF PSY-CHOLOGY, 44 (1932) pp. 491-502.
18. Bonner, Hubert, GROUP DYNAMICS, pp. 102-105, N.Y.: Ronald, 1959.
see also: Maier, Norman R. F., PRIN-CIPLES OF HUMAN RELATIONS, pp. 256-58.
19. Leonard, George B., EDUCATION AND ECSTASY, pp. 122, 129, 132, N.Y.: Delta, 1968.
see also: Holt, John, HOW CHILDREN FAIL, N.Y.: Pitman Publishing, 1964; Chomsky, Noam, "An Interview with Noam Chomsky", David F. Marshall, COLLOQUY, March 1971, p. 19.
20. Garry, Ralph, PSYCHOLOGY OF LEARNING, pp. 72-3, Washington, D.C.: Center for Applied Research in Educa-tion, Inc., 1963.
21. Schwab, Joseph J. and Paul F. Brand-wein, THE TEACHING OF SCIENCE, Cambridge, Mass.: Harvard University Press, 1962.
22. Borger and Seaborne, PSYCHOLOGY OF LEARNING, pp. 230-33 (italics in original).
23. Chomsky, Noam, "An Interview with Noam Chomsky", David F. Marshall, COLLOQUY, March 1971, pp. 18-19.
24. McLuhan, Marshall, UNDERSTANDING MEDIA: THE EXTENSIONS OF MAN, p. 58, N.Y.: McGraw-Hill, 1964.
25. Siegle, Peter, "The Adult Learner", LEADER'S DIGEST, 3, p. 13 (1956), Chicago, Ill.: Adult Education Associ-ation of the U.S.A.
26. Belbin, R. M., TRAINING METHODS FOR OLDER WORKERS, pp. 29-31, Paris: Organization for Economic Co-operation and Development, 1965.
NOTE: Excellent bibliography.
27. Belbin, TRAINING METHODS FOR OLDER WORKERS, pp. 20, 25.
28. Kidd, J. R., HOW ADULTS LEARN, N.Y.: Association Press.
29. BUSINESS WEEK, Aug. 26 (1967), p. 122.
30. Bergevin, Paul, A PHILOSOPHY OF ADULT EDUCATION, p. 13.
31. Knowles, Malcolm S., THE MODERN PRACTICE OF ADULT EDUCATION, p. 85, N.Y.: Association Press, 1970.
32. Kidd, J. R., HOW ADULTS LEARN, p. 118.
33. Kidd, J. R., HOW ADULTS LEARN, p. 124.
34. Rogers, Carl R., ON TEACHING ADULTS: AN ANTHOLOGY, ed. M. V. Miller, Chicago, Ill.: Center for the Study of Liberal Education for Adults, 1960.
35. Clough, M. F., EDUCATING OLDER PEOPLE, London: Tavistock, 1962.
36. Bergevin, Paul, A PHILOSOPHY OF ADULT EDUCATION, pp. 56-7.

8.

Getting Started

OVERVIEW

Our discussions assume that *learning* is something one does, rather than something one receives, that a *Presentation* precedes discussion, and that a trained *Leader* assists the group. The Leader is a fellow learner, friendly and open-minded, interested but relaxed and well prepared to steer the discussion into some of the important areas of the subject by asking suitable questions, and to develop balanced participation, while keeping in mind the needs of group members, particularly their need for examination of values and of individual decision-making. The questions he asks will not have pat answers, and he will encourage group members' *cooperativeness* rather than *competitiveness*. Realizing the importance

116

of the *first session*, he will be particularly careful in setting the tone, in making it easy for members to become acquainted, to set their own goals, and to begin participating.

PREMISES

learning

The discussions presume that *learning* is something each individual *does*—not something that someone else can do for him or to him. Furthermore, we presume that those attending a discussion are interested in some kind of learning, willing to discuss, and willing to grant equality in discussion. It may be felt that these presumptions are too idealistic, and it is true that most groups need help in arriving at this state, but it is not unrealistic to presume at least a minimal level of willingness.

Presentation

The discussion will be based on a *Presentation* of some kind. We do not have a discussion by saying, "Well, let's talk about something or other that we are all interested in." The Leader is prepared to lead a specific discussion, and the group has been prepared by materials provided in advance of the discussion. These materials may vary widely in form. They may consist of printed matter, a lecture, a film, tape, poster, sociodrama, simulation gaming, role-playing or other medium. The material will have solid value, if possible some artistic or literary merit, and will provide a *common basis* for the discussion. A small group of experts, gathered to discuss a common problem, may decide their presentation should be a brief statement by each member, outlining their particular concern, experience, or position on the problem at hand.

Leaders

As you noticed in the discussion at your first session, the discussion proceeded through questioning by the Leader, and through statements, comments and further questioning on the part of other group members. You will remember that we said Leaders are present to help themselves and other members (1) give serious consideration to the presentation and the problems it presents, (2) clarify their thinking and feeling about the problems, (3) decide their individual response. It is not presumed that Leaders necessarily know more about the subject, but that they are trained and prepared to lead this discussion and offer this special kind of assistance to the group.

HOW DOES ONE LEAD A DISCUSSION?

what a Leader *is*

The question of "how to lead a group" can be roughly divided into (1) what a Leader *is*, and (2) what a Leader *does*. When we talk about what a Leader *is*, we are talking about his attitudes and values.

A Leader is, first of all, a fellow learner. He shares this goal with the rest of the group. This is something that involves the whole person. Remembering this, he seeks *responsive understanding* for himself and others. He seeks *freedom* for himself and others, knowing that freedom involves self-discipline. He seeks to create in the group a warm, friendly, open *climate* which will constantly demonstrate a *respect* for each individual and allow the development of a true community, learning and working together. He is willing to work hard in preparation for each discussion, knowing that no matter how well prepared his group is and how capable they are as discussants, he will fail them in his role if he does not provide the guidance all groups need. By his own example he demonstrates his expectations for the group as, in an open-minded, relaxed, but interested and friendly way, he gives serious attention to their ideas, opinions and feelings.

open-minded

What do we mean when we say a Leader is open-minded? Dag Hammarskjöld described what should be meant by the "neutrality" of the Secretary General of the U.N. as follows: "He is not requested to be a neuter in the sense that he has to have no sympathies or antipathies, that there are no interests which are close to him in his personal capacity or that he is to have no ideas or ideals that matter to him. However, he is requested to be fully aware of those human reactions and meticulously to check himself so that they are not permitted to influence his actions. This is nothing unique. Is not every judge professionally under the same obligation?" [1] Hopefully, the Leader has many ideas, and may feel considerable certainty about some of them. He has attitudes toward many things which will be discussed, and values about which he cares deeply. However, he recognizes that he does not know everything, that sometimes in the past his ideas have proven incomplete or inaccurate, or

his attitudes inappropriate, and that this could be so now. He welcomes new information, constantly strives to deepen his understanding, and considers changing his mind as growth or development, rather than a threat to his security. He holds himself in constant readiness to integrate new knowledge with old by revising his opinions, attitudes and behavior to accord with his growing understanding. James Harvey Robinson said, ". . . knowledge is really creative inasmuch as it makes things look different from what they seemed before and may indeed work for their reconstruction." He contrasts this with the un-opened mind, saying, ". . . most of our so-called reasoning consists of finding arguments for going on believing as we already do." [2]

what a Leader *does* What a Leader *does* can be answered in one sentence: A Leader *asks questions*. This is obviously a simplistic and inadequate answer, but it is a truthful one, and important to keep firmly in mind. The Leader will be tempted to make many statements and voice opinions, but this is overwhelmingly the prerogative of the other members. In order to ask questions he must study the presentation and think through its implications very thoroughly—he can never be too well *prepared*. In order to ask questions, he must *listen* very carefully to everything expressed in the group, so that when he is leading he knows where the discussion has been, where it is, and has some ideas as to where it is going. He *remembers* fairly well *who* said what, when, and to whom, and *how* they seemed to feel about what they said and heard. He has learned how to *rephrase* his original questions and formulate new questions on the run, because once the discussion has started his questions are relevant to, and very much a part of, the interaction as developed by the group. He *keeps in mind* the *areas and problems* he feels it is essential for the group to explore at this session, but is ready to change course when he believes it is necessary.

He is constantly aware of what is going on, or the *interaction* in the group, by listening to and observing the group members in order to assist the interest, involvement and productivity of each person. He is aware of *emotion* in the group, so that he may help it serve the members, and he must try to help the group when destructive behavior threatens the individual, the group or the discussion. He is conscious of his *responsibility* to help group members consider their *values* with care and accept the necessity of *decision-making*. Is this a good deal to expect of a Leader who "just asks questions"? Yes, of course—leading takes skill, hard work, and behind it all, suitable *attitudes*.

using names As a Leader, you are aware of each member as an individual, and so will direct most of your questions *to* individuals by *name*. When you do so, in contrast to common pedagogical practice, you will first address the person by name, and then ask your question. The presuppositions in the typical class "recitation" situation are different in many ways from those in a learning-discussion group. In class, the questions are apt to be of the quiz type, and the person questioned is aware that he either knows the answer, or he doesn't.

Furthermore, he is conscious that the teacher will, one way or another, evaluate his answers and thus himself. He also expects the teacher already knows the answer. Since such a class is, in a way, involved in a tennis match with the teacher, the class presumes that if the question is answered to the satisfaction of the teacher, that question will be dropped and a new question served over the net. It is a kind of competition between the teacher and the class.

no pat answers   In our discussions, the questions asked will *not* have *pat answers*. The whole group seeks "satisfactory answers", not just the Leader. It is possible each participant might have a different answer, all equally "correct". The group members know the Leader is interested in them and in what they have to say, but not on the basis of a "right/wrong" judgment. They know the Leader does not know the answer, or he wouldn't have asked the question. The group finds something of interest in the question, and will usually want to think about it or comment in some way on both the question and the various responses. They can also feel quite comfortable in not responding. They feel happy and safe with the Leader and the group, knowing that although others may disagree with their answer, they themselves will retain the group's respect and interest. They will know their discussion is a mutual search for the freeing truth, for guidelines for decision-making of importance to them. They will know their group is a place where they can test their values and the implications of those values in a supportive situation.

WHAT SORT OF QUESTIONS DOES A LEADER ASK?

The questions the Leader asks must first of all be ones in which he is *interested,* which means he *does not know the answers.* He believes they are reasonably important, and he believes the group will share this interest and that their cooperative exploration will provide the possibility of responsive understanding. Secondly, the questions will be designed to *explore* the subject, the reactions, and the possible range of responses.

Asking a question to which you do not know the answer often strikes strangely on the mind of those accustomed to the more traditional methods in education. But, if you know the answer, why ask **discussion, not** the question? This is a discussion, not a quiz—if you do know the **a quiz** answer, even if you try to keep it a "secret", you are right back with the old quiz, and you will have no true discussion, and a discouraged, disinterested, frustrated group of participants. Furthermore, you will have a group that does not trust and respect your leadership, no matter what they may think of you as a person. Instead of taking the responsibility for searching for personal understanding, they will spend their time guessing what it is you want them to say, or waiting until, one way or another, you tell them.

Since all of your discussions will be geared to responsive understanding, you will find many of your questions will be of the "How?" and "Why?" type, and many will actually contain these words. Questions of response often contain the word "you". Many questions will explore meaning, often through the usual means of grouping, differentiating, comparing and relating.

Many of your questions will deal specifically with the understanding of data provided by the presentation and by the participants' responses to it. Vague, overgeneralized questions applicable to any and all occasions will seldom further good discussion. Since you and your group are actively searching, you will try to make your questions as *open-ended* as possible in most cases, to allow the necessary freedom for deepened understanding and active response. This often means avoiding the "boxing-in" of responses, particularly early in the discussion, by such means as the "either-or" question.

cooperation, not competition

Remembering the importance of a warm climate of trust, you will avoid questions which seek to trip up, trick or confuse your participants, or which deliberately try to catch them out in contradictions. At no time should a discussion be considered a competitive sport—it is a *cooperative* venture.

Since the purpose of your discussions is not simply the garnering of stray bits of information, your questions will help participants integrate previous knowledge with new knowledge, and will help them explore their own feelings in regard to this knowledge and its application to their lives. Since sometimes participants do fail to see, hear or remember accurately, some questions will deal factually with elements of the presentation, and here it is possible that you will ask questions to which you do know the answer, but even this can be avoided, if desirable, by asking another member such questions as, "Is that the way you understood that passage?", or "Is that the way you saw that action?", or "Mary, is that what you said a few minutes ago" When there is confusion it will be helpful to refer to the presentation, if possible—you may find you have been misunderstanding the group member, or have remembered incorrectly yourself.

HOW DOES ONE PREPARE FOR A DISCUSSION?

general questions

During your training you will learn how to formulate questions and will have an opportunity to check them out in actual discussion. As you read your presentation, jot down on a piece of paper or a file card questions and comments which occur to you. Are there statements or sections you do not fully understand? Are there any key words about whose meaning you would like to hear some discussion? Do any of the ideas conflict with other ideas you have learned in the past? What sort of action on your part is implied or indicated in response to any part of this reading? Do any of the ideas in one section seem contrary to those in another? What part do you consider most important? Why? If you were to summarize these pages, what part would you be likely to omit? Why? Why are the parts arranged in this particular order? What pleases and displeases you?

Questions of this kind are *general questions* and, as such, *are seldom suitable for use in discussion*. They are offered as suggestions to use in studying the material. When you have finished reading the material for the first time, put it aside for a while—even for a day or so. Give it some thought. You might want to write a brief paragraph stating its general impact on you and listing what you remember as the most important points. You may wish to read other material to deepen your understanding of the subject. You will not do this with the idea of introducing this outside material into the discussion itself. The questions you ask will be based on the presentation, and the contributions of group members, which will be based on their own understanding of that presentation.

notes and marginalia

Although note-taking during the discussion itself is to be discouraged, note-taking during the presentation is very important. The notes should not be in the form of a record of what was said or shown in the presentation, but in the form of comments as they naturally arise. Questions, agreements or disagreements can be noted very briefly. In the case of a written presentation, either assigned in advance or handed out at the beginning of a session, all of the group members, including the Leader, become accustomed to writing marginalia. A well-read text is a well-marked text! Kenneth E. Eble, in a PERFECT EDUCATION, says, "Schools, it seems to me, deviated from virtue for the noblest of reasons when they began buying texts and renting or lending them to students. Thus they ensured that every student would have a book, but also that he would never mark it, never make it his own, and never regard it with real respect." [3] The "nice, clean page" of the old-fashioned school child is anathema to the serious adult reader. You will want to underline things you think are important, makes notes of key words or ideas, cross-references, comments and suggestions. You may use footnotes, brackets, headlines for each page, use a "hi-lighter", several

colors of ink—whatever will help you make your presentation the raw material of discussion. With written material, it is best to do little or no marking of the text on the first reading. With lectures, film presentations and so forth, your notes must be made during the presentation, but learn to be brief, so that you won't miss anything! You will find there are questions about the presentation that you will want to ask your group in order to enlarge your own understanding and help you find your own response.

HOW DOES ONE ACHIEVE BALANCED PARTICIPATION?

Elsewhere in this text we talk about many of the factors influencing participation patterns. In the kind of discussion we are working with, the participation pattern is not left to chance. A deliberate effort is made by the Leader, with the assistance of the group, to achieve *balanced participation,* and to have comments made by individuals addressed to the entire group as a rule. Naturally there are exceptions to this, as questions are often directed by one participant to another in order to question the meaning of the first speaker's statement, challenge the validity of an opinion, or elicit specific help. At the same time, it can be said that group discussion is more productive when the *majority* of statements are made to the group as a whole.

The Leader of a new group is faced with a number of problems in seeking to achieve this, some of which develop out of the individual's personality, or his state at the time of a discussion. The Leader is not going to completely change the participation habits of the individual members, but a remarkable degree of change can take place through the procedures used by the Leader and the group, the climate in the group, including the attitudes of the Leader and the group members.

From the beginning, the Leader uses procedures directed toward obtaining balanced participation. He will try to get all members of the group to *speak at least once within the first few minutes,* if only to say their names aloud in the course of making a *participation chart.* He will try at the very first meeting to elicit more than just a name by asking each member to say some specific thing, answer some specific question, or read aloud some brief statement. Each time a participant makes even a minimal contribution to the group, he is better able to make the next one! The Leader will make this first plunge into public conversation as easy as he possibly can, to assist the shy members for whom it will be quite difficult.

dyads— introductions   One of the simplest ways to get someone to speak extemporaneously to a small group is to have him speak first to only one member of that group. If members are given a few simple questions to ask one another, they will find this quite easy. If they are then asked to introduce their partner, they will not find it too difficult to say the name of the other person and tell briefly what answers they

received to the questions posed. This is easier for them to do than to talk about themselves, and habits of politeness will make it seem natural to speak up loudly enough for others to hear their introduction.

Dyads have several other advantages, one of which is that the group member thus takes a step toward friendship. Each member feels he knows one person in the group to some extent, and may even feel a bit of responsibility for him. Curiosity, if nothing else, will encourage him to listen to the other introductions, and he will feel a bit closer to all these people. Furthermore, this teaches a lesson in *listening*—one of the first skills he must acquire; in order to introduce his partner, he must listen to him.

goal-setting

motivation

goal overlap

positive focus

encourages cohesiveness

tension reduction

If the questions asked in these introductory conversations include query as to the individual's past experience in similar groups, or reasons for coming to this group, this accomplishes a number of things. (1) The individual's motivation to work toward the accomplishment of his own goals is increased first, by stating them himself, and second, by having someone else tell the group about them—this is one of the reasons for the effectiveness of such groups as the Weight Watchers and Alcoholics Anonymous. (2) Since there will be some commonality in their individual goals, they will see the emergence of group goals, thus providing some of the necessary "overlap". (3) It will help the Leader to some extent to see what group members envision as the benefit of the group to them. (4) It focuses the group's attention on the positive gains to be derived from the group, and away from the individual's concern about his ability to perform in this new group situation. (5) Having listened to at least one other person's goals with attention, each member usually has some desire to help that person achieve his goals. (6) It encourages the members to feel more like a group, and less like a number of people relating as individuals to a leader, and reduces the tension present in new groups whose members tend to be anxious about how they compare with others in the sight of the "authority" in the group.

avoid status stress

It is preferable that the questions which the dyads will have to answer be directly related in some way to the group goals or activities. If this does not seem possible, and a less task-oriented, more personal discussion is proposed, it is best to avoid questions

which will lead to stress on status. For instance, it would not be wise to tell the group, "Please introduce yourselves, tell who you are, what you do, what your interests are." This may sound harmless, but often leads directly to oneupmanship. Even if a person of some prestige in the community tries to soft-peddle his stature, either his partner may ask questions which bring his accomplishments to light, or during the introductions someone else may refer to his position, possibly embarrassing the one who, unwittingly, introduced the Deputy Mayor. When making introductions of the more personal type, it is well for the Leader to take the first turn, prior to the discussion in dyads. He can talk briefly with a partner, then introduce him. He should see that he speaks briefly and simply, in a pleasant and very relaxed manner, and that what he says about his partner refers to him as an individual and avoids stressing status. The Leader may say, "This is Tom Jones, who has broad interests in the life of the community. Tom moved here from a neighboring city two years ago, and says he is beginning to feel at home, though he still misses his friends. He has never been in a discussion group like this before, but one of his neighbors told him about this place, and told him how to get over here." Or he might say, "This is Mary Harris, a mother who is interested in learning more for the sake of her children as well as for herself," or, ". . . a man who is very interested in social problems and discussion," ". . . a student who comes from another city but goes to school here, and had a job in the community last summer", etc. Other facts about these people will come out in the course of the group's life together, but a heterogeneous group can contain many knowledgeable, virtuous, hardworking people who would be put off by the flaunting of the status of others, if they felt outranked, and might not say anything for weeks, or might not even return to another session. Following his introduction of his partner, the Leader would then be introduced in turn.

using the participation chart

When the introductions are completed, the Leader will go around the group once again, checking the accuracy of his participation chart by naming each participant. As he starts this, he should hold up his sheet of paper on which he has drawn a participation chart and filled in the names during the introductions. He should tell the group that it would be a very good idea for all of them to have a copy of this "seating chart", also, and check to be sure that all have pencils and paper. This re-emphasizes in the minds of the group members that *names* are to be used, and helps members fix in their minds the names of their fellow members. The Leader may start by saying, "I am Jim, and on my left is. . . ?", waiting for that person to pronounce his own name. He should go around the group slowly enough to allow everyone to write in the names on his chart.

first names

Most groups are happier using first names. A warmer spirit results from this, some forms of status are lessened, and people are usually accustomed to speaking more frankly and openly with those whom they call by their first name. Also it is usually easier to remember first names than last names. Since the Leader is also on a

first-name basis, it is another step toward reducing the threat of authority which the Leader represents initially to any group.

At this stage in the group's life, the Leader naturally will not encourage anyone in the group to actually fill in his participation chart as a record of interaction, but merely to use it to help him remember names. The Leader himself should not worry the group by making any sort of extensive records during the first few sessions. If he has a rather large group, he may want to place a check beside the name of each member when that individual makes his first contribution, simply in order to be sure everyone is involved in the discussion.

LEADER'S OPENING REMARKS

The Leader will indicate by his opening remarks at the first meeting of the group that he expects all to participate, as this is a discussion, not a lecture, and that when all talk, all gain, and all lose when someone does not join in the conversation. He will tell them that they need not raise their hands in order to speak, that they may come in at any time without any sort of signal, and that he hopes they, too, will have questions relating to the subject under discussion.

THE FIRST QUESTIONS

When he begins the discussion he will call on someone he has reason to believe will feel fairly comfortable about speaking up, and he will call on him *by name*. Since he and all the members of the group will have a participation chart, he will set the pattern of using the names of the participants, and group members will soon follow his example. Particularly at the first few meetings, he will see to it that the first question he asks is one on which practically any participant can easily comment, even if only briefly. It should be a good Primary question, designed with this particular group in mind, but one with which he can expect the group to quickly come to grips.

He will ask those who seem shy and retiring very simple questions, requiring only brief responses, coaxing them into the conversation by slow, simple, easy steps. If he finds that there are **overparticipation** members of the group who tend to be overparticipators, he will see to it that they do not interrupt other, less active members when they are talking, and by calling more frequently on other members, he will be able to achieve some balance in the participation pattern from the early days of the group. As the group develops its norms and goals, as the climate becomes increasingly open and friendly, the problem of the overparticipator usually fades.

underparticipation The Leader will occasionally be faced by the participant who, from the first session, asks "please, I like to sit here and listen, but don't call on me to say anything." The Leader must respect the wishes of this individual, but after this person has sat in silence for one or two sessions, the Leader should make an attempt, late in the course of a discussion, to persuade the silent one to make some

brief comment. He may say, "Mary, perhaps you would like to add something to John's statement", being sure that he asks this after a brief, clear statement on which a good deal more obviously can be said. Mary will usually respond in some way. Very often, the person who has asked not to be called on will join in voluntarily at some point in the discussion. Sometimes, in the beginning, such people are afraid simply because they are not used to discussion, fearing it in the way they may have feared quizzes at school in the past, or thinking of it as an interrogation of their personal beliefs and habits. When they realize its true character, they are glad to enter in. They may also feel their ability to think or understand or to say something of value is, in some way, less than that of the other members. This is seldom the case, and if the discussion is properly conducted, they will have ample opportunity to contribute.

PARTICIPATION PATTERN OF LEADER

Another aspect of the participation pattern is the relationship between the Leader himself and the individuals in the group. The Leader will encourage interchange, and discourage remarks directed solely to him. In the beginning of a new group's discussion, a diagram of the participation pattern would show a series of lines, all leading from the Leader to the participants and from the participants to the Leader. This is because most group members will be more accustomed to the "recitation" situation than they are to true discussion. In his opening remarks the Leader will have stressed the fact that they are all here to talk to one another, rather than to him—that his special job is to assist them in this. He will not want to embarrass group members in the early stages of discussion by pointing out to them that they are "making a mistake" in talking to him instead of to the group, but he will encourage participation across the table by saying such things as, "Sylvia, you seem to be agreeing with John's statement, is that so?", or "John, you sound as though you did not agree with Sylvia, why is that?", or "Harry, you mentioned that point a few minutes ago in a different way, would you like to add something to what Sylvia said?", or "Mary, is Sylvia's statement clear to you—I don't quite understand what he means?" In each case if you, as Leader, look alternately at the two people as you mention their names, they will look at one another, and the rest of the group will tend to do so as well.

Furthermore, although it would be rude of you not to look at someone who is speaking, at the same time, if you continue to stare directly at the person speaking, he will not be so apt to look at the others as he will be if you turn your gaze on the group, after the first few sentences. Since it is important for you to be aware of all that is going on in the group, the reactions of the other members to the speaker are something you are obliged to look for, so it is only proper that you also look at them. When you turn your gaze from the speaker to the group, the speaker will follow your example.

silence   If you avoid interjecting a question immediately after each participant has spoken, there will soon be considerably more voluntary interchange on the part of the participants. A moment or two of silence will allow others to pick up the ball. You will let the group know, in these various ways, that this really is their discussion, not yours—you are there to help, but you cannot "discuss" alone!

FOR SOURCES AND FURTHER INFORMATION, CONSULT THE FOLLOWING WORKS:

1. Hammarskjöld, Dag, MARKINGS, trans. Leif Sjöberg and W. H. Auden, p. xix, N.Y.: Alfred A. Knopf, 1968.
2. Robinson, James Harvey, THE MIND IN THE MAKING, Ch. 3, N.Y.: Harper and Brothers, 1921.
3. Eble, Kenneth E., A PERFECT EDUCATION, p. 90, N.Y.: Collier Books, 1966.
SEE ALSO: Adler, Mortimer, HOW TO READ A BOOK, on "marking a text", and other works in the "Recommended Readings" on "Background".

9.
Questions and Answers

OVERVIEW

The Leader's ability to design questions specifically for the different *phases of discussion* is an important and necessary skill. Questions are classified in two categories, *Primary* and *Secondary*. There are *five types of questions, Meaning, Balance, Response, Fact and Concretizing*. All five types may be used as Secondaries, only the first three as Primaries. The Leader is careful to use questions which he can expect the group to be able to answer on the basis of the presentation and their common knowledge, rather than eliciting responses which depend for their value on outside authorities. By the use of questions, the Leader will try to help group members arrive at *individual decisions, not* requiring *unanimity* of opinion, and help the group tolerate *ambiguity,* when this seems necessary.

CLASSIFICATION OF QUESTIONS

We classify questions in two ways: (1) according to relative importance and primacy of use; (2) according to type.

(1) The two categories according to importance and use are:

(a) *Primary questions* are large, important, central questions deriving from the Presentation and the problems there presented. They deserve thorough exploration. You will find that many other questions *cluster* around or are subsumed under these Primary questions.

(b) *Secondary questions* help the group develop in depth understanding and response to the problem or idea exposed or posed in the Primary question. You will find that they tend to arise from or to cluster around a Primary question. Secondary questions may be very important in themselves, but are obviously related to the Primary question for which they form a *cluster.*

The *Leader controls* the use of the *Primary* questions, since they determine the general direction of the discussion. In other words, he asks these questions himself, at the right time. If they are raised by a participant, he will encourage this change in direction only if he believes the group has satisfactorily and productively completed its investigation and response to the previous Primary question. On the other hand, *Secondary* questions often are, and should be, asked by participants of one another, as well as being asked by the Leader.

(2) The five types of questions according to content are:

(a) *Fact:* What was actually seen, heard, in the Presentation or contributions of other group members? What are the actual words in the text? What did the film present to our eyes? What did the speaker say? Who said what?

(b) *Meaning:* What does this word, this statement, this sound, this picture, mean? Within the context of this work, what meaning did its author intend? Within the context of this discussion, what did the group member mean?

(c) *Concretizing* (give a concrete example): What situation in your community is like this? Do you know someone in this situation? How does your neighborhood handle this problem? (Try out the idea or principle in various contexts, see where and how it might apply and why.)

(d) *Balance* or congruence (questions which seek integration, resolution of dissonance, achievement of balance in attitude systems): How does this information fit in with your known facts, previous information, beliefs, feelings and values? Is this your view of the world? Does it present disconfirming information? Does this seem good? bad? desirable?

(e) *Response:* What decision for action must I make? What is important in this to me? What must I do? why? how? What action or behavior becomes necessary?

development of cluster

Secondary questions are those which cluster around a Primary question. In the actual process of preparation for leading, you will probably start by writing down many questions, without regard to whether they are Primary or Secondary and without identifying them as to type. As you work with these questions you will find that they tend to form groups or clusters centering on a major problem or concern. From this cluster, a Primary will emerge. It may be one of the questions you have already written down, or you may realize that over and above this cluster there hangs a larger question which encompasses all the questions—this is your Primary for that cluster. It is important, however, not to make your Primary question a "general question", so broad that your discussion will not be focused sharply enough to make progress through the phases of discussion. Progress toward the solution of your Primary must not require "facts" or information not included in the Presentation or in the common knowledge in the group, but it should require the group to think, to bring into play their experience, knowledge, beliefs, convictions and viewpoints.

PRIMARY AND SECONDARY QUESTIONS

Primary questions are never Fact or Concretizing questions, but may be one of the other three types. *Secondary questions consist of all five types.* The types of questions may be thought of in terms of the phases of the discussion, although they are not always handled sequentially by any individual or by the group as a whole. Discussion

Fact questions

may weave back and forth. Questions of Fact are never asked unless there is an obvious need for them—a member may have forgotten a point that he believes it is important for him to know in order to continue the discussion, and may ask the group's help in recalling it. Or the Leader may find the discussion seems bogged down because someone has a faulty recollection of a fact of the Presentation. In many cases, others will recognize this, and may point out the correct facts, or say, "I don't think that's what he said—when did he say that?" A Fact question is the typical quiz question.

A discussion that goes no further than Fact and Meaning may leave the subject hanging pleasantly on the wall—something to be admired, or to serve for intellectual fun and games, but with no relevance to the lives of the group members. A discussion which adds to the above Concretizing and Balance will move the subject into the here and now of our lives, and requires an examination of attitudes and values. The Response factor is the last element needed to encourage decision-making, a sense of commitment, or a need for action or involvement.

The following cluster is for a discussion in which the group was interested in the problem of "suffering". In order to provide many samples of the various types of questions, this cluster is far longer than would usually be prepared. Many of the Secondaries would be asked or commented upon by group members without the necessity of the Leader actually asking these questions. The presentation was THE BOOK OF JOB.

PRIMARY
How does THE BOOK OF JOB's view of suffering differ from ours?

FACT
How does Eliu explain suffering (32:14)?
Who proposes the view that suffering is punishment for sin?
What did Harry (a group member) say was Job's worst suffering?

MEANING
What was Job's greatest suffering?
What are the various explanations of suffering offered in this book?
If it represents "punishment", who is punished for what? how? what arguments are presented pro and con?
If it is a "test", what is it testing? how? how are the results known? by whom?
If there is no "explanation", what can we say about it?
Why is suffering a "problem" for Job?
Did Job see any value in his suffering?
Does the author see any one answer as the solution to the problem of suffering?
What is the relationship between sin and suffering in this book? In whose eyes? What is meant by "sin" here?
How does Job see the relationship between sin and God? Why?
Does Job's view of suffering change? why?

(NOTE: Many of these same questions could also be asked of statements made by group members, e.g., *"Why does Mary say she sees value in suffering?", "What does Harry mean by 'sin'?"*

CONCRETIZING
Who suffers today? how? why?
How do people you know react to suffering? why? How do they react to physical suffering? to mental suffering?
What sort of advice do they get? from whom? why? What is its effect? why?
How do their reactions compare with those of Job in, for instance, Ch. 30? why?
Have you ever known anyone like Job? like his friends?

BALANCE
What are your personal views of the causes of suffering? why? of the results of suffering? why?
Are people better or worse off as a result of suffering? Always? Never? Does it depend on others' attitudes toward their problem? on the kind of suffering? the degree? their own attitude toward it?
Would reading THE BOOK OF JOB help someone who was suffering? why or why not?

Are there "correct" and "incorrect" ways of thinking about suffer-
ing? what? why?

Do you find Job admirable? why or why not?

How do you differ from Job? in circumstances? viewpoint? view of
God? view of suffering?

Does today's use of tranquilizers affect our view of suffering? how?
what kind of suffering? in whose eyes?

RESPONSE

If you have a friend who is suffering, what should you do? how?
why?

What would you have said to Job? why? What do you believe his
reaction would have been? why?

How do you decide which ways of helping are best in specific
situations?

When you see others suffering, do you assign blame or responsibil-
ity? to whom? why?

Do you feel any obligation toward others who are suffering? why?
who?

How do you think you ought to react to suffering? why? your own
suffering? that of others?

Would you give a suffering person an anesthetic? marijuana?
heroin? tranquilizers? why or why not? under what cir-
cumstances? Would you want these for yourself if you were
suffering? which?

How do you see your position as different from Job's in times of
suffering?

Which of Job's sufferings would be hardest for you to bear? why?
which easiest? why?

What kinds of things cause you suffering? What causes you the
most suffering? why?

Do you blame yourself or others for your sufferings?

Does suffering do you any good? harm? how and why?

What helps you? (makes suffering easier to bear?) Would some
kind of communication with God help you if you were suf-
fering? with other people? why?

The next sample cluster is for a group which has worked
together longer, and is interested in the problems of group goals.
The Leader introduces the word "goal" in the Primary, even though
it is not used in the presentation, a short story by Kafka, entitled
"The City Coat of Arms". Its application here is fairly obvious.

PRIMARY

How do goals affect man's behavior in this story?

FACT

In the story, who believes that "the idea of building the Tower
would never vanish?

How did Mary (a group member) describe the difference between
"real" and "unreal" goals?

What did John (a group member) say about "goals" and "objectives"?

MEANING
: *Why have the people in this story abandoned building the Tower?*
What did the building of the Tower mean to the citizens in the beginning?
Does Kafka agree with his characters that the idea of building the tower would never vanish?
What motives seem to inspire them in the beginning? later on?
What is the Tower?
What seems to be the most essential element in the building of the Tower?
What did the people of the city value most?
Is Kafka's image of man here hopeful or despairing? how? why?
What seems to be the greatest obstacle to its building?
Why did they feel: one simply could not build too slowly? . . . no anxiety about the future of the Tower?
Does Kafka agree with his characters who feel one need not "exert oneself to the extreme limits of one's present powers"?

CONCRETIZING
: *Do you know any group with an announced goal which seems to be behaving this way? What is their Tower? Are they copping out? being realistic?*
Does loss of a goal lead to conflict?
Who today feels they must build?
Is the city in the story like (city in which discussion is being held)? how? why?
If you were appointed Mayor of the city in the story, how would you try to lead these people? why? If you were a citizen?

BALANCE
: *How would you encourage someone to keep working toward some desirable goal?*
If you had written such a story, what would the Tower symbolize for you?

What do you think may be the causes of modern man's frustrations?
How would you account for the changing attitudes of people in the story?
How might you view your frustrations in the light of this story (or this discussion)?
What personal considerations are essential to you before beginning to build something?

RESPONSE *Where in your daily life do you see more need of working together? what could you accomplish in this way?*
Are you trying to build a Tower? do you think it is realizable?
Right now, are you putting something off? why?
What is the greatest obstacle to your building? What are you doing about it?
What would be necessary to help you achieve your goal?
Have you abandoned a Tower? why?
What can you do to help a group of which you are a member reach a goal?

use of cluster

Probably the most important questions the Leader asks are those of Meaning and Response. However, without the support of the other kinds of questions, a group usually will not be able to arrive at meaningful answers to these questions. You will note those two little questions we mentioned before recurring frequently in the clusters given above—"why?" and "how?" Without their use, many discussions will lack much of their potential value.

You will notice that in none of the questions above was material beyond either the Presentation, common experience, or the personal experiences and reactions of group members presumed or called upon. Other kinds of questions might have been introduced in a group with a common background in Old Testament, or in related materials, such as poetry. Productive discussion requires a basis of commonality.

QUESTIONS OF FACT

The Leader's job is not to strive for unanimous agreement at all stages of the discussion, or even for consensus. However, it is obvious that little discussion can proceed unless there is general agreement on the *facts of the presentation*. In order for meaningful discussion to ensue, the group must be willing to accept these "facts", at least on a temporary basis, before they can examine Meaning. A group will often find this acceptance difficult in the beginning, since in many kinds of discussion, the "arguments" are all about "what really are the facts of this case?" A group can be led to see that "argument" is not the way to determine "fact"—for this, inspection or observation of some kind is the remedy. It is entirely possible that in any given presentation, each member could find some "fact"

with which he is in disagreement, but true discussion takes place at the level of ideas and feelings, judgments and decisions. For a further discussion of some of the problems that arise over facts, see Ch. 13, but we will consider a few very common problems here.

The first is a fairly simple matter, since it seldom arises—this is the problem caused by using more than one translation of a particular Presentation. For instance, in a discussion of the Parable of the Good Samaritan, let us suppose that each member had brought his own Bible. One member might say that his Bible translates verse 37 as "He who took pity on him", not as "The one who showed him kindness". Another might say that his reads, "The man who gave him practical sympathy", and another might agree with the first speaker that it "should" be "The one who took pity on him." Another member could state that his copy says "He that shewed mercy on him." [1] There is certainly no great harm, in this case, in the variety of translations, but neither is the discussion advanced by an argument about "which is right". Groups can spend considerable time in innocent ignorant blundering about, and avoid coming to grips with moral, ethical or social issues. It is better if all agree to use the same translation for discussion purposes, though they may wish to read others in preparation as well.

A related and more common problem arises when group members are told that in preparation for a discussion they should read "something about race relations", or "any *one* of the following articles on race relations". At first glance, this would seem to be a way of enriching the discussion, but the group is apt to devote far too much time to arguing and defending their differing "facts". In such cases it is better in assigning the presentation to offer an optional bibliography, but make it clear that the group will use one particular article or book as its "presentation", or two specific ones, if desired, as the basis for the actual discussion.

A far more common and frequently more harmful type of argument might have started in the group about the relations between the Jews and the Samaritans. If this particular reading is the first exposure a particular group has to "priests, Levites and Samaritans" of the period, in a discussion together, it cannot be presumed that a clear understanding of the distinction and characteristics of these groups is "common knowledge". Since only the merest hint is given in this reading itself, a Leader should avoid discussion of this point, however important he may feel it to be. If he does not, he runs the risk of misinformation being circulated and an argument among the group members as to the status and intergroup relations of these people at the time of Christ—an argument which cannot be resolved because "the facts" are not available to the group during the discussion. If a participant makes a statement about this relationship, the Leader might ask the participant what he finds in the reading to lead him to this conclusion, a common way to handle problems of what appears to be "outside information" or, as would seem far preferable in a case as clear-cut as this, simply ignore the information offered and continue the discussion. If the issue should become the focus of attention for more than a few minutes, the Leader should ask the group to defer this part of their discussion until a later time. He may say, "Could we put off a discussion of this point until we have more common information which will enable all the members to participate in the discussion?" If the group seems interested in the subject, the Leader can assure them that at some future date a suitable presentation and discussion will be provided. One of the responsibilities of the Leader is to help the group obtain necessary, relevant information as the basis for their discussions. If the discussion is one in which certain facts will obviously be *key* points, it will be important that the presentation selected offer the most reliable data available.

dictionaries and other reference works

Group members often want to "get at the facts" by suggesting that dictionaries or even encyclopaedias be brought to the meetings to "settle arguments". The subject matter of the Presentation and the group members' contributions should be the meat of the discussion—not dictionaries or encyclopaedias. Most material used for presentations will not contain totally unknown words, and the meaning can usually be determined from an examination of the content, and often more accurately than from a dictionary. Any presentation used for discussion should have enough material and be of sufficient value to warrant the group spending its full discussion time on it, and the problems which it raises. This certainly does not require that it be lengthy. A good discussion will seldom result from a poor or inadequate presentation. A group that spends its time playing hare-and-hounds with "facts" never gets around to discussing the ideas in the presentation and their own reactions to them. A discussion spent entirely on the meaning of a few specific words is quite suitable for a group of linguists or translators, but presumably the goals of the majority of your discussions would be different.

It is to be hoped that if a group member meets a totally strange word in reading he has done in advance for discussion, he will look it up. The meaning of an unknown word will often be made clear in the context of a work, but material for new groups should be chosen with a view to simplicity of wording. It is sometimes necessary for a group to discuss technical material outside of their own field. If terms used are not explained in the material, a glossary should be provided.

quoting outside
materials

Quoting of "outside authorities" is discouraged in our discussion groups. It is one of the ways in which discussion can become that of which it has sometimes been accused—the pooling of ignorance. It may seem odd to say that bringing into the discussion "more information" will result in greater ignorance, but let us look at what can happen.

example: use
of "outside
authorities"

Suppose you are listening in on a discussion of some of the poetry of Dylan Thomas. John has read three authorities in addition to the assigned poems, and Mary has read two others. During the discussion, the meaning of "death" to Thomas comes up, and John tells the group what he remembers of some of the three "authorities" he read. He tells them the names of the authors of two of the books, as he remembers them, but he is not sure of the third. However, he tells the group in some detail his recollection of what he read in one book, and says he is fairly sure of that author's name, a name which impresses the group favorably. This particular author, as John remembers, said that Thomas was "trivial and inarticulate" and his verse was "devoid of meaning". He adds that "Surrealism, where the importance of rational content was discounted is the background for Thomas." He adds that this author "points out that Thomas himself said that 'as far as he knew it had no meaning at all'." When the Leader asks John if *he* can see any meaning in Thomas' statements about death in the poem, John replies that since Thomas himself said it didn't mean anything, he can't see too much point in discussing it.

At this point, Mary says that she did not trust her memory, so she jotted down the names of the authors and their statements which she read. She reads to the group their remarks on meaning of "death" for Thomas. One quotation she reads states that "it means the same thing Shelley meant when he wrote on the death of Keats—that 'He is made one with nature'." Most of the group, impressed by John's extra work, feels no doubt as to the correctness of his statements, and are prepared to dismiss most of the poetry as "meaningless and trivial".

However, Harry says he thinks he read one of John's authorities some time ago, and he doesn't agree with John's version of what he said. He tries to explain to the group his understanding of John's "authority". Harry also thinks John has his authors' names mixed up, but he can't be sure.

Jane then says she likes that second explanation that Mary read. Mary, encouraged by this, points out that "it does seem clear". However, Jim asks Mary if she read the whole book, or only parts of it. Mary admits she read only the parts listed in the book's index on "death", whereupon Jim says that "you have to understand what that author means by many of his terms, or you can't understand his explanations."

Ann, quiet until now, says she read a book recently about Surrealism, that it was very interesting, and seems to fit in with what John was saying, except that she couldn't agree that therefore it meant Thomas' work was "meaningless". She tells the group some of the things that interested her in Surrealism. Jane, remembering Mary's statement about Shelley, says that she really likes Shelley's poetry much better. She is torn between asking the group if they remember that other poem Shelley wrote about death, and asking Ann to tell her more about Surrealism.

By this time, the Leader is dismayed. What has happened to their discussion? The group is "discussing", but they are certainly not pursuing the points the Leader felt should be discussed, and he is rather bewildered as to exactly what it is that they are discussing. He feels "it is the group's discussion, and they should talk about what they are interested in", and yet he feels something is sadly awry. A number of things have happened to this "discussion", and none of them is good.

1. The group is not discussing the Presentation or their own ideas or reactions which they came together to discuss. They have no "common basis" or "common information" for what they have been talking about. The group is being forced to listen to readings, advocacy, debate, and a battle between "your authority" and "my authority".

2. There is no way the group can judge the accuracy of the statements made by John, Mary or Harry, since they do not have access to the material. If the rest of the group even try to enter the discussion they may well be met by, "Well, if you had read this book, you would see it differently."

3. Those members impressed with Mary or John's seemingly greater knowledge have stopped trying to understand the meaning for themselves, being quite willing to rest quietly and have someone else tell them what to think. With the exception of Jim, no one was familiar with the name of either of the authors of Mary's quotations, but Jane will probably remember the one she thought sounded well. She will, that is, if she goes back to thinking of Thomas' work at all. Just now, she is involved in a vague recollection of Shelley, and her interest in Ann's account of Surrealism.

4. Ann, feeling left out of the discussion to which she could contribute nothing, having read only Thomas' poems, decided that if

some members of the group were going to talk about other books, there was no reason she shouldn't do so. She was pleased that her statements on Surrealism aroused the group's interest and felt that now she was part of the group again.

5. The Leader was dismayed for all the above reasons, but he had some more of his own. He, too, had read two of John's authorities and felt quite certain John was misquoting and was also confusing the names of his sources, and that these particular critics were early commentators on Thomas' work, later overruled. He also felt John was overextending Thomas' intent in this isolated statement about his poetry having "no meaning at all", which was not relevant to the "death" question originally. As for Mary's authorities, the Leader thought Jim's criticism might be right, but he wasn't familiar with these sources. Furthermore, he knew that at this rate the group would never get to the planned discussion and would in the long run, be dissatisfied with their own work.

The Leader has allowed the group to get into a hopeless situation. He cannot seek clarification of Mary's statements by questioning other participants as to their understanding of the material, since they have not read it and do not have it before them. Even if one or two had read the same books, such questioning would still leave the rest of the group out, and might result in a " 'tis — 'tis'nt" argument. As to John's authors, what the Leader would really like to do is simply tell the group, "They're wrong!" This, however, would only involve him in what is, for the group, a pointless argument. The only immediate remedy is to drop the pursuit of the "death" theme, and hope the next question he asks the group will be one in which no one has any "quotations" to offer, and in which they will be sufficiently interested to forget John's remarks temporarily. The Leader may also want to stop this discussion a little early and engage the group in conversation about what happened during this discussion.

Unhappily, the above situation is neither unusual nor exaggerated. Was it "wrong" for John and Mary to read these books? No, of course not! Had they read them to see how much help they could get for themselves in understanding Thomas, and then gone back to the poems and thought them through for themselves, they might have arrived at an understanding of his use of "death". Reading one "authority" is seldom wise, but had they read several it would have been an enriching experience. They could have tested their understanding in the context of their previous knowledge and their ideas about the problem, presented their thoughts to the group in the context of the poems, and the group could have evaluated their ideas. John and Mary would have had to back up their statements from the poems themselves, and their understanding of them would have deepened. They could then have gone on to discuss the meaning of "death" to them, and its relationship to Thomas' ideas. Unswayed by undue admiration for John, not overawed by name-dropping, not involved in sympathy for Ann or worried by an insoluble argument between Jim and Mary, not distracted by tangential discussions of Surrealism and Shelley, they could have pursued their common goal of discussion for responsive understanding.

proper use of supplementary materials

You will remember that one of our premises for discussion is that learning is something each individual *does*—not something someone else does *for* him or *to* him. This is one of the principal reasons we do not include *in our discussions* the use of outside authorities. During preparation for discussion it can be very helpful to read supplementary materials, but the value lies in helping you see various aspects of the presentation and problem which you might not otherwise consider, or suggest ideas which might help you in thinking about the issues. If, however, this material is used as a substitute for thinking about and discussing these problems yourselves, it can be harmful.

Elder Olson, writing in THE POETRY OF DYLAN THOMAS, makes a statement applicable to any of our Presentations:

> What Thomas wanted was for the reader to begin with the idea that he *might* be speaking literally; to declare something a symbol or a metaphor only after it was evident that it could not be a literal expression; to find out, in that case, what kind of symbol or metaphor it was; and so go, eventually, *from the text*, to Thomas' meaning. This is the right way to read Thomas, and the right way to read anything; and it is the only right way.[2]

another example

A similar situation can develop in a discussion on a topic in which the group is seriously interested and involved, but with which they are hesitant about making a decision. Suppose you are a member of a group which is discussing a presentation on abortion or population control. There is a great deal of information and opinion available about these vital social issues. If you wished, you might have chosen to read a statement about this subject by a particular authority whom you respect and simply accepted his views. This would have saved you the trouble of thinking about it, or even of studying the presentation. You could have told your group that you had read and accepted a statement by Mr. X, and told them what he said. Questions to you will simply provide answers from Mr. X. Safely armored in the ideas of another, you could go through the entire discussion, parroting his views on occasion, keeping the whole subject safely out of view around the corner of your mind, and never coming to grips with what *you* think of the problem. If you listen carefully to the views of the others, you may acquire a few more ideas, but they will be pasted on top of your armor—never being allowed to come near to *you*. The mere acquisition of the ideas of others can provide a substitute for internalization, decision-making and response.

But that is not thinking—that is memorizing and reciting and, if you memorized it correctly, the group might well have gained Mr. X's views, but that is not discussion—it is a trading of the ideas of people who are not even present. The group wants to know what *you* think and feel about this subject, and you want to know what *they* think and feel. All of you seek to understand for yourselves, through a careful turning over of these ideas in your minds and through an exchange of your own ideas in your own words. This is the way we come to grips with ideas and build a balanced structure of thoughts, feelings, attitudes and values by which we will guide our lives. This requires very real work and sometimes discomfort, but it is far more exciting, rewarding and productive than rote learning—if such should even be called "learning".

Leaders—and outside authorities

If, as Leaders, we introduce the opinions of outside authorities, we will initiate deviation from the Presentation and from the group's understanding and ideas. This is apt to make the group believe we are indicating the presentation was valueless or, at best, inadequate, and that therefore their own thinking about it needs support from outside. We are also introducing the idea that either *all* authorities quoted—or misquoted—have equal value—otherwise some one person in the group will have to be the appointed or self-appointed judge as to which authority is to be preferred. It is far better to rely on the presentation for the facts of the discussion, and the group members as the authorities for their own ideas. As long

as all group members have access to the common material which is the basis of the discussion, all members have an opportunity to investigate its meaning, judge the usefulness of its views, and determine its applicability to their own ideas and actions. If a group member quotes "Mr. X" in answer to a question, ask him if that is what *he* thinks, and if so, why. Tell him that the group is perfectly willing to listen to his own ideas, no matter what their original source —after all, how many people have ever had a really "original idea"? All that you ask is that he support these ideas either from the presentation or from his own experience and thinking about the problems. If John, then, thinks Thomas' poems are "trivial" or "meaningless", the group will be happy to listen to why John thinks so, and can discuss why they agree or disagree with John. John is right there, the group has all read the same poems he has, and they meet on equal ground.

MEANING AND AGREEMENT

Once a group has agreed to accept the words of the Presentation as their "facts" for discussion, the conversation can get on with its exploration of meaning. Here unanimity of agreement is less possible and less desirable, but it is often worthwhile to strive to reach a common understanding as to the meaning of the most important points in the Presentation. The group does not have to feel certainty, either as individuals or as a group, nor settle on the same words, but simply try to reach a state in which most of them feel that "this meaning" is the more probable one. There may still be a mi-

nority who disagree, and their disagreement must be accepted by the Leader and the group—sometimes the minority is right! Research has given abundant evidence of the power of the group to sway the judgment of the member who holds a different opinion,[3] and protection of the minority is an obligation of the Leader.

difference between author's "meaning" and "influences on him"

There is a difference between understanding the author's meaning, and understanding the influences which affected the author and helped develop that meaning in him. The former should be discernible in the text or the film or whatever the medium; the latter may often require considerable "outside information". The matter of Thomas and the possible influence of Surrealism is a case in point. Sometimes a few words of explanation should be included in the presentation *if* there is a special problem of genre or of the period and place in which a work was created, and *if* this is vital to the group's goals in a particular discussion.

core meaning

It is quite possible for an entire group to misunderstand some of the fine points or details of a presentation. Usually this is unimportant. The main points, the heart or core of the matter, is what the group should seek to understand. In reading the work of Dylan Thomas, for instance, a knowledge of Welsh folklore and the Bible will help clear up a number of allusions which might be misunderstood, but a group can grapple with many of his ideas, his world view, his aspirations and beliefs without clearly understanding all these allusions. In the Parable of the Good Samaritan, a group might well misunderstand why a Levite, a Samaritan, and a man on his way from Jerusalem down to Jericho are selected as characters in the story. The Leader, however, should disregard random remarks on these matters and get on with the other important material which is made more explicit. Even in a selection as short as this Parable, a group can find ways to spend time on details or irrelevancies and share considerable misinformation, rather than facing up to problems and responsibilities with which they should try to deal. It is the understanding of the core with which the Leader should help his group work. The "core" may differ somewhat, according to the group and its specific goals, and the selection of the Presentation must naturally be made with this in mind.

Leader's criteria for need for agreement

A group may find even this degree of general agreement difficult at times, and the Leader must beware of a number of things. First, before he persists in trying to find a meaning generally acceptable to the group, he must himself believe the issue at stake is an *important* one. Second, he should have reason to think the *group* feels, or will feel, that it is important. Third, in some cases a word, phrase or section of a written work, film, etc., will be *ambiguous*, either deliberately, or because the very subject matter tends itself to no other handling; this, too, must be recognized. As E. D. Hirsch points out, "Certainty is not the same thing as validity, and knowledge of ambiguity is not necessarily ambiguous knowledge."[4] The fourth, and possibly most important point, is that the Leader must not set himself up as a final authority in such cases—he is not the arbiter in cases of disagreement. His aim is to try to lead the group to an understanding which is satisfying to them, and an interpretation with which many of the group seem to disagree loses a bit of satisfactoriness for those involved. Since he, too, is a "member" of the group, he has the right to their help in his own search for understanding, but it is still possible that he may find himself at odds with the group's understanding of a particular point. Here he must accept the fact that agreement is a goal, not a requirement, in a discussion of meaning, and neither he nor any member must feel coerced to accept the majority opinion in case of continued disagreement.

AMBIGUITY

A film of the late sixties dealing with some contemporary problems ended with the apparent resolution of at least some of the personal problems of the two leading characters. Since the film-maker uses strong situational and symbolic religious emphases, it seemed impossible to avoid the fact that he was making some statement about "religion". Since the situation and symbolism were shown as "Christian", it was possible he was making a specific statement about "Christianity". The total film presented itself to the viewer as moralistic in tone—it said some things are good and some are bad for man to do. However, the ending of the film seemed ambiguous insofar as the specific statements about religion. Some viewers felt the film was "indicting all religion"; others that its maker was "indicting organized religion"; others that it was a criticism of "the hypocrisy of Christians"; others that he was "condemning the religious practices of wealthy, white Americans"; others that he was "upholding true religion", and still others that religion entered into the matter only incidentally, as part of a total social structure which was faulty.

If a group discussing this film presented such a variety of viewpoints in these terms, this would not be a situation in which the Leader should strive to bring about "agreement". It would be necessary, however, to examine what each speaker meant when he said "religion", "Christians", and "religious practices", as well as the modifying terms, in connection with this film. The group could then discuss what they felt would be the film-maker's definitions, so far as they could judge from what they had seen. It is possible the group might reach considerable understanding of some of the film-maker's views on religion, and still not be able to satisfy themselves as to what he might mean by those words. They might have to conclude there was insufficient evidence to resolve their original controversy. They might decide the statements the film made about religion were "ambiguous". If they wished, they might go on to try to decide whether the ambiguity was deliberate, or a "fault" in the film or, if deliberate, why? There might still be members who felt strongly their own interpretations were correct, but if there were evidence for ambiguity, they might grant this as a possibility.

FOR SOURCES AND FURTHER INFORMATION, CONSULT THE FOLLOWING WORKS:

1. Confraternity Edition, NEW TESTAMENT; THE NEW TESTAMENT IN MODERN ENGLISH, translated by J. B. Phillips, N.Y.: Macmillan Co., 1962; THE JERUSALEM BIBLE, Garden City, N.Y.: Doubleday, 1966; THE HOLY BIBLE (Knox), N. Y.: Sheed and Ward, 1950.
   NOTE: The translation presumed used as Presentation, THE NEW ENGLISH BIBLE, NEW TESTAMENT, published jointly by Oxford University Press and Cambridge University Press, 1961.
2. Olson, Elder, THE POETRY OF DYLAN THOMAS, Chicago: University of Chicago Press, 1954, p. 62.
3. Eisenson, John, J. Jeffery Auer, and John V. Irwin, THE PSYCHOLOGY OF COMMUNICATION, p. 234 and references, N.Y.: Appleton-Century-Crofts, 1963.
4. Hirsch, E. D., Jr., VALIDITY IN INTERPRETATION, p. lx, New Haven: Yale University Press, 1967.
   see also: Empson, William, 7 TYPES OF AMBIGUITY, 3rd ed., N.Y.: Meridian Books, 1955, for discussion of ambiguities as "hidden riches". Black, Max, THE LABYRINTH OF LANGUAGE, N.Y.: Mentor, 1968, pp. 156-69, for discussion of ambiguity as "fault". The brief discussion of dictionaries on pp. 164-65 is also of interest.

SEE ALSO:

A MANUAL FOR CO-LEADERS, Source Books, Vol. 1, Chicago: The Great Books Foundation, 1965. The Great Books Foundation offers an excellent Leader Training Course to prepare Leaders for the Great Books Discussion Program. The authors wish to acknowledge their debt of gratitude to the Foundation, its personnel and materials for much background help, particularly in the area of the development of "Meaning" questions, and the problems of "fact" versus "outside authority".

Cohen, L. Jonathan, THE DIVERSITY OF MEANING, N.Y.: Herder and Herder, 1963. This work provides a very helpful philosophical approach to the problems of meaning, concepts and language, reviewing a wide range of viewpoints.

Gowers, Sr. Ernest, THE COMPLETE PLAIN WORDS, Baltimore, Md.: Penguin Books, 1954.

Blankenship, Albert B., CONSUMER AND OPINION RESEARCH, N.Y.: Harper and Brothers, 1943.

Payne, Stanley L., THE ART OF ASKING QUESTIONS, Princeton, N.J.: Princeton University Press, 1951.

NOTE: As the Leader trains himself to devise clear, simple questions, he will find the use of a good dictionary and thesaurus helpful, as well as such works as:

Bernstein, Theodore M., THE CAREFUL WRITER: A MODERN GUIDE TO ENGLISH USAGE, N.Y.: Atheneum, 1965.

Strunk, W., THE ELEMENTS OF STYLE, rev. ed., E. B. White, N.Y.: Macmillan, 1959.
   see also: Works suggested under "Background" in "Suggested Readings".

10.
Preparing To Lead

OVERVIEW

The selection of the right *Presentation* is important to the discuss of the discussion. The Leader thinks through the phases of the discussion, sometimes in terms of *general questions*. He begins to formulate his *discussion questions*, being careful of their *length*, *avoiding* such *problem questions* as "yes/no", "either/or" and rhetorical questions, and keeping them *brief, specific, open-ended, clear, simple* and *exact in wording*. He begins to train his group in *goal-setting*.

148

THE PRESENTATION

There is a limit to how much time we can expect group members to spend in preparation, or how much time we can spend with a Presentation given at the time of a class or meeting. Presentations should be rich enough for discussion, but brief enough to allow time for all to be prepared and for a discussion of adequate length.

A Presentation should not be thought of as merely a stepping-off point for the discussion, but should have value in itself. Until a group is trained to judge a Presentation, the Leader should be responsible for its selection. Good discussion material usually contains more ideas than facts, develops at least one idea rather fully, contains a definite viewpoint, is a well-crafted, artistic example of its medium. Usually unsuitable are such things as newspaper reports of events, most textbooks, and research reports. There is a great deal of excellent discussion material available in a wide range of subjects in collections of articles and essays, short stories, poetry and drama. Films, lectures, photographs, tapes, the theater, even posters, slides, music, advertisements, games and simulations, case studies and field trips or combinations of any of these media can provide adequate input for a discussion. Many discussions founder because of insufficient information, poorly designed or selected Presentations. Groups which have worked with good material will be dissatisfied with poor Presentations, and the Leader will find his job much more difficult if he has chosen the wrong material for his group. The selection of the best Presentation for the particular group at the particular time deserves careful study.

GENERAL QUESTIONS

The Presentation, in whatever form, is an attempt at communication. Its creator is trying to get some ideas out of his head and into yours. One way or another, this communication will concern itself with important questions with which we struggle most of our lives: Who am I? What are other people like? What can I know, and how, and what should I do with this knowledge? How can I be happy? What ought I to do, and why? How should I chose to spend my time? There are many questions of relationship: between man and man, man and God, man and society, man and the world. Chapters 7 and 9 also provide further suggestions for general questions. At one time these were considered "philosophical questions", suitable for discussion by philosophers or students in a philosophy course. It is readily seen, however, that their ramifications appear in all fields of knowledge, and when ignored imperil the individual and society.

phases of discussion You will usually find it helpful to start your preparation by following the general approach of the phases of discussion or the problem-solving patterns. You might first ask yourself, "What are the problems posed by this work? How is the problem analyzed?

What solutions are proposed and what related problems are involved?" When you have some ideas on the particular problem or problems with which the author is working, try to write some questions which narrow the problem to those aspects he covers in the material. Try to "think yourself into his shoes" as you do this, and phrase the question in terms which you believe would be meaningful to him, and then to the group. You might go back to something you have recently discussed in training and see if you can write some questions to help understand and answer the "general questions".

Do not forget that you are looking for questions to which you do not know the answer. At this first stage you are trying only to understand the problems raised, and to understand them first of all as the Presentation seems to do. Simply jot down the questions in the form in which they first come into your mind, without rewording them for improvement, or arranging them in order.

Now you are ready to go on to the solutions of the Presentations, if any are proposed. What part of the problem does a solution try to resolve? What other parts of the problem are left untouched, or changed in some way by this? Does the creator of the Presentation seem happy with his proposals? What satisfies or dissatisfies him about them? How does the solution relate to the basic problem or problems as he defined them? Try not to quarrel with the Presentation at this stage of your work, but simply try to understand it. If its creator were present, what questions about his problems and their solutions would you most want to ask him?

By now you will want to compare this information with your previous knowledge. The first step might be to think of simple, hypothetical or real situations in everyday life which present the problems with which the author deals. How would the author explain them in his terms, and what solutions would he pose? Sometimes, when you start working with these questions, you discover further gaps in your understanding of his terms, or his analysis of the problem or his solution, and will want to go back to noting down some more questions in your first two groups.

Now you are ready to understand just what this new information will mean to you and to the members of your group. Will this information be disconfirming in some way? Are ideas presented which are apt to meet with disagreement in the group? Why? What alternatives may they suggest? What problems and discomforts might some of these solutions pose for you or other group members? How might you or they apply these new ideas? How will they affect your feelings, your beliefs, your behavior? How would such actions fit in with your previous behavior? How do you feel about it when you think of putting this decision into action? Will the group be divided on these things?

Leader attitude Let us always remember that in our questioning we are striving for responsive understanding for ourselves and the other members of the group. In our discussions we will not be dealing in small talk or trivia—we will be talking about matters of importance to the members of the group. Our questions must never seek to trick people, to make them look foolish. They must be asked in a spirit of trust and with the knowledge of our own fallibility in mind. We are trying to do our work in friendship and understanding.

FORMULATION OF QUESTIONS TO BE USED IN LEADING

G. M. Young said, "The final cause of speech is to get an idea as exactly as possible out of one mind into another. Its formal cause therefore is such choice and disposition of words as will achieve this end most economically." [1]

key words In your choice of words, it is often best to phrase your initial questions of Meaning with the same *key words* used in the Presentation. If you start to substitute your own words at this point in the discussion, you are already interpreting for the group. You are saying, "This is what *I* think this word means." For example, in a discussion of the Parable of the Good Samaritan, you might want to find out what Jesus meant by "neighbor". You might ask, "What does Jesus mean by 'go and do as he did'?" or, "How does Jesus answer the question, 'who is my neighbor?'" If, instead, you were to ask, "What does Jesus mean by telling us to be a neighbor by helping those in need?", you have already done some of the interpretation, and probably limited the possible responses. Let us see how such a discussion might go:

LEADER (being careful with the disposition of words): *Mary, what does Jesus mean by "go and do as he did"?*

MARY: *I think he means he wants people to be a neighbor to everyone they meet.*

HARRY: *I don't think we have to be a neighbor to everyone, only to those who need our help.*

MARY: *But the story shows this man meeting someone— not going out on purpose to see who needs him.*

LEADER: *Mary, what does "be a neighbor" mean?* (Leader here is going back to the phrase Mary used in her first response.)

MARY: *Well, the lawyer talks about "kindness", and Jesus seems to be agreeing that that is the right answer.*

LEADER: *Harry, do you think "kindness" and "loving your neighbor" mean the same thing in this story?* (Leader has decided that since two questions are apparently being pursued at the same time—"What does *being* a neighbor mean", and "*Who* is my neighbor?"—it is best to seek an answer to the first before continuing, but he is still working primarily with key words actually used in the text.)

open-ended

The Leader is also being careful with the disposition of words in trying to keep the questions open-ended. At this stage in the exploration of meaning, he tries not to force a particular interpretation, and to accurately reflect the meaning that participants seem to be giving. As the above discussion continues, Harry might answer "yes" to the last question, and then the task would become to determine how Harry and Mary and the other members understood the word "kindness". It would then be necessary to further explore with the group whether there is any difference implied in the Parable between "loving your neighbor" and "kindness".

honest questions

In trying to make our questions "open-ended", we will try not to tie them to a pre-determined answer. One way of knowing whether your questions are really "honest" or not is to see if you could answer them yourself in at least two different ways. If the Leader asked, "Mary, does Jesus want us to love our neighbor?", Mary can hardly answer anything but "Yes", and no one has really learned anything. If the Leader asked, "John, does the lawyer really want an answer like this?", we have loaded the question by using the word "really"—we have implied that the "right" answer is "no". If the Leader "really" wants an answer to this question, it would be better to ask, "What kind of answer does the lawyer expect?", or "What kind of answer do you think the lawyer might have expected?", or we might go about it by asking, "Why did Jesus rephrase the lawyer's question?" Phrasing a question in the negative often has the same result as loading it with such a word as "really". For instance, if the Leader asks, "Doesn't the lawyer want a different kind of answer?", we are implying the answer "yes", or if the Leader asks, "Doesn't being a good neighbor mean being kind?", we again imply the expected answer. At this point in a discussion the participants have little to say but, "Well, yes, sure . . ."—and will probably not even go on to add, ". . . but . . .". A question such as, "Isn't being a good neighbor really not 'passing by' people in trouble?" manages

. . . vs. loaded questions

. . . and questions in the negative

152

to combine a number of faults. The question is obviously loaded by the word "really" and by the negative "isn't", and also implies a definite interpretation.

A common device used by some teachers is to phrase a question in the negative to bring out "points" the teacher himself wishes expressed. He may say, "Isn't there one more thing you want to add to that?", or "Wasn't there a particular word in the reading that is important here?", or "Aren't there some other things we should take into account?" These are obviously questions to which he has a predetermined answer which he is just waiting to hear. As Thelen says, "Inviting the group to guess what the leader has in mind is possibly a useful teaching device in situations in which the members acknowledge their job to be one of learning to think 'like teacher'. It turns the discussion into a game. . . ." [2] The Leader will simply have to face the fact that some of his pet ideas are not going to be expressed! A great deal can be done with skillful questioning, but the Leader must resist the temptation to be so "skillful" that he is really leading the group "down the garden path". Again, the Leader should ask questions—not make statements disguised as questions.

problem of double negative

In addition to these dangers with the "negative" question, questions expressed negatively are often more difficult to hear correctly and understand, and double negatives are doubly confusing! It has been shown that questions with a double negative confuse the hearer, and elicit answers which do not reflect the respondent's meaning.[3] For example, the question, "Doesn't the way the lawyer asks the question show that he's not looking for an answer?" is somewhat more difficult to understand than, "Is the lawyer looking for an answer?" Furthermore, the question clearly signals the expected answer. A question which indicates the "right answer" is a rhetorical, not an "honest", question. Even an honest question with more than one negative can be confusing, such as, "Mary, why don't you think 'not being kind' isn't wrong?" will confuse almost anyone.

yes/or/no questions

Primary questions should not be simple "yes-or-no" questions. In preparing questions for discussion you will sometimes find that Secondary questions can fall into this class and be helpful in developing an answer to your Primary question. For instance the Leader asked, "Harry, do you think 'kindness' and 'loving your neighbor' mean the same thing in this Parable?" This question arose naturally in the discussion, since Mary used "kindness" in answering "What does 'being a neighbor' mean?" In preparing the discussion questions, the Leader might have had such a question relating the meaning of "showing kindness" and "being a neighbor". However, in this case, since Harry has already spoken about "being a neighbor" to those who need our help, it is unlikely that he will answer with a simple "yes" or "no". He is more likely to go on and discuss this relationship in some way. The Leader must gauge his group and the individual to whom he asks such a question.

either/or questions

A Leader must also be careful in the use of "either-or" questions. Again, such questions are seldom suitable for Primary questions, but are sometimes useful in Secondaries. If the discussion has progressed with Harry answering the question on "kindness" and "loving your neighbor" by saying, "I think 'being a neighbor means actively doing something—I don't think 'kindness' covers it for me —you can sort of 'be kind', but not really do anything," at this point the Leader might wish to ask, "Is the answer, then, a rule of action or a rule of attitude?" This question *tends to limit* the answers to a choice between the two, and the participant will often feel forced to make this particular choice. In this case, also, it seems unfair to Harry who seems to be saying that it is a rule of action, not of attitude. It would be best for the Leader to continue the discussion by asking instead, "Is the answer, then, a rule of action?" He may go on to ask, "What kinds of actions would be covered in 'being a neighbor'?" If the members do not bring up other possibilities besides overt acts, the Leader might wish to ask, "How do you think the Samaritan differed from the priest and the Levite?", or "Does loving your neighbor mean doing kind acts for him?", or "When the Samaritan left him at the inn, did he stop loving this man?", or "Was it impossible for the man lying in the road to 'love his neighbor'?"

"What is this all about?" questions

In our efforts to make Meaning questions open-ended, however, we must not go to the other extreme and simply ask, "What is this Parable all about?" or "What does this story mean?", or, worst of all, "What can we learn from this Parable?" Many clever but useless variations of this question have been evolved by Leaders who are either afraid of overleading or too lazy to lead at all. This sort of question is "open-ended", but it gives the group no assistance toward responsive understanding. By abandoning the group to its own devices, it results in an unfocused discussion. A great many different answers are possible, such as, "How to gain eternal life", or "It tells us that to love our neighbor is to be kind to people in trouble", or "Our neighbor is the downtrodden", or "It talks about the recognition of the human person", or "It shows us how Jesus felt about priests and Levites", or "It shows the Jews that even though they looked down on Samaritans, the Samaritans were really better people", or "It's a good example of what hypocrites lawyers really are", or "It shows how everybody was out to get Jesus."

In a brief presentation such as this Parable, a Leader would probably be able to go from most of these responses to guide the discussion along fruitful lines of exploration, but each member of the group might mentally be going off in a different direction after such an initial miscellany of remarks. If the Leader selected one response to follow, rather than another, the group would tend to think the response selected was the Leader's version of the "real" meaning of this, and tend to concentrate all their efforts on seeing it his way.

By asking a "What is this all about?" question, the Leader hands control of the Primary to anyone in the group whom he happens to call on, and to those other members who then wish to respond. He is asking that the group determine the direction of a large portion of the discussion and asking them to make this decision on a moment's notice. Remember that the Leader should *control the Pri-*

mary, particularly in a new group. The majority of the group might have been pleased with the Leader's choice of a Primary. Furthermore, in longer or more complicated presentations, a question of this sort is unnerving to the group member, who is there to *find out* "what this is all about", and who may feel very unhappy at being asked to begin with a summary or conclusion.

brevity Correct phrasing of questions includes brevity. A question which is too long, or prefaced by a long quotation or much "setting of the scene", may only confuse the listeners. They are apt to remember only the first or the last part of the Leader's words, and miss the point of the question. As a rough rule of thumb, try to keep your questions no longer than *eleven words*. A question this length can usually be accurately remembered. We will consider the matter of brevity in more detail in Chapter 13.

What happens when a Leader does ask a long question—thirty words or more? The very cooperative participant is trying to mentally repeat the question to fix it in his memory, but as the Leader continues, the task becomes too much for him. He then remembers the first six to eight words fairly well, but feels pretty well lost about the rest. The somewhat less cooperative member is not trying to remember what the Leader said word for word, and therefore may have a slightly better overall idea of at least the first half of the question, or the middle, but isn't sure about the last part. The casual group member isn't listening closely, but he is aware that the Leader seems to be going on and on, and he may well decide that among all those words, the Leader must have mentioned one he himself is rather interested in, so he proceeds to talk about that—relevant or not.[4]

Sir Arthur Quiller-Couch said, "Essentially style resembles good manners. It comes of endeavoring to understand others, of thinking for them rather than yourself—of thinking, that is, with the heart as well as the head. . . . So (says Fenelon) . . . your words will be fewer and more effectual and while you make less ado, what you do will be more profitable." [5] Therefore, in addition to brevity,
. . . and simplicity use your "heart" and speak in the simplest terms which convey your meaning. Sir Arthur was talking about style in writing, but the spoken word requires even more understanding of others, as the hearer cannot look up words he does not understand, go back and reread what seems confusing, or take time to puzzle out what you are trying to say. Furthermore, it increases the possibility of missing part of a question through actually not hearing it, if the question is very long.

In the early stages of a particular discussion, by using primarily the words of the presentation, you are working with terms to which they have already been exposed, to which they have given some thought, and which are "common" to the group. By utilizing positive redundancy, you increase the probability of the question being received accurately. As the group members introduce new concepts into the discussion, it can be presumed that the group understands what they mean in most cases, but if the concept is important to the understanding of the presentation and discussion, or there is a hint of misunderstanding in the group, it is often wise to ask a member what he means by terms he uses. Stuart Chase in THE TYRANNY OF WORDS suggests that we might as well say "blab" when we use a high-order abstraction so far as conveying a clear meaning is concerned.[6] People are frequenlty able to understand a concept about which we want to ask them, but the question must be so worded as to be understandable to *them*.

definitions and concept availability

We must not, however, allow discussion to deteriorate into an endless series of definitions. A fine balance must be maintained between that situation in which group members are talking past, instead of to, each other, because each is using a private definition of the key terms, and an endless and boring attempt at refinement of meaning. The Leader must make the decision here, judging by the complexity of the material under discussion and his estimate of the members' sharing of concepts. Borger and Seaborne point out the importance of this latter factor: "The concepts which a person uses constitute a kind of filter system for the infinite variety and complexity of the information which impinges on him—there is a strong tendency to see and respond to the environment in terms of available concepts."[7] Without shared concepts, discussion is meaningless. Your group will learn fairly rapidly to define when necessary.

This does not mean that the Leader or anyone else in the group is "talking down to his audience". Wise men of all ages have recognized this problem. Thomas Aquinas, commenting on one of Aristotle's writings, said, "A listener's understanding becomes confused, if a person uses a word with many possible meanings and fails to make these meanings distinct. For, when a person uses an ambiguous term without distinguishing the meanings, it is not clear as to what meaning gives rise to his conclusion."[8]

style and simplicity

Whether you are leading a group in a high school, a university, an in-service training program, or the Home and School Association, your "style" should be as simple and straightforward as possible. Complexity is bound to enter the discussion, and is not always a bad thing, by any means. Albert North Whitehead said, "Seek simplicity, and distrust it."[9] "Life, liberty, and the pursuit of happiness" are very simple *words*, but their meaning cannot be reduced to the "clear and distinct ideas" sought by the optimistic philosophers of the sixteenth to eighteenth centuries. Even Descartes, in an early formulation of this hope, said, "I came to the conclusion that I might assume, as a general rule, that the things which we conceive very clearly and distinctly are all true—remembering, however, that there is some difficulty in ascertaining which are these that we distinctly conceive."[10] Twentieth-century philosophers seem to have rather less, than more, faith in our ability to "distinctly conceive" ideas. We must tolerate considerable fuzziness, but not deliberately foster it by asking questions worded in an unnecessarily complex fashion.

generalizations

If we, as Leaders, try to speak as simply and clearly as we can, we will help our groups directly, by presenting them with comprehensible questions, and indirectly by our example. We will help ourselves by thus improving our own communication skills, while helping the group improve theirs. It is a common tendency to hide from thought by screening ourselves with catch-all phrases, labels, and all-encompassing generalizations. We often believe that if we can just put a label on something, particularly an academic label, it is ours, without further thought. Such habits interfere with the kind of thoughtful exploration we are seeking in our discussions, and make discussion itself of little value by actually interfering with communication.

TRAINING THE GROUP

goals   Each of our discussion groups has at least one explicit goal each time it meets: a productive discussion by the group about some matter of significance which will result in responsive understanding.

. . . group   An discussion group is a work group, or a socio-group; it exists to *do* something specific, and its members will not be satisfied unless the group achieves some success in this endeavor. At the same time, discussion groups should have some of the elements of a psyche-group—a group whose members join together for psychic satisfaction, as do friends.

As we have said, it is important that group members clearly understand and agree upon group goals, and that they see these goals

. . . individual as important and achievable. One way in which the overlap of in-

dividual and group goals can be achieved is by involving the members as much as possible in settting group goals. Some discussion of goals should take place fairly early in the group's life. In this discussion, the Leader serves as a liaison person between the parent organization and the group, and may be used by the group as a resource person at this point.

setting of goals

There usually is a considerable area of freedom within which they may discuss and determine their short-range and even some of their long-range goals. Sometimes a new group may have a steering committee, which will get together prior to the first meeting of the entire group. Such a committee would be made up of a representative sample of interested people, who would prepare recommendations to present to the group for consideration, and these recommendations might include such things as short-range goals, topics, materials, and possibly details of recruitment of members or physical arrangements. The Leader will provide guidance to this committee in the selection of topics and materials, but will hope that the committee will have suggestions of its own. When this committee meets with the full group, its recommendations should be proposed as suggestions to which the group may wish to add. The Leader should then conduct this meeting as a *moderator*, and in such a way that the group reaches its decision by consensus, if possible. He must remember to restrict the discussion to those decisions which are within the group's area of freedom.

steering committee

group action decision

In some cases such a steering committee may not be practical, and the Leader may either decide on the materials to be used as well as a good deal of the other detail, or the parent organization may have made most of these decisions. He may be able to propose a selection including more than can be covered in the allotted time, and allow the group to eliminate those items which seem least popular. Since not all materials are suitable for discussion, the Leader will help the group find the best presentations for its purposes. This very discussion of the immediate goals will do much to provide motivation for the group and support for the means of reaching the goals. The more the group's activities are determined from within, the more likely they are to be accepted as real goals, to be worked for and even enlarged.

limited choices

When a group such as we have been talking about meets for the first few times, it is a fortunate group, as it will almost inevitably meet with some *success in achieving its goal* of responsive understanding. The importance of this goal, and the other group goals, should always be present to the mind of the Leader, and should become so to the entire group. The group is more dependent for success in the early days of its life on its Leader than it will be later as it matures. Every effort should be made to help the group improve its performance. *Success energizes* the group in its goal-seeking, while making goal achievement more possible through improved cohesion and communication. This is the dynamic interaction, the spiraling effect of which has such importance in the life and growth of groups.

the dynamics of success

158

FOR SOURCES AND FURTHER INFORMATION, CONSULT THE FOLLOWING WORKS:

1. Gowers, Sir Ernest, THE COMPLETE PLAIN WORDS, p. 9, Baltimore, Md.: Penguin Books, 1954.
2. Thelen, Herbert A., DYNAMICS OF GROUPS AT WORK, p. 315, Chicago: University of Chicago, 1954.
3. Blankenship, Albert B., CONSUMER AND OPINION RESEARCH, N.Y.: Harper & Brothers, 1943.
   see also: Adler, Max K., LECTURES IN MARKET RESEARCH, Jacqueline Marrian, ed., London: Crosby Lockwood & Son Ltd., 1965.
4. Brown, John, "Information Theory", NEW HORIZONS IN PSYCHOLOGY, ed. Brian M. Foss, pp. 118-134, Baltimore, Md.: Penguin Books, 1966.
5. Gowers, Sir Ernest, THE COMPLETE PLAIN WORDS, p. 26.
6. Chase, Stuart, THE TYRANNY OF WORDS, p. 39, N.Y.: Harcourt, Brace & Co., 1938.
   NOTE: However, this does not mean that *no* meaning is conveyed. Robert Herndon Fife, former Chairman of the Committee on Modern Languages of the American Council on Education says, ". . . even words with a wide range of semantic values, often determinable only by the context in which they are used, have a certain semantic focus about which the meanings cluster." Among the first six hundred words in an English frequency of use list are such abstract nouns as "being", "hope", "love", "real" and "truth", all of which are translatable into words which also fall in the six hundred most frequently used words in Spanish, French and German. Easton, Helen S., AN ENGLISH-FRENCH-GERMAN-SPANISH WORD FREQUENCY DICTIONARY, N.Y.: Dover, 1940. Quotation from Fife, p. vii of Easton's work.
7. Borger, Robert and A. E. M. Seaborne, THE PSYCHOLOGY OF LEARNING, p. 187, Baltimore, Md.: Penguin Books, 1966.
8. Thomas Aquinas, "I de Caele, Lect. 22", n. 2, quoted by L. M. Regis, EPISTEMOLOGY, N.Y.: Macmillan, 1959, pp. 151, 497.
9. Curtis, Charles P., Jr., and Ferris Greenslet, THE PRACTICAL COGITATOR, rev. ed., p. 51, Boston: Houghton Mifflin, 1950.
10. Descartes, Rene, DISCOURSE ON METHOD, trans. Charles Adam and Paul Tannery, Vol. VI, 33, Paris: 1897-1913, and Cambridge University Press, ed., THE PHILOSOPHICAL WORKS OF DESCARTES, Vol. I.

11.
Leading

OVERVIEW

The Leader will find that he can avoid many problems and achieve productive discussions by careful *listening, honesty,* a *non-partisan attitude,* the *proper use of the cluster and the phases of discussion,* and the pursuit of *clarity.* He will learn how to judge the amount of *time* a particular group with a particular presentation should spend in the various phases, how to use the *group memory* and when to use *form questions.* He will learn to judge when a group can profit by the use of *content and process observers,* and how such observation should be handled.

AVOIDING PITFALLS

A Leader who has carefully prepared for his discussion, and comes armed with several good Primary questions and adequate and interesting clusters of Secondary questions, can still find himself involved in a disjointed conversation instead of an articulated and productive one. What are some of the reasons for this? Let us look at yet another discussion of the Parable of the Good Samaritan, during which the Leader has asked the Primary question, "Mary, what does Jesus mean by 'go and do as he did?'"

MARY: *I think he means we must be a neighbor to everyone we meet.*

LEADER: *John, what was the question the lawyer asked Jesus?*

JOHN: *He asked him "who is my neighbor"?*

LEADER: *Mary, what was the* first *question the lawyer asked?*

MARY: *Why, let's see—he asked—here it is—"How can I gain eternal life?"*

JOHN: *But Mary, don't you think he knew the answer to that question?*

MARY: *Yes—he told Jesus the answer when Jesus asked him, "what is your reading of the law?"*

LEADER: *Harry, what kind of answer does the lawyer expect?*

HARRY: *It says, "trying to vindicate himself" . . . I'm not sure . . .*

LEADER: *Ann, do you know who your neighbor is?*

ANN: *Well, I guess it's the person who needs help.*

JOHN: *Do you have to help everybody?*

ANN: *I guess everybody I meet.*

HARRY: *About "vindicating", I think the lawyer was being very legalistic, that's the trouble with the Jews, that's what Jesus was trying to change. . . .*

LEADER: *Do you think the lawyer's attitude is only to be found in Jews?*

Well, let's stop and see what went wrong. Before you continue reading, take a pencil and see how many errors in leading you can find; then read on.

Quite a few things *did* go wrong, and it is possible to spot them and indicate what the Leader should and should not have done.

listening

1. The Leader was not listening to his group. We can never emphasize too much the absolute necessity of LISTENING. The kind of listening that seeks to really understand what a speaker is saying is the mark both of a good Leader and a good participant, and is the cornerstone of discussion. Not listening in this way is the

rock on which discussions founder and, for that matter, most conversations. It is not an easy thing to master, and even the very experienced Leader will have lapses, but it is the most important asset a Leader can acquire, and the thing he will constantly strive to instill in all the members of his group, both through example and by training. Until Harry's last statement in the discussion above, the Leader apparently did not hear one thing that was said. The group would have done just as well without any Leader, and might well have done better—at least, some of the participants were hearing each other at times. Harry's last statement did come through to the Leader, because it shook him up! He realized that something was wrong, things were getting out of hand. Because he had lost the thread of his discussion which, after the first answer, really had no thread, he had no idea what to do.

abandoning the Primary

2. The Leader abandoned his Primary question. Having asked a good Primary question, and having received a relevant answer which could have been pursued, he failed to continue, leaving his question unexplored. The many possible questions concerned with what it was that the Samaritan actually did, why he did these things, the idea of "kindness", how this relates to us in our world, what we "must do" and why, were all scuttled—not by the group, but by the Leader! Since the Leader asked this *as* a Primary question, we presume he had prepared some such Secondaries. Of course, if a Leader does not study his material carefully, and think it through thoroughly, it is possible to miss the implications of important questions and to drop them before they can be explored.

misuse of Fact question

3. The Leader used a Fact question at the wrong time. His second question, addressed to John, simply asked for the actual words of the material. There is no reason to ask such a question unless there seems to be some confusion in the group as to what these words were. This inappropriate use of Fact questions reduces the discussion to a quiz. The Leader should presume, especially in such a brief presentation, that the group can easily find or recognize a specific quotation. If he wants to explore the lawyer's questions he should ask, "What was the lawyer's problem?", or "How does Jesus answer the lawyer's question?", or "Why didn't Jesus answer the lawyer's question directly?", or "Why does Jesus rephrase the lawyer's question?" or some such questions which presume, until proven otherwise, that the group can identify the statements of the text.

lack of clarity

4. The Leader's second question was unclear. He was not specific enough in his reference, simply saying "the question", when the fact was that more than one question was involved. The group has enough difficulties without obfuscation by the Leader.

missed Secondaries

5. The Leader did not follow through on the relevant points raised by the group. When Mary first answered, she used the word "neighbor", certainly an important term in this presentation, and yet the Leader did not follow through to help the group explore this concept. He does not give Harry or the rest of the group any assistance in seeking to answer his question about "what kind of answer" the lawyer might have expected, nor in answering his question about how we know "who" our neighbor is.

Furthermore, the Leader ignored a relevant and potentially fruitful interchange: John said to Mary, "Don't you think he knew the answer?", and Mary said, "Yes, he told Jesus. . . ." At this point they were trying to speak to the Leader's question of "what *was* the lawyer's question?" Inappropriate as the Leader's Fact question had been, the group was trying to develop a conversation about meaning, and the Leader could have saved the situation at this point by sticking to the issue on which two members were focusing. He might have asked, "How is 'go and do as he did' an answer to the lawyer's question?", or "Why isn't the lawyer satisfied by Jesus' first answer to his question?", or "Why do you think the lawyer's 'reading of the law' did not satisfy him?" To go on to Harry immediately, as the Leader did, even though his question to Harry was a good one and related to his last question, was a poor choice. He could have asked John or Mary the question he asked Harry, "What kind of answer does the lawyer expect?", or a question dealing with "the law" and "eternal life".

poor timing of Response

6. The Leader initiated a Response question before the Meaning had been explored—in other words, he skipped about instead of following a problem-solving pattern, or staying more or less within the proper progress of the phases of discussion. When he asks Ann, "Do you know who *your* neighbor is?", he is asking the group to decide what moral obligations they feel toward others, whom they feel obliged to serve, in the light of this story, before the group has explored the meaning of the story, their feelings about it, and other views they may have on the problem.

dishonest question

7. The Leader asked a loaded question. The Leader's last question to Harry is rhetorical—he expects that Harry will be *forced* to answer "no". Unnerved by Harry's statement, ". . . that's the trouble with the Jews", he has immediately assumed, apparently, that Harry is prejudiced against Jews, and the Leader allows himself to

Leader as partisan

become a *partisan* in the discussion and strike back at Harry. The Leader has forgotten in this case that first he ignored Harry when Harry was struggling unsuccessfully with his question, "What kind of answer does the lawyer expect?", and jumped in too fast, not giving Harry time to think, or helping Harry by asking another, subsidiary question. Harry has therefore probably withdrawn from the discussion temporarily to think about the ideas the Leader's question suggested to him. He may or may not be prejudiced against Jews, but he probably is feeling some degree of irritation at the Leader's treatment of him, and therefore may be either expressing his hostility by adverting to some target "safer" in his mind, or less threatening, than the Leader himself. If he has an idea that this sort of statement may irritate the Leader, he may be deliberately baiting him. In any case, the Leader should find out *what Harry means* by his statement, rather than presuming a meaning. Having found out what Harry means, both by "legalistic" and by "the Jews", he can then explore "what it is that Jesus was trying to change", and how it relates to us. *If* Harry is prejudiced, a direct attack on his attitude of "all

mishandling prejudice

Jews are legalistic", whatever he means by this, will not change Harry. A question such as the Leader's "Do you think the lawyer's attitude is only to be found in Jews?" is only suitable in a situation in which the whole group has clearly enunciated such a stereotype, backed it up, and defined their terms, and though this is possible, it is not probable.

failure of nerve

handling prejudice

8. The Leader did not trust his group. By jumping on Harry with a loaded question, which he doubtless intended to use to "cure Harry of his prejudice", he was playing God. He was presuming that he, and only he, knew (1) what was wrong with Harry, (2) what the group's attitudes were, and (3) how to change Harry. Racial and religious prejudice is common, and difficult to change. Such attitudes develop for a number of reasons, and prejudices are often unconsciously present in individuals. Discussion in small groups is one of the ways in which attitudes actually can be changed, including attitudes of prejudice. In order for this to happen, however, it is necessary for the prejudiced individual—and who is not!—to openly explore the nature of his prejudice in a non-threatening, warm, friendly atmosphere, or climate. He must be allowed to express these feelings without danger of personal attack. Other members of the group must also be able to express their feelings about the matter under consideration. The group should try to explore together the reasons for these attitudes, their congruence with other, related attitudes they hold, and the relation of all these attitudes to the total hu-

man context. No deep-seated prejudice or long-cherished attitude will change radically and suddenly, but people *do* change their attitudes, people *do* learn. The Leader must trust his group when he hears and sees things expressed in the group that he believes are wrong, or bad. This does not mean that he ignores them, but that he helps the whole group explore these ideas and feelings that worry him, not in a punishing or vindictive way, not even with the feeling that "I'm right and they're wrong!", but helpfully and with some degree of humility. He should not plunge in to right all wrongs with the belief that he is the only member of the group who is capable of sound judgment and good will.

improper use of cluster

9. The Leader was not working with his cluster, but was using scattered, unrelated questions most of the time. A question of sufficient importance to be a Primary will have a whole cluster of satellite questions subsidiary to it, all of which will help to explore in depth the Primary. In preparing for the discussion, he will write these Secondary questions in a list, following the Primary, and he will use them, either in the form in which he originally wrote them, or rephrased to fit the discussion in progress, *at the appropriate time.* He will *not* consider this cluster as a rigid "1, 2, 3" list, in the sense that, having asked the Primary, he then goes on to "Secondary question number 1", and then to "Secondary question number 2" and so forth. Just what he asks and when he asks it must be determined during the discussion, and because of what is said during the discussion. In preparing the cluster he does, to some degree, try to think of *possible* answers members might give to each question, and then arrange his cluster to follow through on various possible paths. He also arranges them with a thought as to how his own exploration progressed in trying to think through answers to the Primary. He can never, however, totally predict what will be said. Trying to outguess the group in advance is often a helpful way of preparing questions, as long as it is kept in mind that dozens of equally likely predictions could be made which have not occurred to him. He must also be careful that his "guesses" do not prejudice him so that he thinks he hears the expected answer when a group member is really offering a quite different suggestion.

PROPER USE OF CLUSTER

Let us look at a typical cluster, this time used in a discussion of the first four chapters of GENESIS.

PRIMARY QUESTION: *According to these four chapters, is man responsible for what happens to him?*
SECONDARY QUESTIONS:
Are limits shown to his "command . . . of the whole earth" (1:26)?
If so, what?

Is man shown as absolute master? of himself? of what?

What is God's command of the earth shown to be?

Can we tell from this how man is supposed to exercise his command?

Does the serpent appear to bear any responsibility?

To what extent is God shown to be responsible for what happens to man?

What is the relationship here between freedom and responsibility?

Was man more free before or after he ate the fruit? how? why?

Are limits placed here on man's freedom? how? why?

WHAT LIMITS DO WE PLACE ON MAN'S FREEDOM? WHY?

How do our laws relate freedom and responsibility?

Can you have responsibility without freedom? freedom without responsibility?

What kinds of responsibility do you have? why?

How do we know or judge our degree of responsibility?

> . . . in the use of natural resources? . . . relations with other states or nations? . . . in day-to-day relations with our immediate world?

WHAT MUST WE DO IN OUR "COMMAND OF THE WHOLE EARTH"?

> How do you exercise this command?
>
> What, if any, are our limits in this command?
>
> > . . . in our use of natural resources? . . . in physically changing man?
>
> How do we, or can we, teach our children "responsibility"? What do they "command"? why?
>
> How can we help them grow in freedom?

Such a Primary question as this, together with its cluster, provides ample material for a discussion of at least forty minutes, and probably two hours. A Leader would ruin his carefully prepared cluster, however, if he insisted on treating it as a chronological list. You will notice that no Fact questions are included. In a work as deep and rich as this, it is frequently possible, despite the fact that only a few pages are involved, that some Fact questions will be necessary. Fact questions may also arise in the discussion when other group members are quoted—or misquoted! The Leader who listens carefully, and is well prepared, will know when these are necessary. The Leader will also see that some of these questions will be asked in one form or another by other group members during the discussion.

You will note that all the questions prior to the emphasized, "What limits do we place on man's freedom?", are directly concerned with exploring the meaning of the *presentation*. With this particular question the group begins to relate this new information to previously stored knowledge, to see how the pieces fit together, and to explore their relevant concepts and attitudes. The group may spend considerable time in this Concretizing and Balance area, depending on what has gone before. They then go on to Response with the questions starting "What must we do in our 'command of the whole earth'?"

You will note that the wording of the early questions is specifically designed to make clear to the group that the meaning of the presentation is first being explored here, not their understanding of their life situation. For instance, compare the following:

PRESENTATION QUESTION (Meaning of the Presentation: How does the author of the Presentation answer?)	LIFE QUESTION (Balance, Concretizing, Response; some Meaning and Fact from members' statements)
Is man shown as absolute master?	Is man absolute master?
What is God's command of the earth shown to be?	In what sense does God command the earth?
Can we tell from this how man is supposed to exercise his command?	How is man supposed to exercise his command?
To what extent is God shown to be responsible for what happens to man?	To what extent do you think God is responsible for what happens to man?
What is the relationship here between freedom and responsibility?	What is the relationship between freedom and responsibility?
Are limits placed here on man's freedom?	Are limits placed on man's freedom?

The clue words used in the "Presentation questions" above are "shown as", "shown to be", "from this", and "here". These words clearly indicate to the group the import of the question. Other variations frequently used are the name of the film-maker, for instance, the author, or the work. A trained group will presume the Leader is asking a question of the meaning of the presentation during the early stages of a discussion until the Leader makes it obvious that he is not, but a new group should be helped to understand when this is the case. With a trained group the Leader may say, "John, how do *you* exercise command over the earth?", or "Mary, what is your opinion as to God's responsibility for what happens to you?", or "Harry, how would you describe the relationship between freedom and responsibility?", or "Joe, how do you think Harry sees the relationship of freedom and responsibility?" Here he is asking John a Response question, Harry and Mary Balancing questions, and Joe a Meaning question which is *not* concerned with the Presentation, but with another member's statements. In all the statements responding to these questions, he is apt to find members including the concepts they have seen in GENESIS, plus the amendments they believe their total life experience has shown them. They should be able to do this in their own terms and make specific concrete applications of these ideas.

Particularly with a new group, the Leader should be sure to indicate whether he is exploring the meaning of the Presentation, asking for opinions on situations outside the Presentation, or asking for personal response. Otherwise he will find himself saying, "No, that's not what I meant, Mary, I meant. . . ." This is uncomfortable for the group and disruptive of the discussion.

members assume
leadership
functions

As his group becomes more mature, he will find to his delight that many of his Secondary questions will actually be asked by other group members. As they become familiar with the process of discussion, they will often have such questions in mind during their preparation, and will want to hear what the group has to say about them. As long as they see the relevance of these questions to the Primary question asked by the Leader, they will feel free to bring their questions to the attention of the group at a time that seems appropriate to them. Here they are taking on the leadership function of seeking information, opinion and response. They will trust the Leader to assist them by delaying the answering of their questions if they raise them at an inappropriate time, or to help them explore the answers if they are asked at a suitable time. If, for instance, a member were to have given an answer to the Leader's first Secondary question, "Are limits shown to his 'command . . . of the whole earth'?", and then said, "But I want to know what *we* must do in our command of the earth", the Leader should indicate that it is a good question, but ask that discussion of it be deferred "until we explore the story a bit more." If another member should ask, "Was there a *real* tree, that's what I want to know", the Leader should not allow the discussion to get sidetracked at this point into a discussion of types of "reality", the various trees, and so on since the Primary question on the table is "responsibility". The whole question of why this story is told as it is, or reality, symbolism and so forth, is worth the group's time, but the discussion would again become a "disjointed conversation" if every interesting by-way and sidelight were pursued as soon as it was introduced. If a member should ask, during the discussion of this Primary question, "Why does God say they'll die if they eat the fruit, and then they don't?", the Leader can probably work this question into the discussion quite well, assisting the group in finding answers by such additional questions as "What is the 'death' God says will result?", as being relevant to the idea of "responsibility" and "what happens to man".

how much time
to spend on
Presentation

The Leader will also have to decide how much time needs to be spent on exploration of the meaning of the Presentation. This will vary with the group, the group goals and the Presentation, but it is hoped that any Presentation deemed worthy of their time has sufficient value in itself to be worthy of some discussion.

group memory,
and questions
related to previous
discussions

Each time the group meets it is adding to its common memory bank—the *group memory*—and the Leader and other members will naturally refer to previous presentations and discussions in the course of subsequent ones. There will usually be one or more common threads running through any series of discussions, and the building and comparing which result are valuable parts of the learning experience. The Leader will include in his questions some which refer specifically to other views and ideas previously discussed by the group.

FORM QUESTIONS

There is another category of questions which a group **may** pursue: *Form questions.* Form questions may be questions of Meaning, Concretizing or Balance. They explore the style and tone of the author, artist or film-maker, how he achieves his effects, what devices, techniques and so forth he employs. They investigate the group's reactions, the reasons for their reactions, and their estimate of the reactions of others. The Leader's decision on when to use such questions depends, again, primarily on the group goals. A class or group studying propaganda, political speeches, advertising or similar material usually classified as "persuasive" may want to spend considerable time on such questions, as might a class studying literature. A group studying racial prejudice might find the close examination of selections from the mass media greatly aided by Form questions searching out the often unconscious reflection of attitudes of prejudice.

general questions   A Leader may use such *general questions* as the following in preparing to lead a short story:

How does the (author) convey a sense of (failure, success, delight, sorrow, crisis, etc.) in this?

How does he evoke (pity, joy, sorrow, fear, etc.) in you?

Does the order or length of various sentences emphasize (a certain point) or create a mood? what? why or how?

Does the rhythm or cadence (of this passage) create (the effect mentioned)? do certain words? how or why?

How does "time" operate in this story? why or how?

How does the author convey his standards of "good" and "bad"?

How does the author seek to achieve our belief?

How does the author achieve your reaction of (what has been stated in the discussion) to (various characters)?

> *How does he reveal his own feelings about (these characters)?*

> *What role does (a certain character) play in this work? why? or how?*

> *Whom do we know from the outside only? why? how can you tell?*

> *What basis does the author use to select data for inclusion? (theme? subject? plot? character?)*

What are the turning points in the story? why?

> *Why does he start the story with. . .?*

Why does he end it with. . . ?
Who moves the action? why? how?
To whom is this story addressed? how do you know?
From whose point of view do we see the story?
Why does the author choose this narrator?
Is there more than one narrator? why?
Does the narrator see everything, or is his viewpoint limited? by what? why?
What seems to be the author's prevailing emotion or emotions? How do you know?
Is the story told in a realistic way? why? why not? what kind of realism? how can you tell?
Is there deliberate ambiguity? why?
What kinds of figures of speech are used, if any? What is their effect? on your cognitive understanding? your emotional reaction? why?
Are there elements of comedy? how are they achieved? what is "funny"? why? for whom would this not be "funny"? why?
Are there elements of tragedy? how are they achieved?
Is there suspense? how is it created?
If you were to change this to (another medium: film, etc.) how would you handle it? why? whom would you cast? why?
What particular sounds create an effect? how or why? (this question is usually more applicable to drama and poetry)

In preparing to lead a group in the discussion of material such as a political speech, the Leader might think about the following general questions:

What persuasive phrases are used?
To what human needs or desires do these phrases appeal?
Whom is he trying to persuade? why?
Whom is he apt to persuade? why?
Is he trying to persuade his audience to believe certain things? to take certain actions? to make certain evaluations of others? why?
How does he try to establish validity?
What things are asserted without support? are arguments based on these assertions?
Are euphemisms employed? why?
Are generalizations used? (overgeneralizations?) are they based on inadequate grounds? how can you tell?
Are the same words used to mean different things? why?
Does he use ambiguities deliberately? why?
Are the terms used in some cases vague? why?
Are things stated as "inevitable" which are not so in fact? why?
What phrases seek to disarm the wary?
Does the author use overstatement? understatement? why?

vagueness and ambiguity   Ross, Berryman and Tate, in THE ARTS OF READING, define "vagueness", and distinguish it from "ambiguity": "(A) vague sentence is one whose meaning cannot be specified *at all*, and an ambiguous sentence is one which has more than one specifiable meaning, but no clear indication which meaning is intended. So 'The king yet lives that Henry shall depose' is ambiguous. It has two meanings, and it is not clear which is intended. 'The world is will', with no explanatory comment, is vague; we cannot state *one* clear meaning for it. . . . (T)he use of 'failure', with no explanation of what is failed, makes a sentence vague. Can a man fail at a task he did not undertake? Can there be failure if one neither wanted nor tried to succeed? Does a man fail if he tries to fail? (This could be a paradox. Suppose every young man had to take a test to get into the army. Would those who tried to fail and managed to, be successes or failures?)" [1]

However, vagueness is a matter of degree. As Hirsch points out, "(A) type always has a dimension of vague expectations by virtue of which more than one concrete instance can be subsumed without compelling an alteration of the type. . . . There is nothing vague about a thing, but there is always something vague about a meaning." [2] A certain amount of vagueness is therefore unavoidable in communication. We are concerned with questions exploring what seems to be excessive vagueness, or deliberate vagueness or ambiguity, and the reasons for such handling of his material by an author, artist or film-maker. There are times when it is important for a group to identify and understand the reasons for vagueness or ambiguity in a Presentation, and also to understand its presence both in the individual members of the group or in the group as a whole. Once more, we remind Leaders that the group's goals should guide decisions on how much exploration of this type, or of any Form questions, a particular group should pursue.

USING CONTENT AND PROCESS OBSERVERS

In order for either Process or Content Observers to be of service to a group, it is necessary that (1) the group accept the idea of being observed, and see potential value in the procedure; (2) the observer be acceptable to the group; (3) the observer be somewhat familiar with group processes; (4) he be able to report in a fairly objective fashion what he *sees* and *hears;* if he is to make evaluative statements or judgments, they are to be about the *group,* not the individual; (5) time be allowed for discussion of the Observers' reports; (6) in the case of a Content Observer, he be familiar with the presentation and the immediate objectives and long-range goals of the group.

Observers do not participate in the discussion during the session which they are observing. Listening and watching carefully and making notes for their own reference in reporting to the group, they make qualitative and quantitative estimates on the group operation and performance. Their purpose is to provide feedback which the group can discuss with the aim of group growth and of improving their work together, and therefore they seek the sort of information they would need themselves as a Leader or other group member.

Observers may use anecdotal reports or highly systematized forms to record their observations. Forms may be designed to check or rate items on a qualitative scale or continuum, or to make quantitative records of specific items. An Observer may be asked to look for only one thing during his period of observation, or he may look for many things. An Observer who merely remarks that "it was a good discussion", or "it was a poor discussion", is obviously not providing useful feedback, and therefore he must have some idea in advance of what he intends to look for. The group may recognize, or believe it sees, a particular problem, and ask for particular observations in connection with that. The questions at the end of this section are merely suggested approaches, and many items anticipate problems which a particular group may not encounter, or omit items most needed by another group. Other questions may be developed using such materials as the list of leadership functions or participant attributes. Other means of tallying, such as the Bales' observation categories and participation pattern charts, provide ways of keeping track of the particular contributions of each member on the basis of process. A Leader might be interested in having an Observer simply record the types of responses elicited by his own questions, and such a record might be kept on a chronological basis or on a quantitative basis related to specific questions or specific group members.

The most important thing about group observation and evaluation is that it fit the needs of the group at the time. This requires knowledge of group process, the particular group and its needs, and the various means of providing feedback. It is best if the Leader plan this with his group. The group may not be knowledgeable about process or methods, but they can help in determining their own needs as individuals and as a group. Although in a training group, observation is imposed early and arbitrarily on a group, this is because of the goals of training. A group whose specific goals are something other than leadership training will be apt to be uncooperative or at least uncomfortable with such imposed observation.

SUGGESTED QUESTIONS FOR CONTENT OBSERVERS

The Content Observer is concerned with *what* is said—with the quality and progress of work on the group task. His observations are obviously subjective to a greater extent than those of the Process Observer.

General:
Is progress made in problem-solving and decision-making?
> *Did the discussion move beyond the exploration of the meaning of the Presentation? Does the group try to relate problems to their own experience, so that members think through problems, make judgments, and seek and develop appropriate responses? or was the approach overintellectualized, or noninvolving? If progress was not made, did this seem to be because the Presentation was unsuitable? members poorly prepared? questions inappropriate? was there a reasonable amount of consensus on meaning of core content?*

Did the group achieve some grasp of the meaning of the Presentation?
> *Did the discussion move away from the Presentation too rapidly so that further discussion was on a basis of inadequate information, or so that obvious misunderstandings of the Presentation hampered progress?*

If there was controversy, was it explored to determine its cognitive roots? were misunderstandings of members' statements ignored?

Was there evidence of listening?
Was the group memory used?

LEADER   *Are the Leader's questions concerned with important aspects of the subject under discussion?*

Do his Secondary questions seem helpful in exploring the subject in depth, eliciting statements of "value" and "decision"?

Does he develop or rephrase his Secondaries so that they flow naturally from statements by the group? Are they offered to the group at appropriate times?

Are his questions ones which the group should be able to deal with productively?

Does the Leader allow himself to become a partisan, or does he remain outside the discussion in order to help the group develop all of its ideas? (Does he make statements or phrase questions in such a way as to push his own views?)

Does he err in the other direction and waste time exploring what you consider trivialities?

Does he follow the discussion with sufficient care so that he can pick up ideas expressed early in the discussion and reintroduce them with questions at appropriate later times?

Does he defer good questions brought in too early or at the wrong time and fit them into the discussion later?

Does he avoid the "What is this all about?" questions?

Does he use Fact questions appropriately?

THE GROUP MEMBERS

Does the group evidence willingness to explore the questions in depth?

Does the group make a real effort to deal with the questions asked, or do they tend to slip away from them to irrelevant comment, superficial remarks, or quite different questions?

Are their own questions relevant to the principal matter under discussion, to the last question before the group, or do they take the group off on a tangent?

Are their questions ones with which the group can be expected to deal? or are they "discussion stoppers", leading to long, irrelevant personal anecdotes or appeals to outside authority?

Are questions asked which obviously seek understanding of state-
ments of others in order to further group progress on the
task?
Are they willing to work with questions which force them to examine
their values?
Are they willing to make a personal response?

SUGGESTED QUESTIONS FOR PROCESS OBSERVERS

Climate and Cohesiveness:
Does the climate seem warm, free and friendly, or cold, inhibited and
antagonistic?
Do members "affirm the person" even though they cannot use the
contribution?
Is concern demonstrated for others? for their comfort? for absentees?
Are members truly attentive to whoever is speaking? do members
look at each other? (eye-contact)
Are questions asked by group members which obviously seek un-
derstanding of the views of others, or do they tend to be
primarily designed to trap, confuse, or refute?
If there is conflict, how is it handled? smothered? ignored? denied?
smoothed over? laughed away? accepted and worked with?
Do members help resolve controversy and conflict, or depend on the
Leader?
Do members feel free to ask the group to help with problems?
Do members demonstrate feeling of responsibility for the group and
its work?

Participation:
Does the participation seem fairly balanced? Are quiet members
encouraged? are frequent contributors allowed to interrupt?
are they requestioned frequently?
Is there evidence that status affects participation?
Are the majority of contributions addressed to the Leader? to one or
two members?
Are there side-bar conversations?
Do some members speak only to certain other members (subgroup-
ing)
Is the minority voice given a real hearing?
Does the Leader try to involve everyone in the discussion in a mean-
ingful way? ask questions of appropriate people? just try
to get people to "talk" without consideration of the question
or the group member involved?
Do group members try to involve quiet members in a meaningful
way, or do they rely on the Leader for this?

Communication:
Does the communication level seem high or low?
When there is distortion in communication, do other members try to
help clear it up, or do they depend on the Leader?

*Does the Leader offer assistance in communication problems when
necessary?*

*Is an effort made to see that all members can see and hear one
another?*

*Do members address questions and contributions to appropriate in-
dividuals when suitable?*

Are contributions dialogic or monologic?

Do members try to speak concisely, clearly and simply?

*Do members make a real effort to put difficult ideas into words? to
express emotions and feelings?*

*Do members encourage others in this? do members question one
another for clarification?*

*Are members listening to each other with a real effort at under-
standing? are they content to understand only those with
whom they agree?*

*Are members willing to try different ways of explaining their state-
ments when there is misunderstanding or lack of comprehension?*

Roles and Functions:

*Do group members try to enlarge their repertoire of leadership
functions? (try different leadership functions)*

*If they have usually performed in only one or two interaction
categories, are they trying to make contributions in others?*

*Does the Leader encourage or discourage this? do other group
members?*

*Are a large number of leadership functions shared throughout the
group?*

*Is the level of dysfunctional behavior high or low? If high, is its
immediate, present cause apparent? If high, do you think the
group should discuss this?*

Norms and Procedures:

Do members conform to the group norms?

*Are any sanctions invoked for non-conforming? how? how are sanc-
tions accepted? Does the group reward those who conform?
how?*

*Were any of the group norms specifically mentioned during the
session? why? was there an indication that some norms are
changing, or is there evidence of a desire for such a change?
were reasons expressed? was there disagreement when sanctions (including rewards) were evidenced? majority or
minority?*

*Were there times when subgrouping, role-playing or some other
technique might have been helpful? when? why?*

Does the group accept silence when it might be productive?

Goals, Planning and Motivation:

Did the Presentation seem suitable for the group? for the subject?

Did the group seem to believe the subject was relevant for them?

Was the group really interested in pursuing the problems and issues? Does the group seem fairly united in its goals?

Did the Leader have to urge them on, or simply act as traffic director?

Do you believe other kinds of feedback (through observation, discussion, etc.) would be helpful? If so, what? why?

Was there strong evidence of individual goals which did not overlap group goals? how did group accept this?

Are the physical arrangements suitable for the groups? Are minor or major changes needed? why? Is group size suitable?

Does the group seem hampered by outside forces of any kind? If so, what, and why? Is there evidence that their area of freedom is too small?

FOR SOURCES AND FURTHER INFORMATION, CONSULT THE FOLLOWING WORKS:

1. Ross, Ralph, John Berryman and Allen Tate, THE ARTS OF READING: AN ANTHOLOGY OF THE FINEST LITERATURE OF ALL TIME, WITH CRITICAL COMMENTS, pp. 127-28, N.Y.: Apollo, Thomas Y. Crowell, 1960.

2. Hirsch, E. D., Jr., VALIDITY IN INTERPRETATION, pp. 270, 274, New Haven: Yale University Press, 1967.

12.
Democratic Leader's Goals and Means

OVERVIEW

The discussion Leader's goal is the *freedom* and *growth* of each member of the group, and of the group as a whole. He works to minimize negative influences restricting the ability of the members to think, to feel, to express, to decide—to *be*. His role is to *fulfill those leadership functions which group members are not yet ready to assume*, while trying to help them take on increasingly larger amounts of responsibility. His means are his own attitudes, particularly that of *respect* for the individual, his assistance to the other group members in developing similar attitudes, the development of a healthy group *climate*, the facilitation of *productive discussion*. Throughout this course we talk about "the Leader" and "the group members". We say, "the Leader must . . .", "the Leader should not . . .", "It is the Leader's responsibility to. . . ." We also talk about the necessity for the *sharing of leadership functions*. These concepts may seem in contradiction. However, the resolution of the contradiction is achieved through *training the group*. A mature, trained group *has* leadership—this leadership is shared. It will still usually function best if it retains a titular head, but his role and responsibilities shrink in proportion to his group's growth.

THE SITUATION OF THE GROUP

The concept of democratic leadership often includes a group's self-selection of goals, membership, location and definition of necessary functions and sometimes self-selection of the titular head.[1] The question naturally arises as to whether it is possible to conduct a learning-discussion group, a class or other teacher-learner situation "democratically", and to "share the leadership functions".

The answer, of course, is "yes, but. . . ." Democratic leadership does not mean that the group is a "leaderless" group, that the Leader allows a "tyrant" to take over and run things his way, that the group can decide to be a hockey team, rather than a discussion group, or that principles or goals foreign to human values will become the ruling norms. The limits are set primarily by the stated goals of the parent organization and by the explicit and implicit goals of any particular group established under its auspices. These goals define to some extent the group's area of freedom.

area of freedom

In the accompanying chart you will note that the outermost line (A) designates the limitation imposed by the external situation, including availability of personnel and materials, any limitations imposed by the surrounding or environing community, and by the discussion process established as the general means. Within this area, certain things are blocked off by the authority or determination of others. These blocks further limit the freedom within "A". Block "B" represents any policies and dictated procedures—including criteria for selection of Leaders, or possibly the nomination of the Leaders and other personnel, specific procedures and materials — of the overall parenting agency or program. Block "C" represents local control: any of the above named limitations imposed by a subordinate parenting group affiliated with or forming a department, section, or division of the overall parenting group, and having sufficient autonomy or delegated responsibility to issue directives to the discussion group. Block "C" may, in some situations, be subdivided, but presumably would have similar lines of communication to those shown by the connecting arrows. These lines of communication make possible alteration of the situation in at least one, but

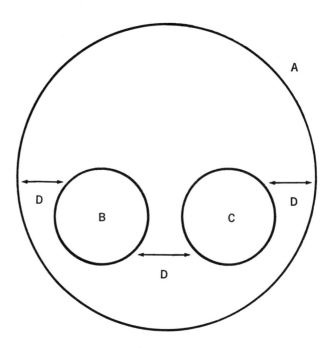

A Limitation of the situation: availability of personnel, materials; limitations of surrounding community; discussion process as means

B Parenting organization or program: policies and procedures

C Subgroup of parenting organization: local control

D Lines of communication: make possible alteration of the situation in either direction

limitations of democratic leadership

usually both directions. The limitations of the group's area of freedom are also the limitations of the Leader's area of freedom for democratic leadership.

All groups have an area of freedom, beyond which they cannot go without losing their identification. For instance, it is possible to think of a number of different kinds of groups, all of which could operate democratically within quite a small area of freedom: a plane crew, a work team in a watch factory, a high school history class. This does not mean that the crew can decide that the stewardesses should take turns being the pilot, nor that the crew can change the assigned flight pattern; it does not mean that the watch factory team can change the design of the watch or decide to just go out and play ball all day; it does not mean that the history class can decide to study algebra and abandon history, nor can they tell the teacher to sit quietly in the back of the room and not interfere. Each of these decisions would be outside their area of freedom. It does mean that within this area of freedom, their Leader will constantly encourage the sharing of leadership functions, freedom and individual responsibility. The Leader who refuses to assist the group in this way will not further group freedom or discussion, and will have either tyranny or anarchy, but not democracy.

The control element in our data processing decision system model of group discussion includes those prior decisions of the parenting organization as well as those of the immediate group. Many of these may be negotiable. When a Leader feels the group's area of freedom, and therefore his own, is unduly small, he should examine all points in the control element, keeping in mind the importance of the group's real goals. He should also examine his lines of communication in relation to the area of freedom, with a view to making or keeping them two-way, rather than one-way, lines.

difference between learning-discussion group and action group in Leader's behavior

Some people advise a discussion Leader to find out as much as possible about the members of his group—their backgrounds, interests, tastes and habits, their jobs, their friends, and so forth. If a Leader took such advice seriously he might begin to feel like a secret agent. One reason for such advice is that the advisors are thinking in terms of decision-making in action groups, particularly in business and industry. A Leader armed with such information and skill in handling people can often resolve tension in a group and successfully lead the group to a decision. Also, he can sometimes protect an individual who has a particular bias because of a personal problem of which the group is unaware, or the Leader can draw out the "true" feelings of someone who is opposing the group for reasons of his own. Such Leaders, because of their position in a company or organization, strive to "win the conference". Such a Leader has a responsibility both to the parent company or organization and to the group itself to create a situation in which all members will be in agreement with a given solution, and sufficiently committed and energized to carry the project through to successful completion. Therefore, when we read remarks such as, ". . . the man who would be an effective Leader can, by careful observation of the behavior of the people . . . and by constant alertness to every clue in their past histories . . . develop an acute sensitivity with respect to human relations", remember this advice is related to group-decision and group-action. The key word here is "effective"—effective, that is, in terms of the necessary result.

Our effectiveness as learning-discussion Leaders is not to be measured by the same kinds of production values and standards as those of a management team or a fund-raising group—our "products" and our "funds" will reside within the individual members. We must learn how to live as a member of this particular group, but the goals do not require group-decisions on group-actions to be carried on outside the discussion group. Such decisions may be made occasionally, but they are not the purpose of the group's existence.

Keeping this in mind, it is still true that the better we understand our group members, the better job we may be able to do. Probably the best way of making the distinction in practice is by the way in which we acquire and use our knowledge of group members. As Leaders we try to encourage openness in the group, so that the knowledge we have of group members is the knowledge group members feel free to share with the group. We need not, as Leaders, seek private information. It is true that members often speak privately to their Leader, divulging information they do not feel free to discuss openly with the entire group. The Leader will not, of course, pass this information on to the group, and he must be careful of how he uses this information. The Leader cannot be totally knowledgeable about all the factors influencing the opinions and attitudes of group members, or even those which influence himself, but he should be conscious of the existence of these influences, and learn what sociology and psychology can tell him about the feelings and behavior of people in groups.

. . and goals   The Leader has taken on a special obligation to help members reach their own goals and those of the parent organization, which may include the acquiring of information, the development of carefully examined attitudes and values, and the living of a meaningful life. This does not mean that he is obliged to do this by

indoctrination or manipulation. As Grace Coyle, an early student of groups, put it, ". . . he does not coerce people to accept points of view or teach them indirectly to be subservient to leadership. Free and understanding acceptance of new values and the participation in new learning provide the essential nourishment to growth." [3]

THE LEADER AND THE GROUP

newcomers
New members, as they seek acceptance and recognition, sometimes present a very limited or even a distorted aspect of their own opinions and feelings. There is a certain amount of "jockeying for position" and a need to "know what the leader is like." [4] Until they believe they understand the group opinion, goals, norms and procedures, and until they feel accepted by the group and understand in some sense their role in the group, they will usually hesitate to do more. The will privately cling to those beliefs and opinions and attitudes in which they feel comfortably safe. They will publicly express only those they feel will meet with acceptance. They will be fearful of experimenting with new ways of thinking, believing or feeling, and will often reject new ideas without even attempting to understand them or "try them on". A new group presents the Leader with all of these attitudes and behaviors, in addition to his own feelings of "newness".

As the individual in the group gets to know the other members and feels better able to judge what their responses may be, he will more readily express his opinions if he believes they will be in accord with either the majority opinion, the Leader's opinion, or the opinion of a subgroup of which he is a member.[5] But he still may hesitate to be the lone voice.

minority opinions
If he finds that his group demonstrates concern for him as an individual and respects his ideas and feelings, regardless of how they may differ from their own, he will be increasingly willing to voice his opinions even knowing they may meet with disagreement. The group should learn to welcome and not fear disagreement.

extremes of conformity and non-conformity
In any group it is possible to find individuals who, for many different reasons, tend toward extremes of conformity or non-conformity, at least in some areas. It is possible that their reasons are based outside the group, but in some cases it may be due to great differences between their background and experience and that of the majority of the group, a factor which could cause them to go toward either extreme. The extreme conformist is usually easily accepted in most groups, and is often unrecognized. The group climate should be such that the non-conformist can also be accommodated, even though he may remain peripheral to some extent.

THE LEADER AND CLIMATE-MAKING

climate defined
The matter of climate-making is so important that some authors say it is the primary function of the Leader.[6] The climate is

the mood, the tone, the atmosphere which prevails in the group. Although the climate of a group may vary to some extent from one time to another, most groups establish a fairly consistent and durable climate which has a considerable effect on the productiveness of discussion. A cold, formal, unfriendly climate will inhibit fruitful interaction and discourage the honest expression of opinion. A chaotic, disorderly climate may allow much interaction and participation, but communication will be low and the discussion is not likely to be fruitful. Although each participant contributes to the climate, one of the Leader's most important services is his help in the establishment of a suitable climate.

freedom

A free permissive climate is desirable—one in which the members feel they may have and express differences of opinion and feeling. In such a climate group members feel warmer toward one another, they are interested in one another as individuals. They have an "at home" feeling, and yet the ultimate result of the group is energizing rather than merely relaxing. They have a sense of comfortable freedom. David H. Jenkins suggests a list of six ways for testing whether freedom exists in a group:

"1. Do the individual members . . . feel free to disagree with each other?

2. Do (they) feel free to disagree with the Leader or with any authority in the group?

3. How frequently are members encouraged to expand a different point of view, to give it a fuller explanation?

4. How often does a person who is expressing a disagreement get interrupted or cut off by someone else?

5. How often is there a sudden change in the direction of discussion by someone?

6. Have the group members been together long enough to understand and appreciate each other and their differences?" [7]

climate and community

Climate will probably be the factor most important in furthering the group's goal of community. A group which feels itself a community is one which has achieved a good climate and a high degree of cohesiveness. After five or six sessions together, a group should feel a fairly strong degree of "groupiness", interest in and concern for one another, and look forward to its sessions together.

the Leader and cohesiveness

Cohesiveness itself is both cause and effect, a dynamic factor which needs a good climate in which to grow but which is also dependently related to the group goals, the task, and the motivation of the group members. Eisenson, Auer and Irwin believe that the Leader can best contribute to group cohesiveness through attention to ". . . keeping the ATTENTION of the group focused upon its task; creating a common ground of INTEREST among members; channeling the strongest MOTIVATION for each member into a desire to achieve the group's goals and support its values; and guiding the

climate and cohesiveness

discussion so that LEARNING will be reinforced." [8] A group can have a good climate, and yet lack cohesiveness. A party, for instance, may take place in a warm, friendly and open climate, and yet lack many of the necessary elements of cohesiveness. And if a group goal of community is disregarded, a group may be cohesive in a rather cold, closed climate as, for instance, in a team of highly competitive salesmen. Normally, however, high cohesiveness and a "good" climate go hand in hand.

climate and internalization of norms

The aims of an educational program include the internalization of attitudes and the development of values, rather than mere compliance or identification with attitudes as they appear in the group. If only compliance or identification results, these attitudes will not be salient in out-of-the-group situations, or will not be lasting. With internalization the content of the new ways is itself satisfying, and new knowledge, attitudes and behavior are of themselves satisfying. They become really one's own, free of the necessity for accompanying social reinforcement.[9] A free accepting climate in which the presence of a "strong leadership personality" is minimized will further internalization. A climate is needed in which the concern is for the individual and his own personal achievement of congruence and balance in freedom, rather than one which seeks quick acceptance of authoritatively presented ideas, discourages disagreement and induces fear of controversy or conflict. The more stable and cohesive the group, the greater the influence the group's norms or standards will have on the individual's behavior.[10]

learning and human relationships

Obviously we cannot create community, a climate of acceptance, or an I-thou relationship by telling a group, "Now, we are all going to love each other!", or "In this group, we are all going to trust one another!" "Love" has become a catch-all word, evacuated of meaning for much of our society. It is currently used to convey absolutely everything with the possible exception of hate. It seems to have joined such words as "commitment", "involvement" and "community". "Trust" is rapidly becoming part of this jargon. Nevertheless, it is a relationship of love and trust and community which we are trying to achieve or establish, and for lack of other words, we must hope that these do convey some meaning. Dostoevski wrote, "Until you have become really, in actual fact, a brother to every one, brotherhood will not come to pass." [11] It is doubtful that learning of value for the living of life can be achieved without this relationship. Again we must state that it is not just what a Leader *does*, but what he *is!*

ESTABLISHING THE DESIRED CLIMATE

What can the Leader do to establish the desired climate? The group's first contact with the Leader is extremely important. The climate which the Leader initiates at this time is apt to remain fairly stable for a long time. Even when a group is looking forward with enthusiasm to a first experience in a particular group, or to a new Leader, they will still be wary and anxious to size up this person who is going to be important to them. In his first experience with them the Leader should seek to remove the element of threat he carries as an authority figure, and to establish a dialogic rather than a monologic relationship. He can do this in part by verbal assurances, by the physical arrangements, but most of all by his attitudes which he will try to convey to them as sincerely and warmly as possible.

Leader models behavior for group

The Leader tries to exhibit those qualities he wishes to see in the group. He shows that he is cooperative, rather than competitive, he focuses his services *to* them rather than *on* them. Because he is, indeed, "involved in Mankinde", he shows his regard for each member of the group as "a piece of the Continent, a part of the maine." [12] Genuine respect helps produce a climate of freedom, thus making available to the individual members an opportunity to "be". In time, "being" leads to creativity and expression. The Leader should be warm, friendly, concerned for each individual, interested, open-minded, trusting, cheerful and enthusiastic without exaggerated emotionalism or sentimentality, relaxed but energetic. He should be permissive without allowing tyranny to destroy the group or chaotic disorder to ruin the discussion. He must be sincere and honest with the group and in the discussion situation, and he must not become a partisan in the group or seek his own ends at the expense of the group. In this way the necessary relationship of *trust* will begin to be established.

confidence

It is important that group members be given confidence: confidence in themselves, that they know how they are supposed to behave in this situation, and that they are able to function to the satisfaction of the group, and that they will personally benefit from contributing; confidence in discussion, as a happy and productive learning experience; confidence in the Leader, that he will provide the necessary assistance; confidence in the group, that its climate will be friendly, open, interested, and concerned with the whole person, rather than just with an intellectual exercise. M. B. Miles says,

education

"Traditionally, education has been concerned often with solely verbal learning, less often with growth in the expression of feelings and (some would say) least often with what people actually *do*. Ideas, values, principles, attitudes, feelings and concrete behavior are involved in 'whole-person' learning. . . ." [13]

practical first steps in climate building

There are practical steps the Leader can take which will assist in climate-making. He should learn the names of all the members of the group from the beginning, and use them whenever he asks a question. As we suggested when we spoke of the dyad introductions for the first meeting, it is important to see that everyone is introduced, that everyone has an opportunity to say a few words from the very beginning, and that they become accustomed to using one an-

names

other's names. In a group of more than six who have not previously met, the use of a seating chart, as described in Chapter 8 should be continued for a few meetings. This gives members a chance to hear each name spoken correctly by its owner, resulting in less mispronunciation.

. . . and addresses

It is often a good idea to see that each member receives a complete list of the names, addresses and telephone numbers of

group members. Someone in the group may volunteer to provide this, or the Leader may do so himself.

absentees
To help develop a feeling of group responsibility it is often a good idea to check absentees and then ask some member of the group to volunteer to call them, telling them what went on at the meeting, that the group missed them and hopes to see them at the next meeting. This method has met with some success even in a city high school with students with a high rate of absenteeism.

physical arrangements
Although groups have met successfully under very adverse conditions, the Leader should do whatever he can to achieve a comfortable and suitable environment for the group. A group is apt to feel somewhat lost, insecure and unwelcome in a room which is too large, but it should be large enough to permit some freedom of movement and rearrangement of furniture when desired. The often mentioned but frequently disregarded requirements of comfortable temperature and adequate ventilation, quiet, and proper lighting should be considered, with particular attention to avoiding glare. It is best if the room has a round table about which the group may be seated. They will have a place to put things and the table serves as a uniting element in the early days of the group's life. The table offers a kind of protection, and group members are apt to be less restless and more relaxed, particularly if there are both men and women in the group. As a group becomes more cohesive, they may wish to dis-

pense with the table, at least at times. Groups which have worked around an oblong table for several sessions and which then have moved to a round table only large enough to provide seating room have often made such comments as, "today was our best discussion", or "there was a real improvement today—let's sit here next time". A program in seventeen high schools in Cleveland, Ohio, reported, "The poorest discussions witnessed were those in which students sat in conventional rows facing front. In such arrangements almost all interaction was between one student and the teacher so that there was no pupil-to-pupil interaction. In the most productive discussions, students were seated in a circle so there was maximum opportunity for eye-to-eye contact and other kinds of non-verbal communication." [14]

The only danger may be that the group will spend too much time on the social-emotional, and too little on the task areas of discussion in what may be a much more relaxed atmosphere. However, the strictly task-oriented Leader is apt to underestimate the amount of social-emotional work necessary for a healthy group. If it is absolutely necessary to use a classroom in which there are fixed desks or chairs, use only the front row, bringing in other movable chairs, or use whatever free space is available to seat a group on the floor. Groups should feel free to experiment with their environment to find the arrangements most suitable for them at any given point, but for the first few meetings it is desirable that the Leader impose what he believes is the best arrangement.

If the Leader is solicitous about the comfort of the group members, they in turn will give consideration to the group's comfort. He should provide ash trays, but if he has group members who object to smoke, try to group the smokers together, "downwind" of the non-smokers. He should offer paper and pencils in the beginning of the group's life. He should make it clear that group members are free to move about as they choose. Some kind of refreshment should be offered, even if it is only a cup of coffee, soft drinks or some cookies. For some groups it is best if this is served at the end of the meeting when the main business is out of the way, but for most groups, particularly when they are new, if this is made available to them from the beginning of the session it will have a wonderfully warming effect. There is something about sharing bread together that has had a unifying effect since the most primitive times, and we have yet to develop a better tribal ritual for this purpose. The "bread" may take many forms, but its presence is not a trivial matter. Occasionally people feel that "refreshments" detract from the necessary seriousness of purpose, but this is the case only if the food or drink becomes a large feature of the meeting or introduces a competitive note, when provided by different group members in turn.

The juice-and-cookies routine of kindergarten vanishes until it reappears as coffee and occasional refreshments in graduate school. That's a long time between drinks! Despite the many problems connected with food and drink in classrooms, and the impracticality of students with a seven-period roster eating or drinking seven times a day, it should be possible to allow more freedom in at least some classes, particularly in schools where modular scheduling is used. In non-academic situations today the coffee pot regularly outranks the chalkboard.

name tags

Some groups feel that name tags or name signs standing on the table in front of the individual members are helpful. Only in the case of a group of ten or more meeting for only one session would we recommend this. The disadvantages usually overcome the advantages.

accepting comments

Thelen reminds us that every comment should receive a constructive response and says, "The easiest way to accept all comments is by seeing how they are related to the topic at hand, rather than to theories of individual personalities and background." [15] In the conduct of the discussions, the Leader shows that he is interested in every member, in every idea and opinion and feeling they wish to express. Because he gives each contribution serious consideration, not indicating shock, distaste, or disapproval, he shows that this is the way people behave in discussion groups. At the same time, when other group members meet a contribution with disfavor, he does not stifle this disagreement, but encourages its open exploration, demonstrating that affirming the person does not necessarily mean agreeing with the person's ideas. Because he wants to be sure he actually hears and understands each contribution, he asks the participant to repeat what he does not hear, and to clarify what he does not understand. He is not afraid of silence in the group, nor is he impatient if a member wants more time to think or does not wish to make any comment when called upon. He has a sense of humor, and realizes that the group needs to break the tension of serious thought, hard work, and a sometimes emotionally charged discussion with occasional jokes or a bit of horseplay. He is sympathetic with, rather than critical of, those who have not had an opportunity of preparing an advance assignment, or who have missed the Presentation or previous meetings.

Leader accepting his own feelings

The Leader will want to continue to develop his ability to recognize and accept the feelings of the group members. In order to do this, he should learn to understand and accept his own feelings, but this should not be thought of as a necessary prerequisite to starting to lead, but as an ongoing process with which the group will help him. This is an area in which many people will find sensitivity training of assistance. The list of recommended readings in the back of this book gives some further suggestions for material which may be helpful in developing empathy, sensitivity and self-awareness.

ESTABLISHING APPROPRIATE NORMS AND PROCEDURES

From the first meeting, the Leader will do well to recommend to the group some minimal guidelines for their discussion. These may be explained to and discussed with the group, or given to the group in written form as suggestions. You and the group may want to add to or change these "rules" as time goes on, but offering initial recommendations or procedural guidelines is not sacrificing freedom to efficiency, but is promoting freedom. Stogdill points out that group members on entering a group feel less "free" when they do not know the "roles and rules", and therefore cannot pursue their individual goals in an unstructured group situation. Stogdill speaks of "freedom for initiative of the group members in interaction", and "freedom from restraint in action toward a goal", and says, "The area of freedom is at a minimum in a group of minimum structure. As the structure of positions in a group becomes more highly differentiated and roles more clearly defined, members experience a greater area of freedom because they know the bounds within which they can act without unfavorable consequences for themselves or the group as a whole. But there appear to be upper limits beyond which increase in rigidity of structure produces no further increase in freedom of action. Too little or too much structure imposes restraints upon the group's freedom of action." [16] There is considerably more involved in learning the "roles and rules" than simply the stated guidelines for handling the mechanics of discussion, as we are sure you realize, but this does help to get a group started, and started along a path which will allow for some measure of success.

roles, rules, goals and freedom

If the group members actually read a few recommendations or "rules" for their discussion out loud, it not only provides a simple means for each member of the group to say something out loud, but gives them confidence that they know to some extent what is expected of them, and also gives them the security of knowing that others share these expectations. Giving the group an opportunity to bring out any doubts they have about rules and talking about them together will give the group confidence that these rules or norms are workable, and seeing them in print, hearing them said aloud, and talking about them will help fix them in their minds, so they will have less worry about remembering them during the discussion. These suggestions or rules should be made brief and simple, have relevance to the particular group and its goals, and convey some of the spirit of the desired discussion.

The first time a Leader meets with his group he should tell them briefly what he understands his role to be. In discussing the rules with them, their own role requirements will be clarified. Lundberg, Schrag and Larsen, speaking of social structures in general, say that "A coordinated system of action is likely to occur where the following criteria are met: (1) the group's positions are highly valued, (2) role requirements are clear and consistent, (3) sanctions are uniformly applied and are supported by group opinion, and (4) the group's members regularly anticipate conformity among their fellows. To the extent that these criteria are not met, non-conformity, group tension, and conflict are the likely result." [17] These criteria and the anticipated results of their application are equally valid for the U.N., the management of a supermarket, a state prison, and a learning-discussion group. As such, they are obviously rather broad generalizations, but do provide a framework for the Leader's expectations.

feedback on norms　　It is wise after the first few discussions to go back over the originally suggested norms, as a group, allowing each member an opportunity to make any comments he wishes on how he thinks the *group*, as a *whole*, conducted their discussion in the light of their goals and planned procedures. This may be an opportunity again for some quiet member, who was probably better able to observe what was going on, to add his comments. It is particularly important at this early stage to avoid pinpointing "offenders" in any way, and the Leader should indicate that any problems that might arise are *group* problems and that he, and all the members of the group, share the responsibility for finding suitable answers and changes in conduct. The Leader should never feel that he sits in judgment on the conduct and behavior of the group or of its members. He must, however, until the group is more mature, feel a special responsibility in the area of diagnostic functions, commitment to group goals, and a greater sense of the group-as-a-whole than is usually possible to members of a new group.

LEADER AS INSTRUCTOR OR CHAIRMAN

When the discussion Leader is also the instructor of the group, or serves as a "committee chairman" for the same group of people in a situation in which they *do* need to reach a group-decision or take some *action as a group*, the group has moved over the line from a learning group to an instructional class or an action-group, and the Leader "moves over the line" also. He *moves over the communication line*, in particular. The Leader may decide to participate in such a situation, in order to offer his own contributions to the group discussion. If, as in learning discussions, the Leader does not express his views or answer questions, there may be said to be a restriction of communication, and therefore a widening of the distance between Leader and group. In the instructor relationship there is also a distance, but of a different type, in that not only is the instructor actively participating by offering communications of his own, but is also judging the communications of others as to their accordance with his ideas. In the committee situation, the Leader changes hats in a way which may or may not partake of the instructor relationship. In both cases, he has the additional responsibility of helping the group become comfortable with his change in roles. If the Leader makes clear to the group the change in roles, rules and the Leader-group communication pattern, the group will have less difficulty.

Some changes in the physical arrangements are often helpful in making evident this change. The Leader-now-instructor for instance may wish to stand, or to sit at a "head table" or desk or, if

there are no other possibilities, even the seemingly pointless operation of having everyone get up and change places can be helpful. Usually the ideal arrangement for discussion is a circle. When the group changes character and the Leader changes roles, it is best to rearrange this "perfect circle", where no one "sits at the head" and no one sits below the salt, and create a physical situation which emphasizes the change. The instructor or chairman role may still be handled democratically, if so desired, but as such his role is still quite different from that of a discussion Leader. In a different way, he is responsible for the quality of the decisions of the group, and for the feasibility of implementation of the decision on the part of an action group. It is important that the group be trained to distinguish the roles and activities proper to these differing situations. The alteration in the role of the Leader causes changes in the roles of all those with whom he interacts in the system. A driver-education instructor may sit down with his students and discuss the problems of air pollution caused by gasoline burning engines, and he may also instruct the class in how to park a car along the curb of a busy street. Their roles and his are quite different in these two situations. In both cases he may be the titular head, he may operate "democratically", and they are a group of students reporting to him. Their roles are interdependent in both cases, but the situation has altered and the differences should be made clear.

FOR SOURCES AND FURTHER INFORMATION, CONSULT THE FOLLOWING WORKS:

1. LEADER'S DIGEST, 1952-1953, p. 18, Adult Education Association, U.S.A.
2. Haiman, Franklyn E., GROUP LEADERSHIP AND DEMOCRATIC ACTION, pp. 79ff., Boston: Houghton Mifflin, 1951.
3. Coyle, Grace, GROUP WORK WITH AMERICAN YOUTH, p. 25, N.Y.: Harper & Brothers, 1948.
4. Thelen, Herbert A., DYNAMICS OF GROUPS AT WORK, pp. 302-303, Chicago: University of Chicago Press, 1954.
5. Gorden, R. L., "Attitude and the Definition of the Situation", AM. SOCIOLOGICAL REVIEW, Vol. 17, pp. 50-58, 1952, reprinted in ATTITUDES, eds. Marie Jahoda and Neil Warren, pp. 240-55, especially pp. 252-53, Baltimore, Md.: Penguin Books, 1966.
6. Haiman, F., GROUP LEADERSHIP AND DEMOCRATIC ACTION.
7. Jenkins, David H., "Planning Conditions for Personal Growth", LEADER'S DIGEST, No. 2, p. 65, Adult Education Association of U.S.A., 1965.
8. Eisenson, John, J. Jeffery Auer, and John V. Irwin, THE PSYCHOLOGY OF COMMUNICATION, p. 265, N.Y.: Appleton-Century-Crofts, 1963.
9. Kelman, H. C., "Three Processes of Social Influence", PUBLIC OPINION QUARTERLY, Vol. 25, pp. 57-8, Princeton, N.J., 1961, reprinted in ATTITUDES, eds. Marie Jahoda and Neil Warren, pp. 151-62.
   see also: Festinger, L., "An Analysis of Compliant Behavior", GROUP RELATIONS AT THE CROSSROADS, 1953, eds., M. Sherif and M. O. Wilson, pp. 232-56, N.Y.: Harper, 1953; Kelman, H. C., "Attitude Change as a Function of Response Restriction", HUMAN RELATIONS, Vol. 6, pp. 185-214, 1953; French, J. R. P., Jr., and B. Raven, "The Bases of Social Power", STUDIES IN SOCIAL POWER, pp. 150-57, ed. D.

   Cartwright, Ann Arbor, Mich.: Institute for Social Research, 1959; Jahoda, Marie, "Conformity and Independence", HUMAN RELATIONS, Vol. 12, pp. 99-120, 1959.
   see also: Hovland, Janis and Kelley, "Group Membership and Resistance to Influence", COMMUNICATION AND PERSUASION, pp. 134-70, New Haven: Yale University Press, 1953.
10. Festinger, Leon, Stanley Schachter and Jurt Back, SOCIAL PRESSURES IN INFORMAL GROUPS, p. 91, N.Y.: Harper & Row, 1950.
    see also: Freedman, Ronald, Amos H. Hawley, *et al.*, PRINCIPLES OF SOCIOLOGY, rev. ed., p. 178, N.Y.: Holt, Rinehart & Winston, 1956.
11. Dostoevski, F., THE BROTHERS KARAMAZOV, transl. Constance Garnett, Part II, Book IV, Ch. 1.
12. Donne, John, DEVOTIONS, XVII.
13. Miles, M. B., LEARNING TO WORK IN GROUPS, p. 33, N.Y.: Teachers College, Columbia University Press, 1959.
14. Fish, Kenneth L., CONFLICT AND DISSENT IN THE HIGH SCHOOL, p. 137, N.Y.: Bruce, 1970.
15. Thelen, Herbert A., DYNAMICS OF GROUPS AT WORK, pp. 302-303, Chicago: University of Chicago Press, 1954.
16. Stogdill, Ralph M., INDIVIDUAL BEHAVIOR AND GROUP ACHIEVEMENT, pp. 207, 210, 211, N.Y.: Oxford University Press, 1959.
17. Lundberg, George A., Clarence C. Schrag and Otto N. Larsen, SOCIOLOGY, 3rd ed., p. 150, N.Y.: Harper & Row, 1963.

NOTE:
For further material on "area of freedom", see Maier, Norman R. F., PRINCIPLES OF HUMAN RELATIONS, pp. 11, 24-5, 198-99, 250-53, N.Y.: John Wiley & Sons, 1952.

13.
Overcoming Problems

OVERVIEW

Well-led groups are usually effective, but some groups may be ineffective or unproductive for most of their life, or may have occasional periods of malaise. There are some problems so common that the Leader may expect to encounter them at one time or another. Problems arise in carrying out *leadership functions*, there are barriers to *communication*, problems in *participation* and problems of *conflict*. The Leader's attitudes and skills can help the group learn to solve these problems and in many cases to prevent them. The two things which probably do most to hinder success in discussion are *lack of clarity* and *lack of charity*. The Leader who takes positive steps to promote these characteristics in his group will find his group experience rewarding.

LEADER'S ATTITUDES AND APPROACH TO GROUP PROBLEMS

The very freedom for individual decision which the Leader tries to foster is itself a source of anxiety to him, as it creates a group picture of ambiguity and uncertainty, of divergent views, and sometimes of conflict. This is often in contrast to the seemingly greater clarity, oneness, and sense of direction seen in a typical classroom where all are usually working toward a grasp of a single correct answer. It is also in contrast with the decision-making stages of a committee meeting or a problem-solving conference in the business world. In these typical action-groups, there may often be divergent views and conflict, but the acknowledged goal of the meeting is the resolution of these differences and the narrowing down to a mutually satisfactory conclusion. At various times during their discussions such groups make small majority decisions which provide visible landmarks. Although their goal is not always easy to achieve, its very existence strongly encourages those present to go through the stages of elimination, compromise and compliance as rapidly as possible.

The leader of such action meetings knows when his job is completed, and usually whether he has completed his own task well or badly. In contrast, the learning-discussion group Leader does not always have this sense of progress, demonstrated by one landmark following another. Neither does he have the sense of completion which accompanies the final decision toward which the action group successfully heads. He therefore has little assurance when his session has ended that he really has helped the group, and finds it difficult to know whether he has accomplished anything or not. The results of his session may be a long while arriving.

self-confidence and listening

Leaders of discussion learning groups often are concerned about various kinds of problems in their groups, and sometimes worry unduly about their ability to "handle" them. The two things that often cause Leaders the greatest difficulty are lack of *self-confidence* as a Leader, and lack of careful *listening*, the latter often being a function of the former. Thelen adds that the Leader suffers from "anxiety . . . over the feeling that the group is incapable, over the ambiguities and lack of certainty that are so inevitably a part of discussions prior to decision. In many cases these anxieties are needless, and . . . can be dispelled by placing one's faith in tested methods, and in the ability of people to learn these methods."[1] He goes on to point out the importance of the Leader to the group, and the fact that the very importance of good leadership makes it imperative for the Leader to develop in his group the sharing of leadership functions.

Thelen points out three principles the Leader should keep in mind in situations in which the group blames the Leader for its failures: "(1) the Leader does not have to take responsibility for everything that happens, (2) the Leader has only one purpose—to help the group, (3) the Leader has to accept his own skills and limitations as realities in the situation." [2] The Leader's attitudes and his approach to the problem are as important as what he does, and an attitude of trust and respect will guide him best, if he can manage to see the situation as it really exists. He must examine his own feelings of frustration and irritation, attempting to determine their real causes, and he must try to look at his group with a genuine desire to help them identify and solve their problems.[3]

A group in difficulties may believe that the answer to their difficulties lies in a need for further direction and assistance from the Leader. A Leader may be questioned by a new group as to why he doesn't participate in the discussion. The briefest explanation is best in most groups. They can understand if you tell them that you enjoy participating, but feel it best to do so in a group which you do not lead. You may tell them you have found that when the Leader participates, the group does less discussing, and that it is difficult for you to see how the discussion is moving and to help the group if you are actually a partisan. This does not mean that you are refusing them "further direction and assistance", but that it must come in a different way.

COMMON PROBLEMS IN TASK LEADERSHIP FUNCTIONS

shared leadership functions; member as Leader

During the course of a discussion, the actual "leading" of a particular phase may easily pass from the appointed Leader to another member. The appointed Leader still maintains his role, his "distance" from the group, or his "difference" from the other members. He is still basically in control of the discussion, and has the right to re-enter the actual leadership at his discretion. For example, if a member asks another participant a question, for that moment *he* is "leading". Furthermore, he may continue with a series of questions involving more than one other member, without offering an opinion of his own during this interchange. A visitor entering the group during this time might easily infer that the questioner is the appointed Leader. If the discussion is going well, and in a direction the Leader believes acceptable, there is no reason for him to interrupt the process. He will be pleased to see this assumption of leadership functions by his maturing group. The well-trained group will not expect him to say anything at all during such an interchange, and will continue the discussion, trusting the Leader to interrupt only if necessary. Furthermore, the questioner who has moved temporarily into a leadership role feels its responsibilities, and will increasingly have the good of the group and group goals in mind.

In such a situation, the temporary "leader" knows he does not enjoy the immunity from "answering" that the appointed Leader has, and he knows other members may request him to explain his views on the subject under discussion, a request they would not make of the Leader. The questioner feels safe because he knows that in this situation the Leader has temporarily moved into an "observer" role, from which vantage point he can be aware of the total group in a way in which he, the questioner, cannot. The questioner feels free, therefore, to pursue his individual interest and his personal goals, knowing that the Leader will see to it that other interests in the group are sufficiently protected, if not by other group members, then by the Leader himself.

drift

When a Leader hears lively discussion going on without his assistance, he is sometimes tempted to relax. Before he is aware of it, the group may have drifted away from the proposed subject. The process usually has several stages. First, having asked a good Primary question, the Leader may find that one of the group members picks it up and goes on with a good Secondary question of his own. Another member, answering this question, may then go off tangentially, and the subject of this tangent, rather than that of the Primary or Secondary question itself, may become the subject of the discussion. The group is now far from the subject and is the victim of drift. This will often make those members interested in the basic

lack of progress

subject of the discussion unhappy, and even those who are a part of this drift may well regret it later, feeling "we really didn't get anywhere with that discussion." In the second place, such drift often prevents participation on the part of those who were prepared for the discussion based on the Presentation, but not knowledge-

unbalanced participation

able in the area of the drift. Unbalanced participation follows, which is unfair to those not actively participating, and also to the total group, which now lacks the contributions of these quiet mem-

damage to climate

bers. The third problem arises when the Leader tries to get the discussion back on the track, after having let it drift for a bit. Even though the group recognizes his obligation to do this, they may feel a mild jolt at this change of direction, become overly aware of the Leader, and experience discomfort; the drifters themselves usually feel some guilt or resentment. The Leader must remember his responsibilities, listen carefully at all times to the discussion, and gently return the group to the main path if they wander too far down side-roads.

valuable side-roads

There are occasional instances where drift is allowable and even desirable. Sometimes what seems like a "side-road" may in reality be a different and very useful approach to the same problem. The Leader should keep in mind the Primary which the group is exploring and see in what way the discussion now going on may be relevant to that issue. He also may find that the particular side-road on which they are traveling is actually of more interest and value to the group as a whole, and if it is relevant to the subject of the presentation and the comments of members up to the time of the drift, it may be more valuable to continue this particular discussion, even if it means that the original Primary is not completely explored.

amount of drift tolerable

The amount of drift which is tolerable or desirable for a group depends primarily on the group goals, the length of the group life and the number of times it meets. A mature, cohesive group with a productive history and future meetings in view could tolerate considerable drift during several meetings. Drift may sometimes represent good work on long-range overall goals at the expense of a particular short-range goal, and thus be a desirable thing. A new group must often depend on its Leader to make such evaluative determinations; a mature group can come to grips with and solve this problem for itself.

more than one discussion at a time

There may come a time in the discussion when you feel you simply do not know what the group is talking about. Unlike drift, where the group is somewhat limited in its digression, this situation is characterized by confusion. The cause is usually that a number of different issues are being discussed simultaneously by subgroups. This does not mean that more than one person is talking at the same time, or that there are side-bar conversations, though these may develop if the condition persists. The group may present an external picture of an orderly discussion, but is actually quite disorderly. The cure is to simply ask the group, "Where are we?", or "What are we talking about?" The group will then try to focus on its main point of concern, or if they seem unable to do so, the Leader may remind the group of the Primary under discussion and of the last point in the discussion where the group seemed united. This does not mean that he needs to summarize at this point, but simply restate the questions or a few key words.

summarizing

There are times in some discussions when a brief summary may be necessary, hitting the highlights of the points discussed in terms of questions, issues and group progress. Sometimes when the Leader asks the group, "Where are we?", a group member will do this summarizing, but if not, it is sometimes better for the Leader to do it, rather than risking plunging the group into further confusion by asking one or more members who may have been actively or passively involved in one of the subgroup discussions. Even a well-trained group can occasionally find itself in this difficulty.

when to depart from plan

We have talked about the importance of having a cluster of questions available on several points, while remaining flexible in its use. Sometimes a group of Secondaries must be abandoned or their use deferred. It is a frequently observed phenomenon of the thinking process that in seeking to grasp meaning or understanding, we move along in jerks and jumps, rather than in a smooth glide. We often go from a baffled and confused state to a sudden illumination—the "Aha!" phenomenon—and this happens in group discussion,

the "Aha!" phenomenon

also. It is one of the rewards of leading to see comprehension suddenly light up the face of a member, or to see the whole group move forward when a clarification or a new idea is put forth.

the Leader, surprised

This sudden movement forward can often be as much of a surprise to the Leader as to the group, and although it has been said that "in skilled performance there are no surprises", it can present a challenge to the Leader. This "discovery" may mean that he has to throw away a number of questions which he has prepared, and start on a new line of inquiry. He may find that this new line actually fits in with some Secondary questions he prepared under a different Primary, or he may find that he has nothing at all on the subject.

shifting Secondaries

criteria for shift

If he feels unprepared with questions, he is faced with a decision: shall he follow the new inquiry, recognizing that he will be feeling his way, or shall he drop it, and go on with another Primary? He must base his decision on (1) the importance of the issue raised and his belief that it will be of interest and value to the group; (2) his ability to carry on a discussion for which he is not prepared. The second point will depend to some degree on his knowledge, experience, ease and confidence in leadership. If he feels at all competent, it is probably best to go with the new idea, if he is satisfied that it meets the above criteria. A. Lawrence Lowell tells a story of a Parisian during the upheavals of 1848 who saw a friend marching after a crowd toward the barricades: "Warning him that these could not be held against the troops, that he had better keep away, and asking why he followed these people, he received the reply, 'I must follow them. I am their leader.' " [5]

working without a plan

The first step is to be sure you understand the new idea as presented by the group. Question the original speaker to see how he has found this in the presentation or developed it from comments of the group or from his own knowledge. How does it relate to other points brought out in the discussion up to that time? Does it fit in with, or contradict, some of the main ideas so far developed? Try to be sure that it is not a false lead, a seemingly easy answer which is no answer at all. Actually, this is seldom the case if the majority of the group have registered real interest and satisfaction with it, but be sure that you understand it clearly and can pursue its probable applicability. You will then be able to continue with the discussion, using this new insight to assist in the solution of the basic problem or problems under discussion. You may find, of course, that it changes the character of the problem. Remember that if your group has been discussing together for some time, they will not look to you for all the questions, and doubtless some members will immediately raise questions of their own, spurred on by the group's "new idea".

difficulties with the Primary

It is possible that you may have a good Primary question and a suitable cluster of Secondaries, and yet find that your discussion is not going well because the group just does not seem to be interested in this question. Despite your best efforts at selecting a question which you thought would be significant for this group, you may find that you, and perhaps one or two others, are the only ones seriously interested in it. In this case, it is not necessary to plow on, disregarding the feelings of the group. Here you will discover the great advantage of being well enough prepared so that you have a choice of several Primaries with clusters.

It is possible that, once you have worked through one of your other questions, the group may see the interest and relevance of your first Primary, and return to it voluntarily. Let us suppose a Leader working with the first four chapters of GENESIS had started his discussion with, "According to these chapters, how much responsibility does man bear for what happens to him?" and had received little response, despite efforts at rewording the question or trying the Secondaries. Having given this question a fair try, he may drop it, and simply start on another Primary, such as, "Why were Adam and Eve driven out of the Garden?" (3:23). He can go on to ask, "How is this 'sin' described?" or "How did they disobey", or "How is their disobedience described?", depending on the sort of answers he received in the beginning. He can then ask, "What is the 'death' which God says will result from eating the fruit?", and "What is the meaning of 'you shall . . . know good and evil?" It is not unlikely that during this interchange someone may advert to the earlier question of "responsibility", and the Leader may find he can use a combination of his clusters from both these questions.

Suppose, on the other hand, the Leader has asked as his second Primary question, "What kind of God is described here?", and then "How do Adam and Eve think of him before they eat the fruit?", "How does Eve talk about God in 4:1 and 25?", "How would you describe their relationship with God?", and then gone on to examine the relationship between Cain and God and Abel and God. If a member had introduced "man's responsibility" in the middle of the discussion of these questions, it would probably be best to ask that the question be tabled or delayed temporarily. The Leader would do better to continue this question on *God*, continuing through, perhaps, God's "marking" of Cain, before turning back to the question of *man*.

However, it is *not usually necessary* for a Leader *to abandon a Primary* question. Unless the Leader is given to strange enthusiasms, his interests will usually parallel the group's to some extent and his judgment of the importance of the problem or issue involved will give him considerable guidance. The Leader is far more likely to abandon a good Primary too easily, believing, because the group is relatively quiet, that the question is "no good". Most groups take some time to warm up, and a bit of quiet thoughtfulness is wholesome. A Leader is also tempted, when his Primary **adding-on and** question does not meet with an immediate response, to "add on". **"doctoring"** He might ask, "What kind of God is described here?", and then rather nervously continue to add what he trusts will be helpful clarifications of his question, such as, "I mean, in these four chapters", or "You know, what can you tell about God from just these four chapters of GENESIS?" or "Well, how does he differ, for instance, from the kind of God your friends believe in, or you believe in?" This does more harm than good. Prepare your questions carefully, go over their wording, try to make them as short and clear as you can, state them in a confident, direct, optimistic way—and trust your group. The first, second and third persons on whom you call may all request that you "ask someone else", though this is not really likely, but do not be too easily discouraged, and do not go back and "doctor" the question. You may decide, of course, that your question really is not clear. If so, indicate to the group that you are going to ask a slightly different question, and rephrase the entire question.

Almost always someone will try some sort of answer rather quickly, if only to "help out the Leader". As your group grows to trust you more, you will seldom have difficulty obtaining some sort of answer to your first question within a minute or two. Actually, it is a rare group which can tolerate more than three or four minutes of silence at *any* time. The group will learn that you may ask Mary to answer the first question, and then ask exactly the same question of John, regardless of Mary's answer, and then of Harry, too. The reason is that your Primary questions are such that they could not be answered in a few words, or totally explored by a single member. You might want to say, after Mary's answer, "John, how would you answer that question?", or "Harry, do you agree with Mary's answer?", or "Ann, would you want to add something to Harry's statement?" The Leader is not indicating dissatisfaction with the first answers and members will recognize this by the reactions of the Leader and other group members. This is not to suggest that the Leader poll the entire group for their answers to a question before going on with the discussion. Very often, if Mary has asked in the beginning that the question be passed to someone else, the Leader will do well to come back to her after one or two others have answered, and ask if she has anything to add. She will have been thinking and listening and may want to come in by that time.

challenging the question

You will remember that one of the Secondary questions in the dialogue in Chapter 11 was "What is the relationship here between freedom and responsibility?" We said that at this point we were still concerned with the meaning of the Presentation, as opposed to the "life question". It is possible that a member might challenge the Leader on this question, saying, "That question doesn't make sense in this context—the text says nothing about 'freedom' or even 'responsibility', and to the writers of the Old Testament the concept of 'free will' or 'freedom' as we think of it, would have been meaningless." What is the Leader to do in a situation like this? First, the Leader should remember that it is wholesome for the group to feel free to challenge the Leader's questions, and it is something which he should encourage. Sometimes a Leader will talk to a new group at the first meeting about this possibility, and tell the group that he hopes they will feel free to voice their disagreement with the way his question is phrased. He may say, "If you believe that my question indicates a misreading of the presentation, or a misunderstanding of the remarks of a member, please feel free to say so." A Leader must remember that he, too, is limited by his own mental set, his available concepts, and that participants may be able to "see" things he cannot see.

The challenging statement in the above paragraph has an

"outside authority" problem, in that the member has said, "the writers of the Old Testament . . .", and if the group has not had a presentation which offered this "information" about philosophical concepts and Old Testament writers, this cannot be presumed to be "common knowledge". However, the Leader need not point this out, in all probability, since the preceding statement, ". . . the text says nothing about 'freedom' or 'responsibility' " provides the member with an adequate basis for his challenge within the Presentation. The Leader may do one of several things. He may ask the member to rephrase the question in terms which he feels are legitimate for him in this context. Or he may decide to eliminate the question until later in the discussion and then ask it in terms of the life situation today, or he may ask the member if he will still allow the question. If necessary, he may go on to ask that the question be allowed on the grounds that, although the words are not used and the concepts may be "alien" to the work, these are concepts familiar to the group, and you are interested in seeing how we apply our mental approaches to this material.

concept availability

Susanne Langer has said, "The way a question is asked limits and disposes the ways in which any answer to it—right or wrong—may be given. . . . A question is really an ambiguous proposition: the answer is its determination. There can be only a certain number of alternatives that will complete its sense", and she goes on to point out that our questions and the way we formulate experience are "determined . . . by the *basic concepts* at people's disposal." [6]

The Leader must keep in mind that concepts available today were not necessarily available in the past. Also that concepts available to him are not necessarily available to all group members, and vice versa. In addition, it is possible for someone to understand a concept without granting that it is useful or "true". If, for instance, the Leader finds he has a member who does not believe in "free will", it is possible that the Leader and the member simply do not have "shared information" as to the meaning of "free will", and that talking about it with some other words may clear up the difficulty. On the other hand, it is also possible that a group member may be able to define and explain the concept as well as, or better than, those in the group who do believe in its existence, but simply say that he doesn't, just as someone might explain the concept "unicorn" and say that he doesn't believe it exists, or "phrenology" or "astrology" and say that he doesn't believe it is a "useful" concept.

when question is by-passed

If, in answer to the Leader's first question about "What kind of God is described here?" he receives only a brief comment such as, "I don't think I like this God very much," or "I don't think this is a God they are talking about—he's too human," the Leader may examine the reasons for this reaction before going on to ask another participant. He has received an honest answer, apparently, and although it is a Balance-type answer to a question which the Leader intended as a Meaning question, it would seem a rejection of the member if his answer were rejected by the Leader. The Leader can pursue the question on the basis of Meaning by asking "What things about this God are dislikeable?", or "In what way is he shown as 'too human'?" The member has tried to answer the question, and although his remarks are not what the Leader expected, serious attention should be given to his reply. "Liking" and "not liking" responses too early in a discussion can bypass the necessary examination of the actual meaning of the Presentation, but the Leader should accept them as contributions to the group effort, and "affirm the person" in his handling of a response which he feels is inappropriate. He can then work his way back into the exploration of meaning.

dislike of Presentation

Occasionally when the Leader asks a member the first question, instead of answering he will state, "I didn't like that film", or "I can't see any value in discussing this!" The Leader can either say, "I'm sorry, but perhaps you could help us start answering this question, anyway", or, if he feels it is wiser, he can say, "I'm sorry, Mary. John, would you like to give us your answer to the question?" If he wishes, he may say, "I find the problems it points up interesting, and I'd like to hear your views on them. We'll start with finding out the viewpoints expressed in the Presentation." It is not a death-blow to the discussion if the Presentation itself did not find favor with the group. Toward the end of the discussion it would be worthwhile to discuss why group members did not like the Presentation, but such a discussion in the very beginning is seldom useful and usually does not serve the goals of the group. The group's idea could be, "Well, we didn't like this film, but there were some ideas in it, and let's see if we can enjoy trying to understand and respond to them." Or, they might feel, "These slides are no good, but we like our group, and we like talking to one another."

"Speak for yourself . . ."

There is sometimes a tendency on the part of members to think they can speak for the group, saying, "We all know that . . ." or "Nobody believes that . . .", or "I'm sure everybody here agrees . . ." This can be harmful in a number of ways, and is to be discouraged. For one thing, even in cases where everyone *doesn't* agree, those who feel they are a minority will often hesitate to say so in the face of what has been enunciated as "the group's opinion". Furthermore, if this sort of groupthink is encouraged, individuals can leave a group with some pretty odd ideas at times, believing that "everybody thinks so, so I guess it's true." As we have seen, group cohesiveness tends to encourage normativeness, or adherence to group norms, in opinion and behavior, and is one of the values of group discussion, but the other side of the coin can be dangerous, and individual freedom must be encouraged. Remind members to speak only for themselves. It is, however, permissible for an individual to react to what *seems to him* to be a group opinion or attitude. For instance, John might say, "It seems to me that all of you are saying 'man is the absolute master in his command of the earth'—am I understanding you correctly?", or "I'm not happy about this discussion at this point, because you all seem to be saying that man has no right to interfere with nature—is that true?" On the other hand, suppose John had said, "We all agree that man is

group pressure

the absolute master, so what does that mean we have to do—about making the world better, or whatever?", or "Everybody knows this is just a story, this business about Cain and Abel, so let's concentrate on the definite statements about 'God'." In such cases it is the Leader's job, *if* no one else makes such a move, to say, "John, we don't know whether everyone else feels this way, but you are telling us that *you* do—is that correct?", or "John, I don't know whether you can be sure of what all the group members think—perhaps you would like to ask some of them. . . ." The Leader helps the group understand that any member may hold an opinion which differs from other members' opinions, and that, conversely, any member is allowed to question *why* someone holds a particular opinion.

HELPING THE GROUP OVERCOME SOME PARTICIPATION PROBLEMS

The Leader will constantly encourage, by facial expression, voice tone and inflection the idea that every comment made by a group member is for the benefit of all the group, not for him alone. Once an idea is out there in the group, it is everybody's idea, to look at, think about, turn this way and that, question and comment on. In a new group, after a question is answered and the member stops talking, the tendency of the group is to look at the Leader. It is also not uncommon for another participant to make some comment on, or ask a question about the statement just made, but in doing so to look at the Leader, rather than at the one who has just spoken. The Leader, naturally, looks first at this new speaker, but he should then turn that comment or question back to the first speaker. Suppose Mary had just said, "Well, if man is really in charge, I guess that means he is responsible for making the best future he can—there isn't anything to stop him!" John may look at the Leader and say, "Yes, but if there isn't anything to stop him, he can decide that genocide of a particular group, or euthanasia for all the mentally defective will contribute to the 'best future'—I don't know about that. . . ." If the Leader continues to look at John and says, "Yes, that's a problem, how do we decide that?", John and the Leader will be involved in a discussion. It is better for the Leader to simply turn his attention back to Mary and ask, "Mary, how does he decide what is 'the best future'?" Mary and John will probably then talk to each other. If they still address their remarks to the Leader, he can redirect even more strongly by using the name of the previous speaker. For instance, he could have asked, "Mary, can *you tell John* how man decides what is 'the best future'?", nodding toward John as he speaks to Mary.

It is helpful for the Leader to remember that this is the *group's discussion*, not his, despite the degree of control he exercises through his questions. His desire is to fade into the background as much as possible. If he keeps this idea before him, the group will recognize the value of this principle, and increasingly act upon it.

We have talked about some of the causes of over- and under-

unbalanced participation

participation and indicated some of the ways in which these problems can be avoided and ameliorated. Many Leaders seem to feel somewhat helpless when confronted with an aggressive overparticipator, but there is no need for this. The Leader should recognize, as always, that this is the group's problem, not his alone. Few groups are satisfied with a discussion in which one or two people do all the talking, and are willing to help see that participation is broadened. As the group grows and becomes more cohesive, members take an increasingly larger part of the responsibility for handling this as well as other problems. With a new group, the Leader's most useful tool is his habit of calling on people by name to answer questions. Because he retains his role as titular head, and because the group quickly becomes accustomed to his addressing questions to individuals, he also has what might be called "the right to interrupt". Since he is not making contributions to the discussion himself, the group readily accepts his interruptions. They will listen to him because he speaks so seldom and so briefly, and only to encourage the development of the discussion, rather than to make his own points.

"the right to interrupt"

When the Leader interrupts someone who has spoken too frequently or at too great length, he certainly avoids doing so in a punitive or disagreeable way. He tries to select a moment when there seems a reasonable break or transition in the speaker's comments. He may break in cheerfully with a question addressed to someone else, or may pick up a point in the speaker's line of thought and ask another member what he thinks of that idea. For instance, if John, a frequent monopolizer, has been talking, the Leader may say, "John, that seems to agree (or disagree) with something Harry said earlier—Harry, would you see this as the best way to handle (the drug abuse problem, a guaranteed income, poverty in our community, etc.)?" However, you do not want to create a continuing dialogue between John, the overparticipator, and Harry. Harry will tend to direct his reply to John, who will simply continue where he left off, in most cases. Instead, other group members should be encouraged to involve themselves in the discussion.

Often John will welcome this shift, but if he is excited about his subject, he may not see this as an opportunity to let others join him in conversation. If he immediately re-enters, the Leader can smile and say, "Excuse me, John, we'd like to hear from Mary on this", or "Mary tried to get in earlier—she had a comment, I believe." Sometimes Leaders make the mistake of continually requestioning the most articulate and talkative members. It is easy to do this, even when conscious that this member has done more than his share of talking. Sometimes the Leader does it because he hopes to turn the discussion toward a new point which will involve others, and he will interrupt the speaker to query him about this new direction—thus prolonging his contribution. Sometimes it is because the Leader knows that, whatever the question, this particular member will make

an effort to respond. Remember that often quiet members have a good deal to contribute, but need encouragement. Certainly the more talkative members should be discouraged from interrupting, whereas the Leader and the group may tolerate interruption of the talkative by the non-talkative, thus helping the group arrive at its norms in this matter.

There are a few other ways the Leader can help with the problem of overparticipation. First, he need not always sit in the same place, and if he sits next to one of the overparticipators, he may lessen his contributions somewhat. This is partly because the places immediately to the left and right of the Leader are the "blind spots"—the Leader is less apt to call on those whose eye he does not catch. Furthermore, seated beside such a member, a Leader sometimes can use non-verbal communication to inconspicuously slow down his too-ready replies. In part, the member's decreased participation may be a function of his consciousness of the leadership functions when in such proximity to its exemplar. The second approach is not always successful, but in some groups can work. The Leader addresses his first question to the talkative member, and gives him some initial encouragement. Having been allowed to make a fairly lengthy statement at the beginning, he may be willing to wait quite a while before coming into the discussion again.

HELPING THE GROUP OVERCOME SOME COMMUNICATION PROBLEMS

transmission
problems

We have seen that a communication may fail to be received or may be distorted due to external distractions, internal bodily sensations, or selective perception. Selective perception may be due to contrary motivation or to a number of functional factors, including personal abilities or disabilities, personality, emotion, and social norms. We have noted that one's own system of meaning, however characterized, transforms the impinging event by translating it to deliver to us some significance. We have noted that the sending of meaningful or significant messages of emotional content is particularly difficult. What clues do we have to lessen problems of transmission?

encoding for
positive
redundancy

Information, or communication, theory speaks of "positive redundancy". Although the word "redundancy" usually implies unnecessary and therefore undesirable verbiage, information theory's positive redundancy aids understanding. Messages are redundant if they contain less information than they could—in other words, if a shorter message could contain the same amount. The common pattern of the English sentence is the actor-action simple declarative. It normally exhibits positive redundancy, but in doing so becomes easier to hear and to understand. One problem in spoken communication is that there is often "noise contamination", and not all the sounds are actually heard. Anticipation of the probable makes it easier to guess those vowels or words not actually heard. This is true because of syntax and sentence structure. The simple question which inverts the declarative sentence exhibits the same quality. The parts of the sentence are so related that having heard one part, you can fill in the other. Even if we actually hear all the sounds in a sentence which lacks positive redundancy, it is often less comprehensible—it may be like a puzzle which we have to figure out.

For instance, in the example of, "According to these four chapters, how much responsibility does man bear for what happens to him?", there is positive redundancy. This question contains sixteen words. By lessening redundancy, we can eliminate all but four: "chapters man responsible happens", or even, "responsibleman". We would have saved twelve to fifteen words, which we could then use to provide more information in a message of the same original length. However, if we added twelve different words of information, less would actually be received correctly or intelligibly. The telegraphic style contains the kernel, the true "information", but the redundancy in the original twelve words clarifies the message for the receiver, and the extra "non-information" helps to order the words in a more comprehensible pattern. The listener is more apt to hear, understand and remember such a sentence. On the same basis, both Leaders and other group members would do well to avoid the "trick" sentence, with a surprise ending, or an unusual or complex inversion of order. For instance, "How much responsibility does man bear, according to these four chapters, for what happens to him?", or "Concerning what happens to man, how much responsibility does he bear, according to these four chapters?" are both more difficult to grasp than the original question. Leaders sometimes cheat when trying to make their questions brief, and try to pack in more than they should, or forget that a fifteen-word sentence of common words and groupings can be preferable to a shorter but more "difficult" one.[7]

amount of new information

Three other hints also come from information theory. One concerns the total number of relatively new words, ideas or information that is put into any given message. Statements of equal length can obviously contain unequal amounts of new information, and Brown hypothesizes that the difficulty of recognizing or identifying a stimulus is proportional to its information content, meaning, of course, new information. Information, by definition, is "new".

and memory

A second hint concerns the receiver's immediate memory span, that is, how long he can remember how much immediately after hearing it. Brown [8] reports that the answer to "Does the memory span vary with the information content of the stimuli?" is "only slightly". It is true, of course, that a meaningful sentence is easier to remember correctly than the same number of nonsense syllables or even of words in random order, but it is equally true that if the length of the sentence is "too long" the receiver is certain to reproduce it incorrectly. In discussion members are seldom asked to "reproduce" questions, but it is preferable if they are reasonably reproducible. They will have more difficulty remembering correctly *any* lengthy discourse, or of being reasonably sure of what was said in any burst of conversation. The Leader must remember to keep his questions brief, and, as we said in Chapter 10, the rough rule of thumb is about eleven words.

limit number of choices

A third point, on which apparently insufficient research has been done to develop sound principles, is the number of choices offered in any given communication. If a given communication opens up one or two choices to the receiver his choice reaction time is much shorter than if a larger number are offered. The quality of the choices has some bearing on this, as some possible lines of thought or avenues of decision might have immediate appeal and some none at all, but if they are fairly similar in this respect, the receiver will be "lost" somewhere along the line when more than two choices are offered. When the Leader has occasion to use an "either/or" question, it is best to limit the number of choices to two.

denotation and connotation

We have talked about the problems that can arise because people mean different things by the same word. Not only do they intend a different denotation, but sometimes, though they share a symbol structure as to the denotation of most words, there may well be differences of connotation. The denotative meaning is the literal, external referent, or the dictionary meaning. Here, even such words as "table" and "word" vary widely in the possibilities of varying denotation. Connotative meanings are those affectional subjective meanings that huddle about a word in our mind, the symbolic references evoked which can both amplify and cloud our communication. Fortunately it has been found that very often connotations are similar for similar people. "Similarity" in this case need be only that of living in the same culture or society.[9] The more similar they are, the more their connotations will agree, of course. However, it is often connotation that causes breakdowns in communication. We are prone to assume that our neighbors' words and ours carry the same connotation.

You will remember John and Mary and Dr. Hess at their dinner party, when Mary may have been frightened by the word "revolution". There is, of course, nothing frightening in itself about a word. Its denotative meaning is given in one dictionary as, "state of revolving; rotation, circular motion of a body on its axis or round a centre; period of rotation; cycle; continued course; radical change of circumstances, attitudes, conditions, etc.; forcible overthrow of political system; attempt at this." Which of these meanings might Mary have in mind? Probably one of the last three. But, even so, why should the mention of the word at a dinner party frighten her? Most probably because of its connotations. Few people would have such reactions at the mention of the word "table", but a child in an arithmetic class who has not done his homework may flinch when the word "table" is mentioned, even though his usual associations with the word are in terms of "eating". The use of the word in context varies its connotative freight.

fear

When people are frightened, they may be unable to communicate clearly. They are more apt to concentrate on one part of the

mental set

message than another, their mental filters are working in what may be a distortion of their normal functioning—they flunk exams, rush into instead of away from danger, charge their best friends with dishonesty. No one is suggesting that if you hear someone in the local supermarket yell "Fire!", you should go over and ask him his definition of the word, but during discussions it is often wise to check your own reactions to words which seem important, and then check both their denotative and connotative meanings with others. Had Mary come into the conversation at that point and said, "When you say 'revolution', it frightens me—what do you mean?", the productivity of the conversation would have been improved. Of course, Mary might have been more frightened, rather than less, by the time the dinner conversation ended, but all would probably have benefited, and Mary would have deepened her understanding and been able to think more clearly, having both expressed her emotional reaction and explored the meaning of the offending word.

When the word "revolution" came up it is quite possible that John and Dr. Hess had quite different pictures flashing across their mental screens. John, interested in European history, might have been thinking in terms of the Reign of Terror in France in the eighteenth century, or the European revolutions in the nineteenth century. The professor may have been thinking in terms of technological revolution, or the knowledge revolution in his own particular field. S. I. Hayakawa suggests some ways of handling the "terminological tangle". He says that it is very important to listen to the other person's terminology without "unreasonable demands", and says the "specific unreasonable demand is the demand that everybody else *should* mean by such words . . . what I would mean if I were using them". If a person's use of a word makes little sense to us when we first hear it, or if we immediately are aroused by it in some way, "we should at once be alerted to special attentiveness". If the speaker uses a word in a way which makes an unfamiliar classification, for instance, it is "a sure sign not that he is ill-informed but that he has a way of classifying his data that is different from our own". He says that we live in a competitive culture which encourages us to try to get our own ideas across to other people and that we "tend to find other people's speeches a tedious interruption of the flow of our own ideas." [10]

Groups should avoid the bad habit of instantly pouncing on every unfamiliar word, or unfamiliar use of a word. Sometimes ensuing remarks will make the speaker's intent clear, at other times the word may be very unimportant in relation to what he is saying. On the other hand, the careful Leader can help his group avoid serious problems by encouraging definition when needed. He will listen for signs of misunderstanding in the group due to what may be different usages of the same word. If the word is important in the discussion, he may ask the participants what they mean by that word. He should always indicate by his manner that more than one usage is possible, which is true of a great many quite important words. He should never patronizingly imply that the speaker does not use the word correctly, but that the group is not sure they understand him correctly. If the speaker actually is misusing a word, he himself may or may not realize it, but the group should be able to continue the discussion, bearing in mind the several definitions present among them for certain words. Connotations are not always made visible when people define their terms, since they usually present a denotative explanation. Careful listening sometimes reveals connotations, however, as these terms are used in the discussion. When relevant, these may also be explored.

politics, religion, values

Politics and religion are known as the two topics people shouldn't discuss. However, they are two of the topics people do—and should—discuss. Surely, one part of the problem lies in differing uses of such key terms as "democratic", "freedom", "liberal", "for the good of the people", "God", "conscience", or "sin". In addition to meaning and usage, there are other communication problems when dealing in such areas where people's *values* are deeply involved. In today's society, discussion of social issues becomes increasingly difficult as various factions and sectors of the population develop highly specialized vocabularies and rhetorics. These often pose the same kind of communication difficulty encountered with technical jargon in interdisciplinary discussion, with an added emotive factor. Much patience is required in trying to bridge the Communication Gap, often a contributing factor in other "Gaps" such as the "Generation Gap" and the "Credibility Gap" of the 'sixties.

Part of the difficulty is that the neologisms of many groups consist of specialized meanings for common words of everyday speech. Accompanying this use is a reluctance to define the terms, due in part to a belief that too much "definition" is a contributing factor in our social problems and that a reliance on "logic" and the "lessons of history" has operated against the "human" solution of problems. It is often useless for a Leader to ask someone using language in this way to explain his meaning or to use other terms. It will usually be equally useless to try to explore the grammar or syntax of statements of this type, or to seek explanation through consistency of use in a series of statements. Discussion groups containing one or more members using specialized or "private" languages of this sort will have difficulty, but if group members are encouraged to persist in their discussions despite inevitable misunderstandings, the communication level will often rise. Sometimes otherwise non-violent people will deliberately "do violence" to language and its traditional patterns in an effort to force others to rethink old problems. Such groups must anticipate slow progress and will need to spend proportionately greater amounts of time in the social-emotional area at the expense of the task area.

Leader and the language of the group

Although we have said that the Leader does not necessarily know more about the subject than the participants, we have also said that he is "prepared to lead *this* discussion". This phrase includes the presumption that the Leader will have familiarized himself with the anticipated language of the discussion, which means both the language of the presentation and of the group members, insofar as he can anticipate what that language will be. This requires forethought and preparation. Whether the group is heterogeneous or homogeneous in its culture the Leader should feel obligated to have at least some grasp of the terms and special meanings he may expect to find used by the discussants. He should try to keep his own vocabulary at the simplest level consistent with the language of the group, but when working with a group of specialists he should not hesitate to use technical terms in their speciality. This requires both care and tact. In preparing his questions he may avoid any technical terms not used in the presentation, but he must be alert to terms used during the discussion by the group members. As a non-specialist in a group of specialists he must avoid pouncing on technical terms and requesting explanations when the term is such that he should presume all group members are acquainted with it. This sometimes requires more than superficial knowledge, since a particular discipline, specialty or culture group may be divided within itself on the meaning. When this is the case, he should be familiar with the various possible meanings and alert for clues in the discussion which might indicate conflicting uses of the term. He should also avoid using an everyday word which this particular group uses in a specialized sense, unless the context makes clear the intended content.

Reuel L. Howe's list of barriers to communication includes language, images, anxieties, defenses and purposes. He grounds most of the barriers in man's "ontological need", "the need and concern which each individual feels for his own *being*". He believes that everyone, burdened with a sense of guilt and aware of his finitude, suffers from anxiety—feels threatened. "Our self-concern not only sets us apart from our brothers but also makes it difficult for us to communicate with them or to hear their cry in behalf of their own ontological concerns." In our efforts to affirm ourselves, we sometimes threaten the being of others. He says that if true communication is to occur, "each must accept his own and the other's need for affirmation." [11]

No single discussion can lift such barriers, affirm the being of each member or enable him to "hear the cries" of the other members. The Leader must accept the fact that this is a slow process, that some members can move more rapidly than others in this direction, and that he will rarely see a dramatic change. What he can, and should see, however, is a gradual warming up unfolding in the warm and open climate of his group. He may also be encouraged by the knowledge that his group may provide the only situation in which this can happen for many of these individuals. For many people such a group is the only place in which people will give serious, concerned attention to his attempts to express his ideas, his beliefs, his yearnings for something else, something more, something better—the only place where someone will really listen to him. Some individuals will continue to attend such a group for months, seemingly little interested in what is going on, saying little, apparently receiving no benefit from the experience, and yet you may later learn that the group is extremely important to them and has made a real difference in their lives.

BUILDING AND MAINTENANCE

At the beginning of this chapter we said, "The two things which probably do most to hinder success in discussion are lack of clarity and lack of charity." By "charity" we mean that quality of human concern, that desire and ability to affirm the person, that dialogic relationship which is the force at work in much of the "building and maintenance" functions of leadership. As we have pointed out, some people are usually more adept at these functions than they are in the task of problem-solving functions. Sometimes their comments may seem, to the person intent on the problem-solving or task aspects of group work, irrelevant or unnecessary. Satisfying and productive interpersonal relationships are facilitated by the occasional tension-relieving joke, the conciliating remark, the gesture of friendliness and understanding, the supportive statement. As a Leader you should keep attuned to comments of this sort. Contributions serving these ends are valuable and necessary, and the Leader who shows his own appreciation by a warm look or a brief remark indicates to the group that this, too, is part of what the group needs.

Leader's "remarks"

You will note that we have said "brief remark", where heretofore we have stressed the Leader as "asking questions". What kinds of remarks are allowable? This is a rather delicate point, as "remarks" by the Leader can be harmful, and since they are often a temptation for the Leader, he must be wary of allowing them to grow up to be speeches! The Leader must keep in mind that when he makes a remark about anything in the discussion he is not doing so with the intention of agreeing, disagreeing or adding opinions. His remarks must be in the nature of what is perhaps best described as "interested, encouraging vagueness." He is indicating to the participant that he is listening, that he is eager to hear more, that he seeks to understand what is being said, that he is happy about their happiness or concerned about their worry. These remarks fall into the building maintenance department, or the social-emotional leadership functions.

Sometimes this restraint is very difficult for an animated, usually enthusiastic person. Watch the speech habits of your friends, and you will find that during most conversations many indications of agreement or disagreement will be shown by the listener. He may nod his head in approval, shake it in disagreement, make comments such as "Oh, I agree!", or "Yes, indeed!", or "Of course not!" These remarks are not for the Leader! Often an interested listener will say such things as "Right, right", or "Unh-hunh, un-hunh" without intending agreement, but simply as an indication that they are hearing and understanding. This, too, the Leader should avoid, since the tendency of his hearers is to believe he is reflecting the opinions of the speaker—agreeing with a particular member. It takes time and practice for many people to learn to indicate interest and enthusiasm wthout indicating approval or disapproval of what is being expressed, but it can be done. The object is to affirm the person without necessarily agreeing with his ideas or demonstrating that you disagree with them. The Leader may encourage a hesitant participant by such remarks as, "I see . . .", or "I understand . . .", or occasionally with a new group the Leader may make a short statement reflecting a bit of what a previous group member's statement expresses. This mirroring on the part of the Leader should be kept to the minimum necessary to train his group to take over this function. Group members will learn to rephrase statements they think they may have misunderstood, and give them back to the original speaker for an accuracy check, or sum up a few remarks and check with the group for any important omissions or misinterpretations.

HANDLING CONFLICT AND CONTROVERSY

When tempers rise in a group and open hostility is shown, thoughtful discussion can evaporate in the heat. A mature group will often rally round to ease the situation or to make productive use of the emotional content. On the other hand, this may not happen quickly enough to save real unpleasantness or the group may depend on the Leader to handle the situation. Table pounding, preaching or joining in the argument are temptations to the Leader, but hardly helpful to the group. A reconciliation of some kind is the end desired, for the sake of the individuals involved as well as the group and its discussion. The Leader himself may feel pretty irritated by what is going on, but must remember that those in combat are unhappy and a punishing attitude on his part will cause further difficulties. There are a number of things the Leader can do. He can temporarily bury the conflict, hoping that it will simmer down of its own accord, or he can try to resolve it by working it through or by some face-saving techniques.

If he chooses the former, he can use a tension-relieving remark, such as "Well, no one can say we're not *involved!* But maybe we'd better get a little less involved for a while!", or "I must say we have a high interest level here, but I think we'd better come down lower for a bit." This will usually serve to turn the anger of those involved at least partially away from each other and probably toward the Leader in a modified form. However, this approach is not as helpful to the people involved or to the group as a real effort at resolution or at face-saving, which can make everyone feel better in the long run, and also reorient the group toward the discussion.

The simplest face-saving method, and one which is often successful, is simply to treat the conflict as though it *were* controversy, but to get into it yourself by asking a question. Do not lecture or scold, but try to shift the argument back to the subject matter, without ignoring the fact that these individuals are angry. You may ask, "Mary, just what is it that you disagree with in this idea?", or "Mary, are you in disagreement with *all* the points just stated, or only some of them?" It may be best to search back rapidly for some point in the present interchange at which the partisans were or seemed to be in agreement. You can ask, "John, excuse me, but would you go back to the point you raised earlier about so-and-so? I know you are not in agreement at this moment, but I think that idea is worth pursuing further." Or, "Mary, we seem to be stuck here, but I know you thought John's idea about so-and-so was a good one—perhaps we could approach this problem again from that view." Or, "Harry, you and John were in agreement that such-and-such should be done, but not in *how* it should be done. Is there some entirely *different* way, which we haven't considered yet, to get at solving this?"

It will be noticed that most of these suggested types of "questions" obviously violate our recommendation for brevity. In order to help his group, the Leader may deliberately lengthen his statements, putting himself center-stage for the moment, to draw off the fire and give others a chance to think. The members so addressed will often be glad to escape their present discomfort, and will grasp at any straws you hand them. Once some minimal response has been given by those involved in the argument, it is best

to turn the discussion to other group members and go back to a question or a point in the discussion where less friction was involved, or to go on to another point entirely. If the subject is changed radically, there is danger that the combatants may be made to feel more shame-faced than is necessary, but the focus can be shifted.

Another face-saving approach is to address your question to the member who seems to be "losing" the fight and, picking up one of his points that seemed to have possible value for the discussion, but which is not the crucial point on which the present argument is based, use it in asking a question of some member *not* involved in the conflict. Again, you are treating the conflict as though it were a controversy, but momentarily excluding the principals. Bring them back into the discussion with some low-keyed question as soon as you feel it safe to do so. There are any number of emotionally-charged current problems which can give rise to heated feelings once the discussion gets past the early stages, and the Leader should be alert to signals of anger or distress, even when these are kept on the level of politeness and low, modulated tones.

The face-saving suggestions are premised on the fact that until a group has become cohesive and developed a climate of trust, anger can damage the group as well as the discussion. As groups mature they can tolerate a far more agitated and agitating climate and still engage in extremely productive sessions. A learning-discussion group is not a sensitivity group, but the discussion of matters of vital concern to the discussants involves the emotions. People are often afraid to express their negative emotions of fear, grief and anger, and are disturbed by hearing others give expression to these feelings. The Leader should not bait the group members, nor try to force them into situations of self-revelation. At the same time he should help them realize the necessity of accepting the emotional content of attitudes and values. His own attitude of acceptance will help his group to be accepting, and his own non-partisan status will help them to feel protected. Group members can then begin to think and feel their way through the reasons for their anger or fear of a particular idea or person.

One of the advantages of the Leader who deliberately abstains from contributing his own opinions to the discussion is his ability to give assistance to a group in conflict. It is not that he does not have feelings about the subject under discussion, or that he is not as strongly partisan as any of the parties in a dispute, but that these feelings are not expressed in the group. Since he has not openly taken sides, he is free to continue in his role as guide, and the group will accept his guidance. Even when the group is quite aware of the Leader's feelings and opinions, a trusted Leader who remains overtly non-partisan over a period of time will be accepted by the group in this facilitating role.

controversy   When the disagreement in the group *is* controversy, the most obvious difference to the beholder is that these people are enjoying themselves and progress toward resolution of some kind seems

216

likely. The Leader has the easier job of helping those in disagreement to explore their differences and the causes of them. The Leader, by close listening, can often help group members find the exact point on which the disagreement turns, and then one of two things may happen. Either those who disagree may see their disagreement dissolve or, once this point is located, may still hold to their own opinion, but can agree to do so more comfortably. The Leader is not there to force people to come to an agreement, or to encourage the group to force agreement upon a minority, but to help individuals to be sure of where their disagreement lies and, if possible, why.

meaning
Some of the common causes of disagreement are the meaning of words, the content of concepts, and generalizations covering different sets of items. Careful listening may show that a seeming disagreement is really a misunderstanding of a word to which people are attaching different meanings. Irving J. Lee points out some fascinating facts about words in HOW TO TALK WITH PEOPLE. He tells us that "a seventh-grade class in English was able to make up thirty sentences in which the word 'set' was used differently each time" and that "even 'word' is listed in sixteen different ways in the AMERICAN COLLEGE DICTIONARY." Also, he quotes Charles C. Fries as saying, "Ordinarily we just don't believe without considerable careful examination that for the five hundred most used words in English . . . the Oxford Dictionary records and illustrates from our literature 14,070 separate meanings." [12]

clarification of the problem
A group may find itself arguing about various solutions to a problem when the real reason for the disagreement is lack of clarity about the *problem*. The Leader can avoid this by staying with the first stage of a problem-centered discussion long enough to allow the group to get out on the table the specifications and limitations of the problem. A group may find itself arguing about how to solve the problem of "juvenile drug abuse" and find they are in disagreement as to who "juveniles" are, what "drugs" are being considered and what they mean by "abuse". They may find they also have avoided or omitted any discussion of causes, contributing factors and so forth.

generalizations
When members contradict one another, arguments may arise before it is determined wherein the disagreement lies. If it involves a generalization, those in disagreement may be referring to different groups of objects. They may differ on details, but really agree on conclusions. It is usually wise to investigate the contents of generalizations whenever such differences arise.

"facts"
Many disagreements are disagreements on "facts". We said earlier that disagreements as to "what the facts are" are not settled by discussion, but by investigation. It is pointless for a Leader to allow a lengthy discussion on a matter which is obviously an easily determined fact. In the heat of argument a discussion can deteriorate to the "It is!", "It isn't!" stage. Such disagreements are usually easy to spot, and if the information is not available to the group at that time, the Leader should simply point this out, and go on to something which it is possible to discuss.

However, although some facts are easy to ascertain, others are practically indeterminable. In some areas, such as social studies, often "the most significant facts are violently conflicting opinions", as Larrabee[13] points out. In addition, the selection of facts can be a very personal thing, as one individual may "see" certain facts while another observer "sees" conflicting facts. What, indeed, is a fact? This becomes a philosophical problem. Not all information is quantifiable, not all decisions can be deferred until all the facts in the case can be gathered. An appeal to "common sense" may prove quite inadequate. The best the Leader can hope to do is, first, to help the group realize this perhaps unfortunate plasticity of same kinds of facts, and second, to confine the major part of their discussion to those areas in which they can find some agreement on facts. The major part, however, does not mean the whole, and hopefully groups can learn to tolerate some ambiguity and uncertainty while discussing some points on the grounds of "If . . . then, but if . . . then." This will free group members to seek their own decisions, while exposing them to alternatives both in sets of facts and in possible decisions based on those facts.

dysfunctional behaviors

We talked previously about some typical dysfunctional behaviors which may appear in groups. A Leader is often tempted to try to "diagnose" such behavior, particularly when it seems to cause conflict, and provide or arrange "cures" for individuals displaying it. It is necessary to be extremely cautious in our efforts in this direction, and to remember that in addition to emotion generated in the group, all members have a life apart from the group which inevitably impinges on their life within the discussion situation. Moreover, it is obvious that many of these behaviors can be due to one or more causes besides those we have considered. The well-trained group shares with the Leader the responsibility for recognizing that all behavior is caused in one way or another, and that a punishing type behavior directed against persons demonstrating unproductive or dysfunctional behavior is usually not constructive and can often be damaging. This does not mean, of course, that such behavior should be rewarded by the group. A grounding in the findings of the behavioral sciences will be helpful to any leader of any sort of group, enabling him to better understand people, their behavior in groups, and the probable effects of various experiences in the group on its members. As his knowledge increases, his caution in applying that knowledge will possibly also increase!

Group members often take time to "settle in", and the Leader should not be too hasty in deciding that he has Problem Children on his hands. Some behavior which seems dysfunctional will disappear, being a temporary accommodation to a new situation. The Leader of a new group is better advised to enter upon his job enthusiastically and optimistically, concentrating on the positive aspects of his role and his group, and he will find that most problems he anticipates never appear, or solve themselves with the help of the dynamics of the group.

FOR SOURCES AND FURTHER INFORMATION, CONSULT THE FOLLOWING WORKS:

1. Thelen, H. A., DYNAMICS OF GROUPS AT WORK, p. 313, Chicago: University of Chicago Press, Phoenix, 1963.
2. Thelen, DYNAMICS OF GROUPS AT WORK, pp. 319-21.
3. Mills, T. M., SOCIOLOGY OF SMALL GROUPS, pp. 123-24, Englewood Cliffs, N.J.: Prentice-Hall, Inc., 1967; W. R. Bion, EXPERIENCES IN GROUPS, AND OTHER PAPERS, pp. 29-34; 77-86, 147, N.Y.: Basic Books, 1959; Fritz Redl, "Leadership and Group Emotion", SMALL GROUPS: STUDIES ON SOCIAL INTERACTION, p. 80 *et passim,* eds. A. Paul Hare, Edgar F. Borgatta, and Robert F. Bales, N.Y.: Knopf, 1955.
4. Borger, Robert and A. E. M. Seaborne, THE PSYCHOLOGY OF LEARNING, p. 129, Baltimore, Md.: Penguin Books, 1966.
5. Lowell, A. Lawrence, CONFLICTS OF PRINCIPLE, p. 138, Boston: Harvard University Press, 1932.
6. Langer, Susanne K., PHILOSOPHY IN A NEW KEY: A STUDY IN THE SYMBOLISM OF REASON, RITE, AND ART, pp. 15, 16, 17, N.Y.: New American Library, 1951.
7. Valentine, Milton, "Information Theory and the Psychology of Speech", THE PSYCHOLOGY OF COMMUNICATION, pp. 170, 179-80, eds. John Eisenson, J. Jeffery Auer and John V. Irwin, N.Y.: Appleton-Century-Crofts, 1963.
8. Brown, John, "Information Theory", NEW HORIZONS IN PSYCHOLOGY, pp. 122-31, ed. Brian M. Foss, Baltimore, Md.: Penguin Books, 1966.
9. Osgood, Charles E., "The Nature and Measurement of Meaning", PSYCHOLOGY BULLETIN, 49 (1952), pp. 197-237.
10. Hayakawa, S. I., "How to Attend a Conference", in THE USE AND ABUSE OF LANGUAGE, pp. 70ff., Greenwich, Conn.: Fawcett Premier, 1962, 1966.
11. Howe, Reuel L., THE MIRACLE OF DIALOGUE, pp. 20-26, N.Y.: Seabury Press, 1963.
12. Lee, Irving J., HOW TO TALK WITH PEOPLE, pp. 14-26, N.Y.: Harper & Bros., 1952.
13. Larrabee, Harold A., RELIABLE KNOWLEDGE, rev. ed., p. 63, Boston: Houghton Mifflin, 1964.

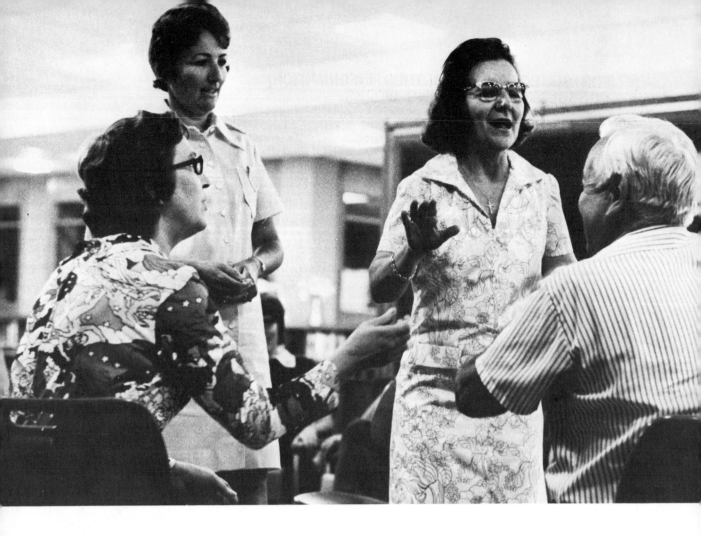

14.
Role-Playing and Other Simulations

OVERVIEW

Role-playing and simulation games are useful techniques for discussion groups. Their chief values are the production of involvement, surfacing of real feelings, and the provision for behavioral experimentation in a safe situation. Role-plays may be loosely or tightly structured and may be used as the presentation or developed at certain points during the discussion. Simulation games are structured and extended role-plays, usually involving competition. Role-plays and other simulations depend for their educational value on the quality of the ensuing discussion.

WHAT IS ROLE-PLAYING?

Role-playing is worthy of special consideration. It is one of the most useful techniques available to groups. Role-playing is an attempt to help members of a group take an issue from a verbal-intellectual level of learning and put it on a level of practice or action. It can be defined as a dramatization of a problem or an incident in the general area of human relations, the acting out of roles in the situation of human relationships.

Dr. J. L. Moreno popularized role-playing at the Psychodramatic Institute in New York. There are two devices used by Dr. Moreno, "Psychodrama" and "Sociodrama". Whereas psychodrama more often refers to therapy, sociodrama is but another term for role-playing.[1]

It should be remembered that one of the premises for discussion emphasized earlier was that learning is something each individual *does*, not something someone does for him or to him. The acting out of roles in a problem situation provides a new and meaningful experience.

ADVANTAGES

The advantages of role-playing are numerous. Problems can be seen from another view and in a different dimension. It gives the suggested solution a way to be tried in a safe, non-failing exercise.

common experience

And it gives to the group a "common experience" as a basis for discussion. Because the experience is not real there is no failure. Matthew B. Miles calls role-playing "a safe learning environment".

safe learning experience

He comments further that it would be better to refer to role-playing as "an irreal experience (a simulated form of realness), one on a temporarily different level of reality." [2]

Of the many advantages of role-playing, the following are among the most important:

involvement

1. It provides a chance to develop a feeling of personal involvement in a problem. It shows what the problem means to an individual person and what it means to the group.

2. It adds a new perspective to the problem. No problem is purely intellectual and no problem can be solved simply by giving an intellectual solution, no matter how well thought out.

3. It helps people gain insights into their own and others' feelings.

feelings expressed

4. It allows many attitudes and feelings that fundamentally affect group attitudes and processes, but are usually left unexpressed and subjective, to be brought out into the open before the group.

freedom of expression

5. It creates a freedom of expression for an individual by releasing inhibitions. Dramatic improvisation helps to generate informality.

6. It is easy to plan, but does demand skill in application.

informality

7. It sparks the imagination, and brings humor to an otherwise drab consideration of life's problems.

USES OF ROLE-PLAYING

Both the Leader and the group will find in role-playing a highly advantageous technique. It generates involvement, and this is, without a doubt, its most important use. When there is a reluctance to express opinions, attitudes and feelings, role-playing will frequently help these come out. When there is need to explore the motives of members of a group, and when adjustments in a group are desired, role-playing is effective.

Herbert Thelen emphasizes that role-playing helps communicate a specific problem so that people will have something real to talk about as the basis for discovering their own problems.[3] Within a discussion, real problems of an individual often come up for consideration. For example, what group is without a member who often refers to his own experience? What group is without a member who will say, "You know, I had a similar situation happen to me last week. My son wanted to borrow the car and I soon found myself in a heated discussion on the teenager, problems, privileges, responsibility—the whole bit." At this point, the Leader can suggest that they role-play the incident.

> *"John, why not show us what took place? You play your part. Someone else can be your son. Any one for the teenager's role? Dick. Good. The two of you can use the next room and go over some of the facts of the incident. Take about five minutes and then return here. You can show the group exactly what you are referring to, John."*

In the discussion which follows the role-playing situation, the group will share their ideas. This will go beyond the actual experience of the players, i.e., the incident of John just mentioned. The different perceptions of the group members will help in setting up various ways to deal with the problem, and will offer several solutions that can be tested. Without making one way look "good" and another "bad", the various approaches to a problem situation can be investigated. It is in this way that role-playing helps us to see many aspects of the problem and many more solutions than those originally offered.

for both action and discussion groups
Role-playing is a technique useful to both an action and a learning discussion oriented group. An action group can use it effectively to overcome obstacles in the accomplishment of a task. A learning discussion group can use it to clarify an issue or help in individual decision-making. When someone has difficulty as to where he stands on an issue, it may help if he instructs two or more members to put forth his ideas in role-playing. He may, with the help of the group, see where his "hang-up" is, where his gaps are, where, perhaps, a buried conflict is influencing a problem. For instance, let us consider the possible case of a member of a discussion group who is not sure of his position on an issue being considered. He thinks one way, but also considers an alternative position. He

would like to make up his mind. The group has been discussing the problem, and he has participated. He still says, "I don't know. I wish I could make up my mind". Two members could role-play the problem, taking the different positions expressed by him. After the episode, he should not be made to express a decision. He should be asked if his problem is clearer now. Groups studying racism have used it successfully to unearth and explore their own attitudes toward inter-racial marriage, and groups studying the problems of abortion have found it very helpful in similar ways.

CASTING ROLES

There are several important things to keep in mind in using role-playing. The casting of roles should be controlled and persons should be selected on the basis of their knowledge and feeling for a situation. Avoid selecting someone who will freeze before an audience, or forcing someone into a role he does not wish to play. This is particularly important if the group has never experienced role-playing before.

PROCEDURES

The character roles should be described briefly and differences specifically pointed out. It is advantageous to stop the scene as soon as it has made its point. Then discuss the scene and the behavior portrayed. Allow the players to react to the role-playing incident first. The players can give an explanation for their actions. The observing members of the group can then follow with their comments.

There will be a temptation at times to load the sociodrama with a message. This would destroy the spontaneity of role-playing and limit the effectiveness of dramatic improvisation. A good rule of thumb in planning and executing role-playing is to aim for stimulation, not indoctrination. Problems should merely be revealed, not answered. Solutions should be tried, not enforced.

If a topic under discussion, for example, is some aspect of the racial problem, the discussion Leader sets up a role-playing situation that takes the problem beyond mere intellectual speculation. The aim is to see the problem in the concrete, to discuss the aspects perceived and even those not seen. If a solution suggests itself, it can be tested and measured appropriately.

TYPES OF ROLE-PLAYING

In setting up a role-playing incident, the Leader has a choice in structuring the situation loosely or not. An example of a loosely structured scene would be the following:

"John, you are a ticket collector at a public swimming pool in the South. Frank, you are the manager of this pool. Negroes have never been admitted before. Mary, Jim, Mike and Alice, you are Negro teenagers who have come to the pool to be admitted."

The situation is simply defined, and the role-players needed are listed. A loosely structured situation designates the characters and allows the individuals to develop their own roles.

Similar situations could be loosely structured along the same lines as the one above. In place of the swimming pool, there could be a school, a lunch counter, a theater, a construction site, and so on. The important thing is to allow for a wide improvisation. The results of the sociodrama will depend on the maturity and experience of the members.

tightly structured   If a tightly structured situation is desired, then the situation and roles are detailed, as for example:

SITUATION: *Confrontation between whites and blacks at a municipal swimming pool in the South. Previously only whites frequented the pool.*

ROLES:
Manager, *65 years old, white male, prejudiced and proud and antagonistic, wants the old ways when people knew their place.*
Ticket collector, *a young adult, white. Though prejudiced, wants to avoid a scene, and especially wants to avoid any violence.*
Teenagers, *one boy and one girl, both black militants, insistent upon their rights and not at all opposed to physical confrontation.*
Teenagers, *one boy and one girl, both black members of a non-violent movement, insistent upon their rights and advocates of non-violence.*

Obviously there can be various degrees of structuring and any member of the group can set the amount of structure desired. Let us look at another example of structured role-playing:

SITUATION: *The introduction of a program in black culture in a large suburban public school.*

ROLES:
Chairman of the board of education *for the school district. Personal data: former principal of a large public school. Good administrator.*
Self-image: strong.
Attitude toward community: conscious of community pressures.
Attitude toward school: feels schools are important, but ineffective to cultivate value formation.

Question to be considered: Where will the finances come from to support the program?

Parent:

Personal data: housewife, black, three children in school.
Self-image: good
Attitude toward community: interested in community affairs and active in civic issues.
Attitude toward school: supportive of school, but pessimistic that a black culture program can be acceptable, or find wide support.
Question to be considered: I want to be helpful, what do I do?

Parent:

Personal data: housewife, white, two children in school. Board member of the PTA.
Self-image: good
Attitude toward community: a realist. Interested in bringing about recognition of the black culture as an important contribution to the making of our American society.
Attitude toward school: supportive of school. Feels need of in-service program for teachers necessary for an effective program.
Question to be considered: What reaction will there be among the parents if a program is set up?

Community Leader:

Personal data: alumnus of the school. Lawyer, politician, white.
Self-image: strong.
Attitude toward community: involved and concerned. Has support of community.
Attitude toward school: feels that the school is the main channel through which peace and understanding between black and white can become a reality.
Question to be considered: Can I count on the support of the board members?

Principal:

Personal data: five years of experience as principal, M.Ed. in administration.
Self-image: strong.
Attitude toward community: involved and interested in civic affairs.
Attitude toward school: leader in innovative education, but lacks the authority to effect change.
Question to be considered: Will the parents' and community's support be consistent?

Superintendent:

Personal data: 50 years old, Ph.D. in education.
Self-image: adequate.

Attitude toward community: concerned about value forma-tion, but not completely in touch.
Attitude toward school: school must have community support.
Question to be considered: What will the Board members think?

loosely structured

After members of the group become experienced in role-playing, the situation to be played does not have to be tightly structured and can be more spontaneous. With time and experience, a situation can be cited and the members will be able to handle it. For example, someone may suggest a family problem. "Who wants to be members of a family where there is concern about the dating practices of a son?", "Who will be members of a union and those of management in a labor dispute?", "Who wants to be members of a student council dealing with the question of a school paper and supervision?", "Who will be various ministers considering religious differences in a marriage?" The players briefly get together and limit the situation and determine their roles.

"one essential
rule . . ."

In all types of role-playing situations, one essential rule must be kept. When a person assumes the identity of another person, he must play the part completely, to the best of his ability, and not hold back. To do otherwise would only frustrate the entire role-playing situation and make the discussion which follows pointless.

ROLE-PLAYING AND THE GROUP ITSELF

role-playing for
group growth

Role-playing can be used to reflect problems within a group. There is no discussion group that does not experience some internal difficulty: the highly argumentative member, the rambler, the overly talkative, the griper, the side conversationalist, the in-articulate. These are but a few of the moods encountered. Often people are strongly affected by "outside" influences: family affairs, money worries, health, sickness, job reports, studies, examinations. It is not possible to know how any one of these may act on a given occasion. Most people are not deliberately creating problems for themselves or for the group. As does everyone else, they need acceptance, guidance, sympathy and encouragement.

hidden agenda

Problems such as these create the "Hidden Agenda". Leland P. Bradford indicates that a group simultaneously works on two levels. The formal task is the first and obvious level. "It represents the acknowledged task facing the group: to nominate a slate of officers for the local PTA, to plan a meeting or conference, to gain understanding of child behavior, or to study the Declaration of Independence. It is the open and acknowledged agenda for the group." [4] Another level is the unlabeled, hidden concern of the group. "Here are all of the conflicting motives, desires, aspirations and emotional reactions held by the group members, subgroups or the group as a whole that cannot be fitted legitimately into the accepted group task." [5] When a discussion is going on, it is not likely that any one member including the Leader can be conscious of the many things affecting the group. Sometimes all that is needed is an opportunity to realize that hidden agenda do exist. Some groups and Leaders may find it possible and desirable to attempt gentle exploration of the immediate and present causes of hidden agenda.

communication and feelings

Matters of feelings are inextricably involved in most problems of communication. Other than straightforward semantics, feelings serve as one of the root causes for ineffective communication. It would seem that people want to hide their feelings, impose them, deny them, distort them, fear them, hate them, and do practically everything but accept them. One way to learn effective communication is to view the difficulty in a safe situation. Role-playing provides this safety. And yet, it still allows a realness to the situation. One main purpose of role-playing is to view problems and test ideas by putting them into play in a situation as close to the real thing as possible. It can act as a mirror to the group, allowing the group to view not only themselves and their problems, but also to anticipate difficulties involved in relationships among the members.

leadership and Leader

Attitudes of members of a group toward the Leader and conflicts over authority may be projected into many role-playing scenes. In this situation the Leader is cautioned not to be eager to make the transition from a role-playing scene to the actual group itself. By introducing interpretation before the group is ready for it, the Leader may put everyone on the defensive. When the group is ready someone will volunteer the thought or pose the question that will introduce the transition. More than likely a member will say, "Could those persons be saying the very things we feel about our Leader? about our leadership? about ourselves?" The Leader now helps the members of the group to make the transition. He should maintain the group in this inquiry.

TIME AND TIMING

There is a time limit for role-playing. Usually five or six minutes is more than enough to bring out the main issue or issues in a situation. The best efforts are given in the beginning when spontaneity is at its peak. In all cases, however, there should be just enough time for players to present their feelings, opinions, reactions and ideas. When the presentation has approached a climax, when feelings have been sufficiently expressed or a penetrating idea has been made, the play should be cut. In this manner, role-playing becomes a springboard for discussion. Not only are the reactions of the observers given freely, but also the feelings and thoughts of the players themselves are shared when they are most vital.

the large group

If the group is large enough, the same role-playing situation could be performed by subgroups. The differences and similarities then can be shared with the entire group. Another possibility is to repeat the same roles with different actors. In this manner more involvement is had and other possible issues of a problem situation can be brought out effectively to all the members.

VARIATIONS

ALTER EGO: There are many adaptations of role-playing. Variations can be found in much of the literature on groups. One's own spirit of creativity can also provide many more. One rather useful variation of role-playing that can provide insight into a communication problem, and even cope with hidden agenda, is the Alter Ego. For each character in a role-playing situation, an auxiliary person, sometimes called "conscience", is used. It becomes the task of the conscience or alter ego to express the thoughts of the actor when they are merely implicit in the words and actions of the drama, or when he senses an altogether different attitude than that expressed by the actor. This usually takes place when an actor in a role situation represses his feelings or denies them. This will also be true when the role portrayed suggests this kind of behavior. For example:

Actor: *Sorry, I didn't hear you. My mind wandered.*
Alter Ego: *You are just not important to me* (showing boredom and inattention).
Actor: *You're getting on my nerves. You're make me feel terrible.*
Alter Ego: *I'm sensitive and you're so callous.*
Actor: *That's your problem, John.*
Alter Ego: *I don't care about you. Don't count on me.*

People have learned early in life highly subtle and sophisticated ways of conditioning their own and others' giving and receiving. We often fail to understand and appreciate the negative effects of attempted communication. We do not recognize the hidden, underlying messages, both received and sent. Role-playing, with the addition of the alter ego, confronts us with the conditioning tactics usually employed which destroy effective communication. When staging this type of role-playing, the alter ego stands behind the actor or to his side.

POSITIVE AND NEGATIVE ROLES: When it is not possible to assign specific character roles to a problem situation, it is necessary to keep the operation as general as possible. It is best to set up the role-playing drama according to a negative, positive and neutral position. Take the situation of the U.S. involvement in Vietnam, a church's involvement in ecumenical affairs, a sports program in a school system, or civil disobedience. In each of these situations, we can react in varying degrees either negatively or positively and the role-playing can take on this format very comfortably.

After stating the situation as clearly and briefly as possible, the following roles are assigned:

Double positive (++). This reaction is the result of a strong and favorable view of the situation, e.g., U.S. involvement in Vietnam. There is agreement on all points.

Positive (+). This reaction is the result of a fairly positive view of the situation. There will be agreement on a good number of the ideas concerning the situation, but not as strongly favorable as double positive.

Negative (−). This reaction is the result of a feeling of dislike for the situation stated. Since there is a dislike, many of the ideas are disagreed with, or challenged.

Double Negative (−−). This reaction is similar to the negative reaction, but more intense. With a strong dislike for the situation, disagreement with all the ideas is voiced.

Indifferent or Neutral. This reaction is the result of no particular like or dislike of the situation described. The member assuming this role can therefore agree or disagree as he sees fit, since there is no feeling for or against.

ROLE REVERSAL: Role-playing can help those in a group see the "other side" of the story. What is developed through role-playing is both insight and sensitivity. Ordinarily, a problem is viewed from one viewpoint, namely our own. To a certain extent, all of us are subjective and prejudiced on many issues. By playing a black man in a racial-conflict situation, a white person can begin to appreciate what the black man experiences when he is discriminated against. Often this is referred to as "role reversal". By taking each other's part, aspects of the situation can be seen in a new light. A person sees himself as another understands him. This type of role-playing, the role reversal, is most effective in a conflict situation: parent-child, minority-majority position, white-black, employer-employee, foreman-worker, teacher-pupil.

AVOID OVERACTING

Matthew B. Miles singles out the "fun" aspect as a particular quality of role-playing. It gives a chance to unbend, and it can be "an emotionally releasing and recreating experience." [6] What is essential to remember in role-playing, however, whether according to the "positive and negative" roles or any other variation, is that the person play the part convincingly. Above all, overacting must be avoided. In particular the person who plays the double negative or double positive role has to be careful not to fail by overacting. There is a little ham in all of us, and it allows us to enjoy such experiences as role-playing. If the acting-out is overdone, then both the enjoyment and the possibility of a new learning experience is lost.

In assigning roles, use a form of the verb "to be". Do not say, "Mary, will you play the mother?", or "Harry, will you act the role of the father?", or even, "John, you'll take the father role." Instead, say, "Mary, will you be the mother?", or "John, you're the father", and so forth. Directions given in this way help the role-player *become* the role, rather than pretending or acting the role.

SIMULATION GAMES

Another kind of role-playing is that involved in simulation games. As the term is used today, simulations are working models, research or educational tools or devices, which reproduce important elements of reality. Richard Dawson says, "The important factor is that the components and variables being investigated through the model respond in a manner comparable to that of the behavior of the real system." [7] Some authors consider gaming to be a term applied to some types of "simulations in which human actors participate . . . generally in a competitive situation".[8] Simulations of various kinds are being used with increasing frequency as educational or training techniques. A few may be used as a means of testing, as in the case of the in-basket exercise,[9] or are used primarily for research, but the majority are useful in education. As such, their value is largely dependent on the quality of the discussion following the playing of the game.

history

The grandfather of all simulation games seems to be chess, with the great-grandfathers such games as draughts or checkers. Even at the time of Napoleon, games used as training devices for the military were elaborations of chess in the form of various board games. These were followed by sand table games and map games, which fell in two general categories: (1) the rigid war game, with control by rules, and (2) the "free" war game, with control by a director. With the introduction of the free game, discussion following the game became an essential part, opening up new possibilities which greatly increased the value of simulation games for education.

rule games and free games

political and management games

Current simulations are relatives of the war games, and include political exercises such as crisis gaming, business or management gaming and the construction of possible futures. Business or management games are often "rule games" rather than free games. Sidney Giffin says, "The business exercise has much the same advantages over simulations of other social subjects that economics has over other social sciences; it has money as a measuring device—the score can be kept on an accounting basis." [10] The purpose of crisis gaming is to help players work through possible international conflicts in an effort to resolve problems without compromising vital national interests or resorting to warfare.[11] Most business and management games require that the players already be knowledgeable in the discipline, but the presupposition is that gaming will increase their knowledge and judgment.

The authors of the Carnegie Tech game were seeking to develop four specific management skills which they felt were universally recognized as important: (1) to abstract, organize, and use

ROLE-PLAYING ARRANGEMENTS

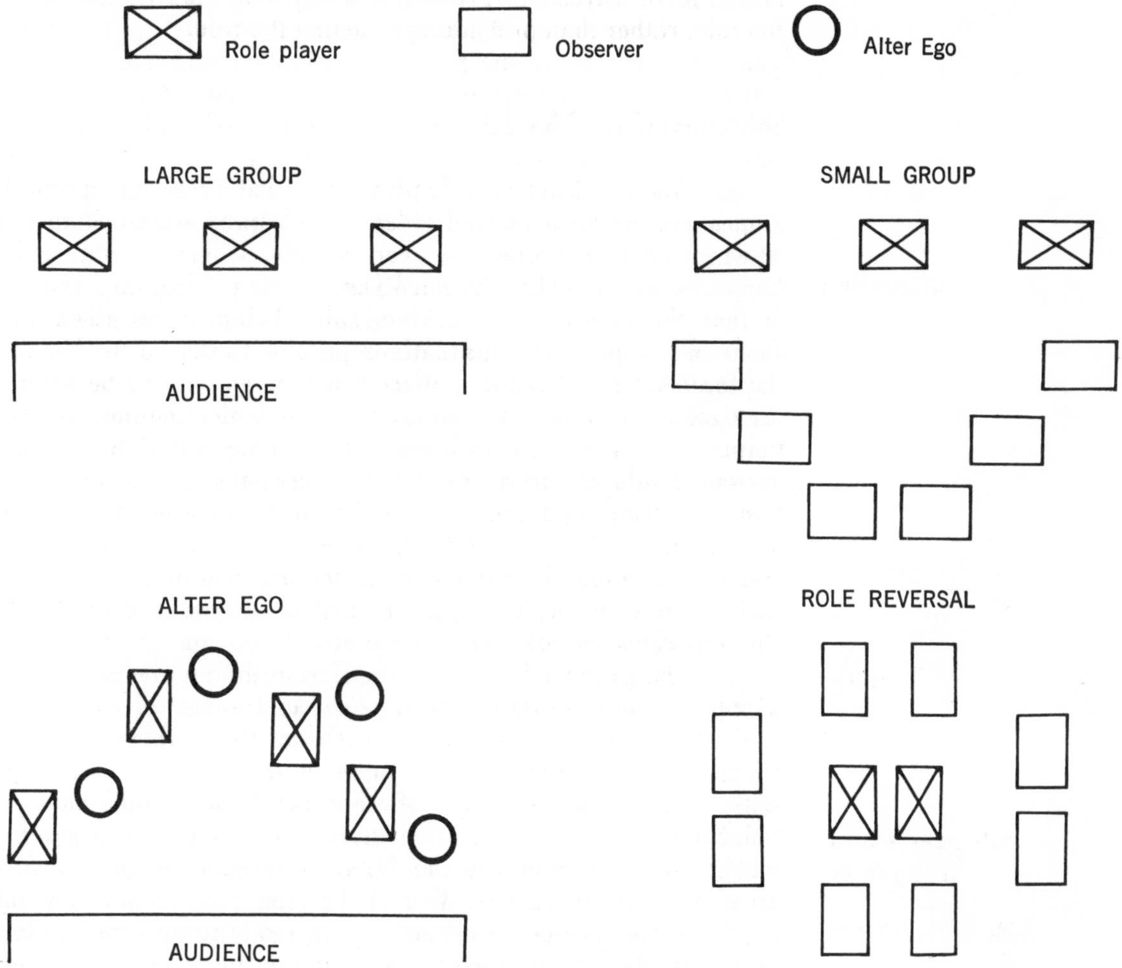

⊠ Role player	▢ Observer	◯ Alter Ego

LARGE GROUP

⊠ ⊠ ⊠

▢ AUDIENCE

SMALL GROUP

⊠ ⊠ ⊠

▢   ▢

▢ ▢

▢ ▢

ALTER EGO

⊠ ◯ ⊠ ◯

⊠ ◯ ⊠ ◯

▢ AUDIENCE

ROLE REVERSAL

▢ ▢

▢   ⊠ ⊠   ▢

▢   ▢ ▢   ▢

information from a complex and diffuse environment; (2) to fore-cast and to plan; (3) to combine the role of generalist and specialist; and (4) to work effectively with other people.[12] With the possible exception of item "3", these features usually are incorporated to some extent in all simulation gaming.

educational games   Educational games must always be selected or designed to suit the level of knowledge of the participants, but some simulation games commercially available can be used at different grade levels with considerable value, even when certain elements inherent in the game must be largely ignored at the lower levels.

Major differences between the role-playing we have been considering in the first part of this chapter and gaming are the time involved and the more obviously competitive nature of the gaming situation. In other kinds of role-play, we have suggested a time limit of five or six minutes, whereas gaming usually goes on for a longer period of time, and in some elaborate types is extended over a period of days. Also, in many simulation games there are interventions from "outside" in the form of "events" introduced by a game director or by the previously planned scenario or game constructors. Some of these events are determined by chance, others by the judgment of the game director or the original game planners, and are based on such things as "but, what if . . .?" or "if x, then y". In gaming the roles are "played out" either to the point where someone or some team "wins" or until a predetermined time limit, at which point the results are examined.

discussion

Two vital elements involved in role-playing and other simulations are (1) decision-making, and (2) communication. The educational value of all simulations fails if these two aspects are not explored in the discussion. Almost all games, and certainly all conflict games, produce communication problems and the ensuing discussion can investigate causes and possible solutions. As in any role-play, players start with different assumptions, and part of the games consists in trying to improve our assessments of the other parties, as we discussed in Chapter 3 in connection with the communication situation. Following a role-play or simulation game, a discussion by both players and observers is most essential. Members playing roles in both the loosely structured and tightly structured sociodramas may tell or not tell their roles before they begin the role-play, but they definitely should explain the role after the performance. The discussion will show what the problem means to an individual and what it means to the group. Insight is gained into one's own feelings and those of others. Questions which have proven helpful are: How did you feel in your role? As an observer, what would you have done differently? The general question underlying others in the discussion is, What could be learned from this situation?

as presentation

preparing
questions

If the role-play or other simulation is pre-planned to be used as a presentation, the Leader can prepare many of his questions in advance. Since he is writing or selecting the scenario, he knows the problem and the roles. However, he must be particularly careful in discussions following such simulations because of several variables: (1) the role-players may change their roles in some way, omitting or adding important elements; (2) he must listen and watch the role-play carefully to rephrase his questions and to formulate new ones to accord with what was said and done; (3) since the role-players will be the first to speak following the role-play, he will not, in this case, begin the discussion with a Primary, but will start at the feeling level with the role-players, using questions such as those proposed in the preceding paragraph, or "Were you comfortable in the role?", "Was there something you wanted to do or say which you felt the role did not allow?", and so forth. In this case, the discussion will *lead up to* the Primary rather than *on from* it. The Leader will find that much of the discussion will be self-generating because of the high degree of involvement on the part of both the role-players and the rest of the group.

role-play during the discussion

When the role-play is introduced during the course of the discussion, the Leader will probably find that many of his previously planned Balance and Response questions will be relevant to the role-play, or that some questions which have already been discussed need to be re-examined in the light of what the role-play and its response have brought forth in the group. He must be aware of the same three elements mentioned in the last paragraph in connection with the phrasing of his questions.

results to be expected

It would be expecting too much to attribute to the use of these techniques the overcoming of deep resentment or resistance. What is accomplished is a better understanding of the dynamics of interpersonal relations. A deeper understanding of problems and a reinforcement of principles taught in the more traditional ways usually results from the involvement obtained as situations literally "come alive" and discussions relate directly to feelings experienced by the participants.

FOR SOURCES AND FURTHER INFORMATION, CONSULT THE FOLLOWING WORKS:

1. Moreno, J. L., PSYCHODRAMA: COLLECTED PAPERS, N.Y.: Beacon House, 1944.
2. Miles, Matthew B., LEARNING TO WORK IN GROUPS, p. 192, N.Y.: Teachers College, Columbia University Press, 1959.
3. Thelen, Herbert A., DYNAMICS OF GROUPS AT WORK, pp. 192f., Chicago: University of Chicago Press, 1954.
4. Bradford, Leland P., "The Case of the Hidden Agenda", GROUP DEVELOPMENT, pp. 60ff., Washington D.C., National Training Laboratories, 1961.
5. Bradford, Leland P., "The Case of the Hidden Agenda", p. 60.
6. Miles, Matthew, DYNAMICS OF GROUPS AT WORK, p. 193.
7. Dawson, Richard, "Simulation in the Social Sciences", SIMULATION IN SOCIAL SCIENCE: READINGS, p. 3, ed. Harold Guetzkow, Englewood Cliffs, N.J.: Prentice-Hall, 1962.
8. Dawson, Richard, "Simulation in the Social Sciences", p. 9.
   see also: Knowles, Malcolm, THE MODERN PRACTICE OF ADULT EDUCATION, p. 293, N.Y.: Association Press, 1970.
9. Frederiksen, Norman, "In-basket Tests and Factors in Administrative Performance", SIMULATION IN SOCIAL SCIENCE: READINGS, pp. 124-37, ed. Harold Guetzkow, Englewood Cliffs, N.J.: Prentice-Hall, 1962.
10. Giffin, Sidney F., THE CRISIS GAME: SIMULATING INTERNATIONAL CONFLICT, p. 49, Garden City, N.Y.: Doubleday & Co., 1965.
11. Giffin, Sidney F., THE CRISIS GAME, p. 71.
12. Cohen, K. J., et al., "The Carnegie Tech Management Game", SIMULATION IN SOCIAL SCIENCE, pp. 104-23, ed. Harold Guetzkow.
NOTE: For further information, see listings in "List of Suggested Readings".

List of Suggested Readings

This is not exhaustive, neither is it necessarily the best list of books for your individual needs. Inspection of these works will give you a general survey of the materials available. Leadership of group discussions is an interdisciplinary field; few can hope to become thoroughly grounded in all its aspects, or adept at all types of leadership. The list is grouped under headings, but the groupings are somewhat arbitrary and there is considerable overlap.

BACKGROUND

THE ARTS:

Beardsley, Monroe C., AESTHETICS: FROM CLASSICAL GREECE TO THE PRESENT: A SHORT HISTORY, N.Y.: Macmillan, c. 1966. Useful and thought-provoking for the Leader as he formulates questions in a number of fields.

Cady, Arthur, THE ART BUFF'S BOOK, Washington, D.C.: Robert B. Luce, Inc., 1965. Subtitled "What Artists Do and How-They-Do-It", it directs the student through a series of exercises. Breezy, brief and amusing, it conveys considerable information on drawing, painting, and various other things, including the "movies".

Cooper, Grosvenor, ed., LEARNING TO LISTEN: A HANDBOOK FOR MUSIC, prepared with Humanities staff of the College at the University of Chicago, Chicago: Chicago University Press, 1957 (Phoenix Books). Brief, simple guide.

Heyer, Robert and Anthony Meyer, DISCOVERY IN FILM, N.Y.: Paulist Press, 1969. A wide-ranging approach to the educational possibilities of film at the secondary school level and above. Related readings, comments, illustrations and cross-references make it far more than a description of recommended short films.

Lavin, Edward and Terrence Manning, DISCOVERY IN ART, N.Y.: Paulist Press, 1969. A beautiful and sensitively arranged collection of contemporary art and related short readings. Designed for student use, but equally helpful for the Leader.

Maurello, S. Ralph, ed., INTRODUCTION TO THE VISUAL ARTS, N.Y.: Tudor, 1968. Very well illustrated, brief explicit text, describes "mechanics" and principles of painting, drawing, prints, mosaics, ceramics, decoration, etc.

Payne, Richard J. and Robert Heyer, DISCOVERY IN ADVERTISING, N.Y.: Paulist Press, 1969. High school text imaginatively handling exploration of propaganda, communication and values in today's society as demonstrated by advertisements reproduced from the press and accompanied by related readings and commentary.

Piper, David, ed., ENJOYING PAINTINGS, Baltimore, Md.: Penguin, 1964. A variety of authors bring a variety of ways to "look" and to "see".

Robinson, W. R., ed., MAN AND THE MOVIES, Baltimore, Md.: Penguin, 1967. Good collection of articles and essays approaching the study of film from a variety of angles. Helpful bibliography.

Stephenson, Ralph and J. R. Debrix, THE CINEMA AS ART, Baltimore, Md.: Penguin, 1965. Helpful in acquiring some grasp of techniques and technicalities. Illustrations and many specific examples provide reference text in many elements of film.

THE WRITTEN WORD:

Adler, Mortimer J., HOW TO READ A BOOK: THE ART OF GETTING A LIBERAL EDUCATION, N.Y.: Simon and Schuster, 1940. Recently reissued, this is an old favorite in many circles. Adler's tendency to compartmentalize is sometimes troublesome. The following reprint provides sufficient information for many readers.

Adler, Mortimer J., "How to Mark a Book", abridged from THE SATURDAY REVIEW OF LITERATURE, July 6, 1940, in READER'S DIGEST, Aug., 1940.

Altizer, Thomas, Wm. A. Beardslee and J. Harvey Young, TRUTH, MYTH AND SYMBOL, Englewood Cliffs, N.J.: Prentice-Hall, Inc., 1962. Good collection of articles on understanding mythic and symbolic elements in various media.

Hill, Knox C., INTERPRETING LITERATURE: HISTORY, DRAMA, FICTION, PHILOSOPHY, RHETORIC, Chicago: University of Chicago, Phoenix, 1966. Elementary text, with examples showing "what to look for". See also Ross, Berryman and Tate.

King, Martha L., Bernice D. Ellinger and Willavene Wolf, eds., CRITICAL READING, Philadelphia: J. B. Lippincott, 1967. Although intended primarily for English teachers in lower grades, has considerable material of value for general reader and educator. Three articles are particularly helpful: Robert Ennis, "A Definition of Critical Thinking"; Helen M. Robinson, "Developing Critical Readers"; Josephine A. Piekarz, "Attitudes and Critical Reading".

Ross, Ralph, John Berryman and Allen Tate, THE ARTS OF READINGS: AN ANTHOLOGY OF THE FINEST LITERATURE OF ALL TIME, WITH CRITICAL COMMENTS, N.Y.: Apollo, Thomas Y. Crowell, 1960. Despite its pretentious title, very worthwhile.

THE WRITTEN WORD: SOME SPECIALIZED WORKS:

Carroll, John B., "Words, Meanings and Concepts", STUDIES IN EDUCATIONAL PSYCHOLOGY, ed. Raymond G. Kuhlen, Waltham, Mass.: Blaisdell Pub., 1968.

Useful reference on "concepts"—could as well be listed under "Communication".

Empson, William, 7 TYPES OF AMBIGUITY: A STUDY OF ITS EFFECTS IN ENGLISH VERSE, N.Y.: Meridian, Noonday, 1955. Although quite technical, of use in many kinds of literature.

Goodman, Paul, THE STRUCTURE OF LITERATURE, Chicago: Phoenix, University of Chicago, 1954. Examination of elements of classic plays, novels and poems aids reader and viewer in understanding cognitive and emotive content of literature and its relation to form.

Hirsch, E. D., Jr., VALIDITY IN INTERPRETATION, New Haven: Yale University Press, 1967. Deals with principles of valid interpretation, problems of genre, distinctions between meaning and significance, interpretation and criticism. Discusses and disputes theories which deny possibility of validity, and sees his work as "a contribution to general hermeneutic theory."

Larrabee, H. A., RELIABLE KNOWLEDGE, Boston: Houghton Mifflin, 1945. ". . . (O)ur task is not to select the single method (of securing reliable knowledge), but rather to know how to make the best use of any or all of them to the maximum degree of profit in terms of understanding" (p. 61). Geared primarily to social studies, offers simple introductory exposition of logics, scientific method, semantics, classification, causal analysis, definition, statistics. Interesting exercises, and still useful, despite being dated in part.

Sherwood, John C., DISCOURSE OF REASON: A BRIEF HANDBOOK OF SEMANTICS AND LOGIC, N.Y.: Harper & Row, 2nd ed., 1964. Simple review, helpful in working to formulate "clean" questions. Designed for use in English Composition classes, includes an explanation of the Venn diagram and list of "common fallacies".

THE BEHAVIORAL SCIENCES

GENERAL:

Berelson, Bernard and Gary A. Steiner, HUMAN BEHAVIOR: AN INVENTORY OF SCIENTIFIC FINDINGS, N.Y.: Harcourt, Brace, 1964. An abridged version is also available. It might be well to purchase the abridged and consult the full edition in the library when necessary. Useful, though possibly overly self-assured, reference work. Will need frequent updating, but is fairly exhaustive survey of the literature. Particularly useful are sections 8, 9, 10 and 14.

CULTURAL ANTHROPOLOGY:

Argyris, Chris, UNDERSTANDING ORGANIZATIONAL BEHAVIOR, Homewood, Ill.: Dorsey Press, 1960. A "management" classic, this work has much of value for any group leader.

Brown, Ina Corinne, UNDERSTANDING OTHER CULTURES, Englewood Cliffs, N.J.: Prentice-Hall, Spectrum, 1963. Examination of patterns of life and speech in other cultures provides insight in working with our own cultural characteristics.

Cantril, Hadley, THE PATTERN OF HUMAN CONCERNS, New Brunswick, N.J.: Rutgers University Press, 1965. Interesting cross-cultural study by the sociologist-psychologist who has done a good deal of work in the field of perception. Not strictly "cultural anthropology", but serves same purposes in viewing life of many groups, and by comparison making our own "patterns" more visible to us.

Hall, Edward T., THE HIDDEN DIMENSION, Garden City, N.Y.: Doubleday Anchor, 1966. (See note under this listing in section, "Communication, Non-verbal".)

Hall, Edward T., THE SILENT LANGUAGE, Greenwich, Conn.: Fawcett Premier, 1959. (See note under this listing in section, "Communication, Non-verbal".)

Mead, Margaret, CULTURE AND COMMITMENT: A STUDY OF THE GENERATION GAP, Garden City, N.Y.: Doubleday, 1970. Comparative study of intergenerational problems and resulting educational problems in various changing societies.

SOCIOLOGY:

Berger, Peter L., INVITATION TO SOCIOLOGY: A HUMANISTIC PERSPECTIVE, Garden City, N.Y.: Doubleday, Anchor, 1963. Delightful non-textbook style, with author's own personality, beliefs and principles deliberately exposed, this book is worth at least a partial reading even by those who need no "invitation".

Nisbet, Robert A., THE SOCIAL BOND: AN INTRODUCTION TO THE STUDY OF SOCIETY, N.Y.: Alfred A. Knopf, 1970. Good, recent standard textbook.

(See also works in sociology listed under "Small Groups".)

PSYCHIATRY:

Frankl, Viktor E., MAN'S SEARCH FOR MEANING: AN INTRODUCTION TO LOGOTHERAPY, N.Y.: Washington Square Press, 1959, 1963. Autobiographical account of life in Nazi concentration camp, followed by summary of Frankl's psychotherapeutic approach and bibliography of works in English on Logotherapy and *Existenzanalyse.* Frankl's thesis: "the striving to find a meaning in one's life is the primary motivational force in man" (p. 154), opposing this to the Freudian pleasure principle and Adlerian "will to power", and going beyond A. Maslow's hierarchy of motives in his stress on fulfillment through meaning.

Frankl, Viktor E., THE WILL TO MEANING: FOUNDATIONS AND APPLICATIONS OF LOGOTHERAPY, N.Y.: Plume/New American Library, 1969. Frankl compares his approach to that of the more traditional therapist, and discusses his more optimistic view of man and his possibilities.

Harris, Thomas A., I'M OK—YOU'RE OK: A PRACTICAL GUIDE TO TRANSACTIONAL ANALYSIS, N.Y.: Harper & Row, 1969. A careful reading will provide help in some communication problems. His use of the term "transactional analysis" is allied to that of Berne's, and not to be confused with the theories of perception considered by such authors as Kilpatrick or Cantril in "transactional psychology".

Rogers, Carl R., ON BECOMING A PERSON: A THERAPIST'S VIEW OF PSYCHOTHERAPY, Boston: Houghton Mifflin, 1961. Although Rogers writes of the client-therapist relationship, his thought has had considerable influence on those who work with other types of small groups. (See also listings under "Small Groups", and "Education", as well as article listed under "Communication".)

PSYCHIATRY, THE THERAPY GROUP:

Adler, R., "A Reporter at Large: The Thursday Group", NEW YORKER, Vol. 43, pp. 55ff., Apr. 15, 1967. A rather negative and cynical account. You will find it interesting, restful reading on a day when you don't want to work, but do want a bit of painless learning.

Bion, W. P., EXPERIENCE IN GROUPS, N.Y.: Basic Books, 1961. Early classic in relationship between emotionality and "work" in groups, polarization and needs of the group. Implications have affected many aspects of group work.

Yablonsky, Lewis, THE TUNNEL BACK: SYNANON, N.Y.: Macmillan, 1965. Lengthy description of rehabilitation of drug addicts, employing "group discussions". As with Alcoholics Anonymous, Recovery, Daytop etc., this is somewhat far afield from most groups you may lead, but you will find it interesting and a hurried reading may give some insights on emotion in groups, salience, etc.

PSYCHOLOGY:

Adorno, T. W., *et al.,* THE AUTHORITARIAN PERSONALITY, N.Y.: Harper, 1950. Classic and influential study of value in working with intergroup relations, authority problems in groups, and problems with "the closed mind".

Erikson, Erik H., CHILDHOOD AND SOCIETY, 2nd ed., N.Y.: W. W. Norton, 1963.

Erikson, Erik H., IDENTITY: YOUTH AND CRISIS, N.Y.: W. W. Norton, 1968.

Foss, Brian M., ed., NEW HORIZONS IN PSYCHOLOGY, Baltimore, Md.: Penguin 1966. Somewhat slanted toward learning theory of behavioral psychology—B. F. Skinner, Watson—but interesting look at some recent research. See especially pp. 7-13; 97-151; 167-82.

Garry, Ralph, PSYCHOLOGY OF LEARNING, Washington, D.C.: Center for Applied Research in Education, 1963. Importance of interpersonal relationships in learning, pp. 72-77. Also brief statements of principles of teaching procedures, some of which is applicable to training groups.

Guilford, J. P., THE NATURE OF HUMAN INTELLIGENCE, N.Y.: McGraw-Hill, 1967. Though deriving from an interest in testing, has wide range of applicability in attempts at improving educational approaches. Stress on creativity.

Jourard, Sidney M., DISCLOSING MAN TO HIMSELF, Princeton, N.J.: D. Van Nostrand, 1968. Avowedly working toward a "humanistic psychology", helping man become all he can rather than manipulating him for other societal goals. Well organized and readable. Bibliography and index helpful.

Kilpatrick, Franklin P., ed., EXPLORATIONS IN TRANSACTIONAL PSYCHOLOGY, N.Y.: New York University Press, 1961. Excellent collection of papers by Ames, Cantril and others in theories of perception.

Köhler, Wolfgang, GESTALT PSYCHOLOGY: AN INTRODUCTION TO NEW CONCEPTS IN MODERN PSYCHOLOGY, N.Y.: Mentor, 1947. Subtitle no longer applies, but is useful review of Gestalt principles in perception, education, etc.

Laing, R. D., THE POLITICS OF EXPERIENCE, N.Y.: Ballantine, 1967. A radical British psychiatrist discusses "normalcy" as today's term for the alienated man, taught by society to avoid confronting himself and others in truth.

McKellar, Peter, EXPERIENCE AND BEHAVIOUR, Baltimore, Md.: Penguin, 1968. Different perspective from above listings.

Maslow, Abraham H., TOWARD A PSYCHOLOGY OF BEING, 2nd ed., N.Y.: Van Nostrand, Reinhold, 1968. Another member of the "humanistic psychology" group, involved in the "encounter movement".

Tibbetts, Paul, ed., PERCEPTION: SELECTED READINGS IN SCIENCE AND PHENOMONOLOGY, Chicago: Quadrangle, 1969. Interesting and varied collection differing in points and view, and not replicating material in Kilpatrick, q.v.

SOCIAL PSYCHOLOGY:

Argyle, Michael, THE PSYCHOLOGY OF INTERPERSONAL BEHAVIOR, Baltimore, Md.: Penguin, 1967. Short useful work by researcher in small group field.

Churchman, C. West, THE SYSTEMS APPROACH, N.Y.: Delta, 1968. A work from the field of management which gives simple and clear presentation of the systems approach to problem-solving.

Inkeles, Alex., "Personality and Social Structure", SOCIOLOGY TODAY, eds.

Robert K. Merton et al., Vol. II, N.Y.: Harper Torchbooks, 1959. Brief review of the literature to date of publication, suggestions concerning theory of relationship of personality characteristics and participants' behavior in social systems.

Krech, D., R. S. Crutchfield and E. L. Ballachey, INDIVIDUAL IN SOCIETY, N.Y.: McGraw-Hill, 1962. Basic textbook in field, particularly good on "attitudes" and "small groups".

Maier, Norman R. F., PRINCIPLES OF HUMAN RELATIONS, N.Y.: Wiley, 1957. Primarily concerned with management's need to manipulate people to serve its own ends, but is excellent book of its type. Outline of "Group-Decision Procedure", pp. 198-203 very helpful. A preliminary reading of pp. 322-24 and 312 and 153 will establish author's viewpoint.

Newcomb, T. M., R. H. Turner and P. E. Converse, SOCIAL PSYCHOLOGY: THE STUDY OF HUMAN INTERACTION, N.Y.: Holt, 1965. Excellent standard textbook, small groups, attitudes, attitude change.

SOCIAL PSYCHOLOGY, ATTITUDE CHANGE:

Bennis, Warren G., Kenneth D. Benne and Robert Chin, THE PLANNING OF CHANGE, 2nd ed., N.Y.: Holt, Rinehart & Winston, 1969. Very useful and basic work.

Borger, Robert and A. E. M. Seaborne, THE PSYCHOLOGY OF LEARNING, Baltimore, Md.: Penguin, 1966. Although more appropriate listing might be under "Education" or "Psychology", is helpful in relating "learning" to idea of "attitude change".

Brown, J. A. C., TECHNIQUES OF PERSUASION: FROM PROPAGANDA TO BRAINWASHING, Baltimore, Md.: Penguin, 1963. Excellent though occasionally slanted survey, which sometimes oversimplifies or draws deductions from or makes generalizations from insufficient evidence, but avoids the overawed witch-hunting of such popularizers as Vance Packard.

Hovland, C. I., I. L. Janis and H. H. Kelley, COMMUNICATION AND PERSUASION, New Haven: Yale University Press, 1953. From the Yale program, reports of research and findings in attitude and opinion change. See also listings under Muzafer Sherif and the following.

Hovland, C. I. and I. L. Janis, PERSONALITY AND PERSUASIBILITY, New Haven: Yale University Press, 1959.

Jahoda, Marie and Neil Warren, eds., ATTITUDES: SELECTED READINGS, Baltimore, Md.: Penguin, 1966. Excellent collection of articles, many of which are not otherwise readily available. Most of the best known men in the field are represented, most articles have their own bibliographies, as well as classified bibliography for work as a whole.

Mann, John, CHANGING HUMAN BEHAVIOR, N.Y.: Scribner's, 1965. Especially Chapters 2, 5, 7, 8, 9. Useful glossary.

Sherif, Muzafer and Karl I. Hovland, SOCIAL JUDGMENT: ASSIMILATION AND CONTRAST EFFECTS IN COMMUNICATION AND ATTITUDE CHANGE, New Haven: Yale University Press, 1961. Another in the Yale series, directed toward examination of how people develop reference scales and anchors (reference points) and make judgments on social issues. See especially "Summary and Implications", pp. 176-207.

COMMUNICATIONS

Berelson, Bernard, and Morris Janowitz, eds., READER IN PUBLIC OPINION AND COMMUNICATION, 2nd ed., N.Y.: Free Press, Collier-Macmillan, 1956. Limited direct value to Leaders, but excellent for further exploration in its field.

Berlo, David K., THE PROCESS OF COMMUNICATION: AN INTRODUCTION TO THEORY AND PRACTICE, N.Y.: Holt, Rinehart & Winston, 1960. Interesting, useful, lives up to its title. Exercises helpful.

Black, Max, THE LABYRINTH OF LANGUAGE, N.Y.: Mentor, 1968. Explores many facets of possible communication problems.

Carpenter, Edmund and Marshall McLuhan, EXPLORATIONS IN COMMUNICATION: AN ANTHOLOGY, Boston: Beacon Press, 1960. Varied and interesting collection of essays originally published in EXPLORATIONS. Several short essays by McLuhan contain much of his basic thinking, sometimes overly expanded in his later works.

COLLOQUY, March, 1971. This issue of a monthly publication concerned with "Education in Church and Society" is devoted to some useful articles in communication.

Eisenson, John, J. Jeffery Auer, and John V. Irwin, THE PSYCHOLOGY OF COMMUNICATION, N.Y.: Appleton-Century-Crofts, 1963. "Basic psychological factors in group communication", pp. 227-52, and "Psychology of group discussion", pp. 253-70, are particularly helpful.

Hayakawa, S. I. "Meaning, Symbols, and Levels of Abstraction", READINGS IN SOCIAL PSYCHOLOGY, eds. Theodore M. Newcomb et al., N.Y.: Henry Holt & Co., 1947, pp. 190-203. Useful excerpt from his early work.

Hayakawa, S. I., ed., THE USE AND MISUSE OF LANGUAGE, Greenwich, Conn.: Fawcett Premier, 1962. Selected essays from ETC.: A REVIEW OF GENERAL SEMANTICS. See particularly, F. J. Roethlisberger, "How to Attend a Conference", pp. 70ff., and Irving J. Lee, "Why Discussions Go Astray", pp. 29ff.

McLuhan, Marshall and Fiore Quentin, THE MEDIUM IS THE MASSAGE, N.Y.: Bantam Books, 1967. What Eliot Fremont-Smith in a review in the New York TIMES called a "simplified photo-montage comic book treatment of UNDERSTANDING MEDIA. You might try this one first, and if you need further elucidation, read the following listing.

McLuhan, Marshall, UNDERSTANDING MEDIA: THE EXTENSIONS OF MAN, N.Y.: McGraw-Hill, 1964. An extremely "linear" approach to what McLuhan rightly considers our decreasingly linear world. He says, "The present book, in seeking to understand many media, the conflicts from which they spring, and the even greater conflicts to which they give rise, holds out the promise of reducing these conflicts by an increase of human autonomy" (p. 51), and ". . . not even the most lucid understanding of the peculiar force of a medium can head off the ordinary 'closure' of the senses that causes us to conform to the pattern of experience presented." Read the first 88 pages, skim the rest, reading what interests you. McLuhan's "media" are any "extensions" of the human body, including the central nervous system, roads, clocks, and "electric technology", and the "content" of any medium is always another medium (p. 8).

Riley, John W., Jr., and Matilda White Riley, "Mass Communication and the Social System", SOCIOLOGY TODAY, Robert K. Merton et al., eds., Vol. II, N.Y.: Harper Torchbooks, 1959, pp. 537-78. Review of findings to 1959.

Rogers, Carl R., and F. J. Roethlisberger, "Barriers and Gateways to Communication", HARVARD BUSINESS REVIEW, July-Aug., 1952. Very useful.

Valentine, Milton, "Information Theory and the Psychology of Speech", THE PSYCHOLOGY OF COMMUNICATION, John Eisenson et al., eds., N.Y.: Appleton-Century-Crofts, 1963.

COMMUNICATION, NON-VERBAL:

Argyle, M., PSYCHOLOGY OF INTERPERSONAL BEHAVIOR, Baltimore, Md.: Penguin, 1967. See particularly pp. 37f. and 143.

Birdwhistell, R. L., KINESICS AND CONTEXT: ESSAYS ON BODY MOTION COM-

MUNICATION, Phila.: University of Pennsylvania, 1970. Sound and scholarly, but with ability to write for a variety of audiences. Very valuable work.

Goffman, Erving, PRESENTATION OF SELF IN EVERYDAY LIFE, Garden City, N.Y.: Doubleday Anchor, 1959. How we create and project our "masks", how they appear to others, how others appear to us. Goffman's work is very helpful in understanding performance in groups. Rich anecdotal style makes interesting reading, difficult theoretical abstraction.

Goffman, Erving, INTERACTION RITUAL: ESSAYS ON FACE-TO-FACE BEHAVIOR, Garden City, N.Y.: Doubleday Anchor, 1967. Collection of earlier essays, plus one not previously published.

Goffman, Erving, STRATEGIC INTERACTION, Phila.: University of Pennsylvania, 1969. This time Goffman uses the international spy as his sample.

Hall, Edward T., THE HIDDEN DIMENSION, Garden City, N.Y.: Doubleday Anchor, 1966. Social distance, territoriality, architecture, and many other ways in which man uses and is affected by spatial relations are discussed in this very readable work. Useful to those interested in communication, intergroup relations, education.

Hall, Edward T., THE SILENT LANGUAGE, Greenwich, Conn.: Fawcett Premier, 1959. Helps us understand our own behavior and that of others in discussion groups.

THE SMALL GROUP AND GROUP DYNAMICS

Argyris, Chris, INTEGRATING THE INDIVIDUAL AND THE ORGANIZATION, N.Y.: Wiley, 1964. See also Argyris' work listed under "Cultural Anthropology".

Argyris, Chris, INTERPERSONAL COMPETENCE AND ORGANIZATIONAL EFFECTIVENESS, Homewood, Ill.: Irwin Dorsey, 1962.

Bales, Robert F., "Small-Group Theory and Research", SOCIOLOGY TODAY, Robert K. Merton et al., eds. Vol. II., N.Y.: Harper Torchbooks, 1959. Brief review of findings including sources of surveys of literature up to 1959.

Bass, B., LEADERSHIP, PSYCHOLOGY AND ORGANIZATIONAL BEHAVIOR, N.Y.: Harper, 1960.

Berne, Eric, STRUCTURE AND DYNAMICS OF ORGANIZATIONS AND GROUPS, Philadelphia: J. B. Lippincott, 1963. Although concerned with the analysis of a very particular group, a spiritualist's seance, contains much relevant material for all group leaders. Berne's specialized vocabulary is sometimes a stumbling block, but work is interestingly written.

Bennett, T., THE LEADER AND THE PROCESS OF CHANGE, N.Y.: Association Press, 1966.

Bion, W. P., EXPERIENCE IN GROUPS, AND OTHER PAPERS, N.Y.: Basic Books, 1961. Concerned with therapy group, but a classic in some fundamental aspects of group behavior.

Bradford, L. P., ed., GROUP DEVELOPMENT: SELECTED READINGS ONE, Washington, D.C.: National Training Laboratories, 1961.

Bradford, Leland P., Jack R. Bigg, and Kenneth D. Benne, eds., T-GROUP THEORY AND LABORATORY METHOD, N.Y.: John Wiley & Sons, 1964. Subtitled "Innovation in Re-education", this forms a basic collection of papers in the work

and principles of the National Training Laboratories.

Buchanan, Paul, THE LEADER AND INDIVIDUAL MOTIVATION, N.Y.: Association Press, 1962.

Cartwright, Dorwin and Alven Zander, eds., GROUP DYNAMICS, (RESEARCH AND THEORY), 3rd ed., N.Y.: Harper and Row, 1968. A collection of basic papers in the field.

Collins, Barry E., and Harold Guetzkow, A SOCIAL PSYCHOLOGY OF GROUP PROCESSES FOR DECISION MAKING, N.Y.: John Wiley & Sons, 1964. Helpful presentation, with summaries and "lists of propositions".

Gardner, John W., SELF-RENEWAL, THE INDIVIDUAL AND THE INNOVATIVE SOCIETY, N.Y.: Harper & Bros., 1964.

Golembiewski, R. T., SMALL GROUP: AN ANALYSIS OF RESEARCH CONCEPTS AND OPERATIONS, Chicago: University of Chicago Press, 1962.

Hare, Alexander Paul, HANDBOOK OF SMALL GROUP RESEARCH, N.Y.: Free Press of Glencoe, 1962.

Homans, G., SOCIAL BEHAVIOR: ITS ELEMENTARY FORMS, N.Y.: Harcourt, 1961.

Knowles, Malcolm and Hulda, INTRODUCTION TO GROUP DYNAMICS, N.Y.: Association Press, 1959. Though not new, this brief and simple explanation of some of the terminology and principles in the field is helpful.

Lewin, Kurt, FIELD THEORY IN SOCIAL SCIENCE: SELECTED THEORETICAL PAPERS, ed. Dorwin Cartwright, N.Y.: Harper, 1951. Another pioneer whose Field Theory has had important implications.

Lewin, Kurt, "Group Decision and Social Change", READINGS IN SOCIAL PSYCHOLOGY, Theodore M. Newcomb et al., eds., pp. 330-44, N.Y.: Henry Holt & Co.,

1947. Development of such concepts as "unfreezing, moving and freezing of a level", and important early review of research on attitude change in group discussion.

Lippitt, Gordon and Edith Seashore, THE LEADER AND GROUP EFFECTIVENESS, N.Y.: Association Press, 1966.

Lipton, W. M., WORKING WITH GROUPS: GROUP PROCESS AND INDIVIDUAL GROWTH, N.Y.: Wiley, 1962.

McGregor, Douglas, THE HUMAN SIDE OF THE ENTERPRISE, N.Y.: McGraw-Hill, 1960.

Miles, Matthew B., LEARNING TO WORK IN GROUPS, N.Y.: Teachers College, Columbia University, 1959. A "how-to-do-it" on applied group dynamics for use with ongoing work teams. Many exercises described in detail, good bit of theory. Authors state, ". . . sensitivity training (is) a somewhat more personally-oriented approach than the group-relevant one being taken in this book" (p. 229), and " 'T-group' is shorthand for a training group which makes an intensive study of its own ongoing processes" (p. 207). Good for use by team of trained leaders for further work. Discussions involved are for the action-oriented decision-making groups.

Mills, Theodore M., THE SOCIOLOGY OF SMALL GROUPS, Englewood Cliffs, N.J.: Prentice-Hall, 1967. Brief but more technical than Shepherd or Olmsted. Covers a great deal in small compass. Mills has own terminology in some matters, but it is more readily integrated with that of other writers than is Berne's, for instance.

Newcomb, Theodore M., "The Study of Consensus", SOCIOLOGY TODAY, Robert K. Merton, *et al.,* eds., Vol. II, pp. 277-93, N.Y.: Harper Torchbooks, 1959. Development of interpersonal consensus in groups. Subgroup structuring and consensual processes.

Nylen, Donald, J. Mitchell and Anthony Stout, HANDBOOK OF STAFF DEVELOPMENT AND HUMAN RELATIONS TRAINING, Materials developed for use in Africa, Washington, D.C.: National Training Laboratories, Stephenson Lithograph, 1967.

Olmsted, Michael S., THE SMALL GROUP, N.Y.: Random House, 1959. Short, excellent survey, similar to Shepherd, *q.v.*

Petrullo, L., and B. Bass, eds., LEADERSHIP AND INTERPERSONAL BEHAVIOR, N.Y.: Holt, Rinehart and Winston, 1961. Interesting collection of papers on various types of leadership and group behavior.

Rogers, Carl, CARL ROGERS ON ENCOUNTER GROUPS, N.Y.: Harper & Row, 1970. A clear statement from "inside" by a highly respected advocate.

Schutz, W. C., FIRO: A THREE-DIMENSIONAL THEORY OF INTERPERSONAL BEHAVIOR, N.Y.: Holt, Rinehart and Winston, 1958.

Shepherd, Clovis R., SMALL GROUPS: SOME SOCIOLOGICAL PERSPECTIVES, San Francisco: (Chandler) Science Research Associates, 1964. A brief and clear review.

Sherif, Muzafer, ed., INTERPERSONAL RELATIONS AND LEADERSHIP, N.Y.: Wiley, 1962.

Stock, Dorothy and Herbert A. Thelen, EMOTIONAL DYNAMICS AND GROUP CULTURE, No. 2, Research Training Series, Washington, D.C.: National Training Laboratories, 1958. Experimental work and findings.

Tannenbaum, R., I. Weschler and F. Massavik, LEADERSHIP AND ORGANIZATION: A BEHAVIORAL SCIENCE APPROACH, N.Y.: McGraw-Hill, 1961.

Thelen, H. A., DYNAMICS OF GROUPS AT WORK, Chicago: University of Chicago, Phoenix, 1963. Interesting to read, anecdotal approach. Considerable information, but difficult to extract. Good for getting a "flavor" of some experimental work with groups, and some aspects of sensitivity training as well as work with community groups and schools.

Thomas, Donald, "T-Grouping: The White-Collar Hippie Movement", PHI DELTA KAPPAN, April, 1968, pp. 458-60; and Norman M. Paris, "T-Grouping: A Helping Movement", pp. 460-63. These paired articles present opposing views on the value of sensitivity training for school personnel.

Thomas, William I. and Florian Znaniecki, "The Definition of the Situation", READINGS IN SOCIAL PSYCHOLOGY, Theodore M. Newcomb *et al.,* eds., N.Y.: Holt, 1947. Early classic.

Weschler, Irving, THE LEADER AND CREATIVITY, N.Y.: Association Press, 1962.

INTERGROUP RELATIONS

Cantril, Hadley, THE PATTERN OF HUMAN CONCERNS, New Brunswick, N.J.: Rutgers University Press, 1965. (See listing under "Cultural Anthropology".)

Epstein, Charlotte, INTERGROUP RELATIONS FOR POLICE OFFICERS, Baltimore: Williams and Wilkins, 1962. Simply written text used as training manual with Philadelphia Police Department in overcoming racial and ethnic prejudice. Includes exercises, questions for discussion, role-plays. (See also listing for Epstein under "Education.")

Myers, Gustavus, HISTORY OF BIGOTRY IN

THE U.S., Henry M. Christman, ed., Capricorn, 1943, 1960. Good reference work on various types and instances of intergroup conflict.

Simpson, George E. and J. Milton Yinger, "The Sociology of Race and Ethnic Relations", SOCIOLOGY TODAY, Robert K. Merton *et al.*, eds., Vol. II, pp. 376-99, N.Y.: Harper Torchbooks, 1959. Brief review of literature up to 1959.

Dubois, Rachel Davis and Mew-Soong Li, REDUCING SOCIAL TENSION AND CONFLICT THROUGH THE GROUP CONVERSATION METHOD, N.Y.: Association Press, 1971. A careful and usable explanation of an adjunctive technique for adult groups at tension points.

NOTE: Many specialized bibliographies are now available for various aspects of intergroup relations, and we have therefore listed only a few of the perhaps less-known sources.

DISCUSSION

Beckhard, R., CONFERENCES FOR LEARNING, PLANNING AND ACTION, Washington, D.C.: National Training Laboratories, 1962.

Beckhard, R., HOW TO PLAN AND CONDUCT WORKSHOPS AND CONFERENCES, N.Y.: Association Press, 1956. Excellent "checklist" of recommended procedures. Practical, brief. If you are faced with handling a workshop for 100 people for the first time, do it with this book in hand. Is not concerned with theory, method, or content.

Center for the Study of Democratic Institutions, THE CIVILIZATION OF THE DIALOGUE, A Center Occasional Paper, Santa Barbara, Cal., 1968. Papers on dialogical concepts, forms of discussion and/or dialogue, including "The Quaker Dialogue", "The Legal Dialogue", "The Psychoanalytic Dialogue", "The Christian-Marxist Dialogue".

Haiman, Franklyn E., GROUP LEADERSHIP AND DEMOCRATIC ACTION, Boston: Houghton Mifflin, 1951. One of the better works available on problem-solving and decision-making group discussions, but slightly out of date.

Howell, William S. and D. K. Smith, DISCUSSION, pp. 271ff. on "Ethics of Discussion", N.Y.: Macmillan, 1956.

Maier, N. R. F., PROBLEM-SOLVING CONFERENCES AND DISCUSSIONS, N.Y.: McGraw-Hill, 1964. (See note under listing for Maier under "Social Psychology".)

Osborn, Alex F., APPLIED IMAGINATION, 3rd ed., N.Y.: Scribner's, 1963. Of interest particularly for brainstorming discussions.

EDUCATION

Amidon, E. J., and J. B. Hough, INTERACTION ANALYSIS: RESEARCH, THEORY AND APPLICATION, Boston: Addison-Wesley, 1967. Background for the following.

Amidon, E. J. and Ned A. Flanders, THE ROLE OF THE TEACHER IN THE CLASSROOM, rev. ed., Minneapolis: Association for Productive Teaching, Inc., 1967. Practical application of the method of interaction analysis in the teaching situation.

Bany, Mary and Lois Johnson, CLASSROOM GROUP BEHAVIOR, N.Y.: Macmillan, 1964.

Barnes, Douglas, James Britton and Harold Rosen, LANGUAGE, THE LEARNER AND THE SCHOOL, Penguin Papers in Education, Baltimore: Penguin, 1969. Valuable transcriptions of actual communication situations, problems and remedies.

Bruner, Jerome S., THE PROCESS OF EDUCATION, N.Y.: Vintage, Random House, 1960. A small but influential volume. (See also note on Jones, below.)

Epstein, Charlotte, INTERGROUP RELATIONS FOR THE CLASSROOM TEACHER, Boston: Houghton Mifflin, 1968. A helpful book of specific techniques and procedures which do not require radical restructuring of the environment, materials or curriculum. (See also listing for Epstein under "Intergroup Relations".)

Jones, Richard M., FANTASY AND FEELING IN EDUCATION, N.Y.: Harper Colophon Books, 1968. Suggested instructional procedures dealing with affective and imaginal elements, particularly in social studies, using extensive investigation of concrete examples. Interesting to read in connection with the Bruner listing above.

Keen, Sam, TO A DANCING GOD, N.Y.: Harper & Row, 1970. Ch. 2, "Education for Serendipity".

Mager, Robert F., PREPARING INSTRUCTIONAL OBJECTIVES, Palo Alto, Cal.: Fearon Pub., 1962. A clear, programmed text. Very helpful to those who tend to think their subject matter makes objective evaluation of students impossible, or who have difficulty formulating their educational goals or objectives.

Parker, J. Cecil and Louis J. Rubin, PROCESS AS CONTENT: CURRICULUM DESIGN AND THE APPLICATION OF

KNOWLEDGE, Chicago: Rand McNally, 1966. Recommendations for teaching-learning procedures and accompanying curricular adjustments based on the belief that education from kindergarten through university must be something more than, or perhaps even other than, the collecting of data.

Raths, Louis E., Merrill Harmin and Sidney B. Simon, VALUES AND TEACHING, Columbus, Ohio: Charles E. Merrill, 1966. Although these authors do not advocate discussion at the elementary school level with which they are here concerned, they do suggest it is a possible follow-up after the use of their "value-sheets" (pp. 108, 112). On pp. 56ff. they list thirty questions of the type we term Balance and Response, and there are many thought-provoking questions throughout this excellent book.

Redl, Helen, ed., SOVIET EDUCATORS ON SOVIET EDUCATION, Foreword by Fritz Redl, N.Y.: Free Press of Glencoe, 1964. Materials from USSR for teachers and parents. Shows strong group orientation versus "individualism". Deserves thoughtful consideration.

Rogers, Carl R., FREEDOM TO LEARN, Columbus, Ohio: Charles E. Merrill, 1969.

Schwab, Joseph and Paul F. Brandwin, THE TEACHING OF SCIENCE, Cambridge, Mass.: Harvard University Press, 1962. Discusses use of discussion methods in teaching of science—"an enquiry into enquiry". Dr. Schwab has also written an article on classroom discussion published in the JOURNAL OF GENERAL EDUCATION, 8, No. 1 (Oct., 1954), "Eros and Education".

EDUCATION, ADULT:

Bergevin, Paul E., Dwight Morris and Robert M. Smith, ADULT EDUCATION PROCEDURES: A HANDBOOK OF TESTED PATTERNS FOR EFFECTIVE PARTICIPATION, N.Y.: Seabury Press, 1963. A useful how-to-do it, consisting largely of checklists, little or no theory. Discusses planning of adult education approaches, selection of techniques. Concerning discussion methods, for instance, they assume a Leader who is a "trained participant", but not necessarily a "trained Leader", and say, "The entire group should have training in the fundamentals of which leadership is a part." However, no information regarding such training is offered. In part has been superseded by the Knowles listed below.

Knowles, Malcolm, THE MODERN PRACTICE OF ADULT EDUCATION, N.Y.: Association Press, 1970. Contains considerable background material, administrative aids, and recommendations for types of programs. Presumes trained leaders available for discussion groups, rather than offering training.

EDUCATION, ROLE-PLAYING AND OTHER SIMULATIONS:

Bergevin, Paul E., Dwight Morris and Robert M. Smith, ADULT EDUCATION PROCEDURES: A HANDBOOK OF TESTED PATTERNS FOR EFFECTIVE PARTICIPATION, N.Y.: Seabury Press, 1963. See pp. 135-47 for useful checklists.

Chesler, M. and R. Fox, ROLE PLAYING IN THE CLASSROOM: Chicago: Science Research Association, 1966.

Knowles, Malcolm, THE MODERN PRACTICE OF ADULT EDUCATION, good bibliographical listings, p. 293, and references.

Frazier, Clifford and Anthony Meyer, DISCOVERY IN DRAMA, N.Y.: Paulist, 1969. Classroom form of role-playing often known as "improvisational theater", usually using a director and scenario as in gaming. Used for discussions of values, social issues and religious beliefs.

Maier, Norman R. F., PRINCIPLES OF HUMAN RELATIONS, pp. 87-172, N.Y.: Wiley, 1957.

Moreno, J. L., PSYCHODRAMA, Vol. I., N.Y.: Beacon House, 1946.

INCREASING AWARENESS

Gunther, Bernard, SENSE RELAXATION: BELOW YOUR MIND, N.Y.: Collier Books, 1968.

Lewis, Howard R. and Harold S. Streitfeld, GROWTH GAMES, N.Y.: Harcourt Brace and Jovanovich, 1970.

Schutz, William C., JOY, N.Y.: Grove Press, Inc., 1967.

PHILOSOPHY

(A limited number of works are included here because of particular relevance to discussion group work.)

Buber, Martin, I AND THOU, 2nd ed., with "Postscript," trans. by Ronald G. Smith, N.Y.: Charles Scribner's Sons, 1958. A new edition of Buber's important work of the '20's which has had a persistent influence in psychiatry and sociology.

Buber, Martin, "Dialogue (Swiesprache, 1929)", BETWEEN MAN AND MAN, trans. by Ronald G. Smith, Boston: Beacon

Press, 1947, 1955. In the introduction, Buber says of this essay, ". . . (it) proceeded from the desire to clarify the 'dialogical' principle presented in I AND THOU, to illustrate it and to make precise its relation to essential spheres of life."

Kwant, Remy C., PHENOMENOLOGY OF SOCIAL EXISTENCE, Pittsburgh, Pa.: Duquesne University Press, 1965. Develops concept of "community" in reaction to "individualism", and opts to Teilhardian "socialization". Emphasizes what he rather unhappily calls "togetherness", while affirming the "person (as) a center of enormous possibilities", but as unable to realize them without interaction with the society.

Langer, Susanne K., PHILOSOPHY IN A NEW KEY, N.Y.: Mentor, 1951. Although all of this would be useful to the Leader in thinking through presentations and forming questions, pp. 15-33 and 224-47 should be read as they deal with ways of looking at the world commonly encountered in some semi-literate and super-literate participants in groups.

Index of Subjects and Names

and decision-making, 29-31
group problems, relation to, 73-74, 227
need for, in group, 74
observation of "unexpressed", 77-78
and sensitivity training, 80
too much, 74
"emotionality", Bion's concept, 74
encoding, 35, 207-208
environment; *see also* physical arrangements; situation
learning, 5, 113
errors, in discussion; *see* answers; facts; question types: Fact
evaluating, a leadership function, 12
evaluation, 81; *see also* Observers
Bales' categories and, 29
content, 77-78
group self-, 73 (*diagram*), 78, 191
a form of feedback, 71
written, 79
"everybody knows. . .", 203
executive role, 91; *see also* Leader, appointed
eye-contact, and encouraging participation, 128, 188

"face-saving", 214-216
factions, 90-91
facts; *see also* question types: Fact
arguments about, 95, 136-138, 139, 217-218
and attitudes, 19
dictionaries, as source of, 138
learning, 103
old and new, 23
of Presentation, 136-138, 143
problems of, 137-138
fading effect, in communication, 24
fears
and interference with communication, 209-210, 212
of failure, 105, 112
in new group, 128
as ontological concern, 212
and the shy, 128
feedback, 36-37, 71-79; *see also* Observers
Bales' observation categories and, 30
cost, 76
definitions of, 36, 71, 72
delayed, 72, (*diagram*), 73 (*diagram*), 75; *see also* Observers
direct or immediate, 21, 36, 72, 73
during discussion, 36
example, 21
in education, 101-102
as fact-finding in goal-seeking, 72 (*diagram*)
formalized, 75, 81; *see also* Observers
goal-seeking and, 71-72
kinds of, 72
in learning-discussion group, 73 (*diagram*)
group self-evaluation, 73, 78, 191
in a system, 70
timing, problems of, in, 76
Wiener, N., on, 37

feelings, 189; *see also* emotion
and role playing, 220, 221, 227
and whole-person learning, 186
Festinger, L., theory of cognitive dissonance, 23
fight, Bion's concept, 74; *see also* aggression; conflict
filter, mental; *see* concepts, availability of; set, mental
Flanders, Ned A., 77
flight, Bion's concept, 74
forgetting; *see* memory
freedom, 221; *see also* area of freedom; climate
encouraged in democratic group, 118, 121, 180-181, 203
as goal of Leader, 118, 178
Jenkins on, 184
and "rules and roles", 190
frustration, 87, 93
functions of leader; *see* leader, responsibilities of; leadership functions

gaming; *see* simulations
Garry, Ralph, and interpersonal relations in classroom, 105-106
gate-keeping; *see* regulating
(The) General Inquirer, 77
General questions; *see* questions, General
generalizations, 156-157; *see also* prejudice and controversy, 217
GENESIS, BOOK OF, questions on, 165
Gibb, Cecil A., 56
Gibb, J. R. and L. M., 11
Giffon, Sidney, on simulations, 230
goal(s); *see also* motivation
achievement, 158
and area of freedom, 179
frustration, 93
group
characteristics of, desirable, 3
and cohesiveness, 45
development of norms as a, 42
discussion of, 134-136, 158
and individual goals, 3, 45; *see also* goal overlap
of learning-discussion group, 157; *see also* community; responsive understanding
seeking, 71
and Observers, 172-173
problems with, 93
and system, 70 (*diagram*), 73 (*diagram*)
individual, 3, 158-159
and attitudes, 23
and effectiveness, 45
freedom and, 190
frustration and, 93
"life", 23
related to motives, 124
and system, 73 (*diagram*)
Leader's own; *see also* Leader, goals of
for members, 178
Observers and, 176-177
overlap, 45, 124, 157-158
parent organization's, 50
relation to system, 73 (*diagram*)
seeking, 15, 158; *see also* motivation

and freedom, 190
with feedback, 72 (*diagram*)
without feedback, 71 (*diagram*)
setting, 148, 158
shared, 45, 124, 157-158
unrealistic, as stressor, 93
Goffman, Erving, 78
glossary, use of, 139
Great Books Foundation, 147
Greenslaw, Paul S., 70
group(s), *passim*
activities, 49 (*table*)
affiliation, reasons for, 15-16
attraction, dynamics of, 44, 45 (and *diagram*)
boundaries (borders), 5
characteristics, 28-29
circumstances of meetings, 49
classification of, 49
death of, 91
definition of, 4
development, 78-79
"Doctor", 80-81
dynamics of, 44, 45, 158, Ch. 5; *et passim*
effectiveness, 11, 76, 181, 194
emotion, 39-40
difficulty of assessing, 40
elements of, 40
event, 39
environment; *see* physical arrangements; situation
"fallacy", 39
growth, 10, 13, 61, 96, 178, 182-183, 226-227; *see also* group, development
history, 5, 32, 70 (*diagram*), 73 (*diagram*)
hypochondria, 81
as information-decision system, 66-75
leaderless, viii, 55, 179
member; *see* participant; Ch. 2
memory; *see* memory, group
models, 70, 84-87
-discussion, 59-60, 64
new, 11, 60, 123-129, 167-168, 183, 185-186, 218
power of, 203; *see also* conformity; groupthink; minority, protection of; normativeness; salience
product, 51, 103-105
productivity, 45, 91
properties; *see* group, characteristics
psyche-, 156
purpose, 49
salience 43 and cf. 47 n. 23; 185
size, 39, 50-51
large, disadvantages of, 5, 50
small, 4
socio-, 157
syntality, 60, 62 n. 18
as system, 5, 65, Ch. 5 *passim*
task, 16
group dynamics; 85, 96-98, 99 n. 12
definitions, 96
groupthink, 58, 203
"everybody knows. . .", 203
"speak for yourself. . .", 203
growth, 178; *see also* group, growth; Leader and, 183
Guilford, J. P., and problem-solving, 5

shared, 16, 45 (*diagram*)
system, 24-25
Vernon, P. E., and "life values", 23

Wallas, G., and model of creative production, 5

White, Ralph, 54
Whitehead, Albert North, on simplicity,
156
"Who says what to whom with what ef-
fect", 34
"Who talks to Whom", 29, 33, 90
Wiener, Norbert, on feedback, 37

withdrawal, 89

Young, G. M., on speech, 151

Zelko, Harold P., on discussion, 60